BRITISH MOTOR CYCLES

Editors: J. B. ASHBY & D. J. ANGIER

Announcement

We offer this U.S.A. edition of this interesting catalog of British Motorcycles. Every motorcycle and autocycle made in England is described in this book. No comparable book on the subject ever has been published. It will constitute a standard work of reference for the enthusiast, the trade and all those who are interested in motorcycling.

Each machine is dealt with in comprehensive fashion, and full specifications are given for every model. In addition, much data concerning the history and development of the industry is included.

This book, originally published by Pentagon Publications, has been published with the technical assistance of every British motorcycle manufacturer.

Interest in the U.S.A. in British motorcycles is responsible for our publishing this title. We feel sure that our friends and customers will find it most interesting and informative.

Floyd Clymer

NOTE FROM THE PUBLISHER

Welcome to the world of digital publishing ~ the book you now hold in your hand, while unchanged from the original edition, was printed using the latest state of the art digital technology. The advent of print-on-demand has forever changed the publishing process, never has information been so accessible and it is our hope that this book serves your informational needs for years to come. If this is your first exposure to digital publishing, we hope that you are pleased with the results. Many more titles of interest to the classic automobile and motorcycle enthusiast, collector and restorer are available via our website at www.VelocePress.com. We hope that you find this title as interesting as we do.

Copyright, 1951

FLOYD CLYMER

World's Largest Publisher of Books Relating to Automobiles, Motorcycles, Motor Racing, and Americana

1268 SOUTH ALVARADO STREET, LOS ANGELES 6, CALIFORNIA

CONTENTS

A.J.S.	2
A.B.J.	7
Ambassador	9
Ariel	10
Bond	14
Bown	15
B.S.A.	16
Corgi	22
Cotton	24
Cyc-Auto	25
Dot	26
Douglas	27
D.M.W.	31
Excelsior	32
Francis-Barnett	36
James	39
Matchless	41
New Hudson	44
Norman	45
Norton	47
O.E.C.	52
Panther	53
Royal Enfield	56
Scott	59
Sun	60
Sunbeam...	62
Swallow	64
Tandon	65
Triumph	67
Velocette	72
Velo-Solex	75
Villiers	76
Vincent	79

Editors' Note

The British motor cycle industry has in the past built up an unrivalled reputation throughout the world. British machines have come to be the standard by which motor cycles are judged. There can be no doubt that this enviable position is retained today, for the quality and design of British machines has brought them to the top in the leading road races, trials, competitions and scrambles in practically every country. Constant research and development have created an invaluable export market; the industry today makes motor cycles for the whole world.

This book contains a complete picture of the post-war development of British machines, and describes every machine which is listed by manufacturers at the present time. It is hoped that it will prove a valuable work of reference for the motor cycle enthusiast, dealer and manufacturer—in fact for all who have an interest in, or use, motor cycles. Full specifications are included, and prices are given in a supplement. Whilst these may change, it has been felt desirable to include them as a basis of comparison.

Post war development has not involved any fundamental breakaway from traditional design. The changes made in many new models are of a minor nature, but detail improvements have constantly been made and progress in design continues unabated. It may be of interest to note some of the present trends of the industry. Firstly there has been a marked swing over to the production of high efficiency vertical twin machines, a large number of the leading manufacturers now offering one or more of this type. A far wider use of rear springing is another tendency, many models being available with rear springing as standard, or alternatively as an optional extra. The same remarks apply to the telescopic fork, which has become widely popular. Both these features are now to be found on even the light-weight machines. The demands of the competition rider have been met by the introduction of special trials and competition machines from many factories. The adoption of the four speed foot change box is becoming almost universal.

The 250 c.c. machine, especially the four stroke, is disappearing, and the small side valve machine is less popular. In their place, the development of the light-weight machine of 98 c.c., 125 c.c. and 197 c.c. has made the motor cycle, as a utility mount, an attractive means of transport for everyman. The autocycle is increasingly popular, and with the scooter and motor-assisted bicycle is capturing new markets.

Grateful acknowledgement is made to the manufacturers of the machines described, and to the British Cycle and Motor Cycle Manufacturers' Union, all of whom have co-operated in the provision and checking of information.

A.J.S. Model 20. 498 c.c. "Springtwin"

A·J·S

**ASSOCIATED MOTOR CYCLES LTD.
PLUMSTEAD ROAD · LONDON · S.E.18.**

U.S.A. Distributors (Excepting Calif.):
INDIAN SALES CORPORATION
Springfield, Mass.

California Distributors:
COOPER MOTORS
4401 S. Figueroa St.
Los Angeles, Calif.

The Stephens family, later A. J. Stevens and Co. Ltd, first produced a petrol engine in 1897, and shortly after began marketing complete motor cycles, with a good deal of success in sporting events. In the early years of the century, the A.J.S. company continued to develop their original 2¾ h.p. single, although the strong tendency of the day was towards multi-cylinder machines. Perseverance on these lines brought startling success in the 1914 T.T., A.J.S. singles securing 1st, 2nd, 4th and 6th places. This same year saw the taking over of the Graiseley premises at Wolverhampton and a great expansion following the outbreak of the first World War. After the war, the A.J.S. again quickly came to the fore, a 350 c.c. o.h.v. machine ridden by C. Williams winning the 1920 "Junior". In 1921 Howard Davies actually won the "Senior", riding a 350 c.c. model, the only time a machine of this capacity has won the Senior award. E. Williams won the Junior trophy in the same year. Racing and record honours followed thick and fast, whilst favourite production machines of the period included the Big Port, the chain driven o.h.c. single, the 8 h.p. and 10 h.p. Vee twins and the 1930 transverse twin.

A bold bid for sporting supremacy has been made by the post-war A.J.S. team. Most important development has been that of the 500 c.c. parallel twin machine, and several records were made by these "porcupine" twins (so called on account of their spike finned cylinders) ridden by R. L. Graham, with J. M. West and George Monneret at Montlhery in 1948, the figures being:—500 km.: 108.05 m.p.h.; 500 miles 107.01 m.p.h.; 3 hours: 108.54 m.p.h.; 4 hours: 107.44 m.p.h.; and 5 hours: 107.14 m.p.h. In all, 18 worlds records were broken. R. L. Graham, star A.J.S. rider, was top of the World's Championship table in 1949, his successes including the Swiss and Ulster Grand Prix. The same rider, after appearing an almost certain victor in the 1949 Senior T.T., was stopped by magneto trouble in the last few minutes. Graham's 1950 successes included 'firsts' in both 350 c.c. and 500 c.c. classes of the Swiss Grand Prix.

The A.J.S. has taken a lion's share of the premier trials awards in recent years, the high spot, being perhaps, B. H. M. Viney's performance in the International Six Days Trial of 1949.

A.J.S. machines for 1951 run to 10 models—a 498 c.c. o.h.v. single, the same model with a spring frame, a springer and a rigid 350 c.c. o.h.v., rigid and sprung 350 c.c. and 500 c.c. Competition models, and the 498 c.c. vertical "Springtwin." The tenth machine is, of course, the famous model 7R o.h.c. racing machine. Further refinements in the 1951 range include a light alloy cylinder head of new design on all single cylinder models, and the redesigning of the rear suspension units on the spring frame models.

A.J.S. MODEL 16M. 347 c.c. o.h.v.

These machines are powered by a high efficiency single port, o.h.v. push rod engine (69 mm. bore × 93 mm. stroke) employing duplex overlapping hairpin valve springs and low clearance wire-wound anti-slap pistons with two piece crankpin and three row roller big end bearings. Lubrication is by the dry sump method, employing a duplex rotary reciprocating plunger pump. A Burman 4 speed positive stop foot change gear box is provided, with a four spring clutch. The primary drive and the dynamo drive are contained in an oil bath chaincase. A redesigned Amal carburettor has been fitted.

A Duplex cradle type frame is employed with Teledraulic front forks, with non-bottoming oil damping.

The brake shoes are now provided with adjustable thrust pads and on all machines smoother front wheel braking has been secured with the incorporation of a longer anchor arm. Other detail modifications are : redesigned front and rear mudguard of deep section, with a stiffening rib. The tool box has been repositioned to allow of better mounting for panniers, and exhaust pipes have been provided with greater clearance for cornering. New and wider rear hubs have been fitted with detachable races.

A.J.S. 16MS. 347 c.c. o.h.v. spring frame.

These machines are similar to Model 16M but the Duplex cradle frame incorporates full Teledraulic oil-damped rear suspension, a swinging arm of massive construction pivoting in a self-lubricating bush in a light alloy casting. The range of movement at the wheel spindle is 3". A valanced rear mudguard is supplied on these models.

A.J.S. MODEL 18. 498 c.c. o.h.v.

The 498 c.c. models are counterparts of the 350 c.c. machines, but with an engine of 82.5 mm. bore × 93 mm. stroke. A five spring clutch in place of the four spring on 350 c.c. models, and a 3.50" × 19" rear tyre instead of a 3.25" × 19" as on the 350, are the only substantial differences.

A.J.S. MODEL 18S. 498 c.c. o.h.v. Spring Frame.

Similar to Model 18, but with full rear suspension and valanced rear mudguard.

A.J.S. MODELS 16MC (347 c.c.) and 18C (498 c.c.) Competition Models.

These competition models include further detail refinements to the completely redesigned 1950 model, and will make an immediate appeal to the enthusiastic clubman.

The major modifications to the standard single cylinder machines are as follows:—

Special shortened frame with wheelbase of 52½", and ground clearance of 6¾". Undershield is fitted.

Narrow section aluminium alloy mudguards.

Front wheel: 10 gauge spokes with 3.00" × 21" tyre.

Rear wheel: 6 gauge spokes fitted with 4.00" × 19" tyre.

KE 805 rear spindle and security bolts.

Small capacity (2¼ gallon) petrol tank.

4 pint oil tank with repositioned filler neck.

Racing type Lucas waterproof magneto.

Wide ratio gearbox with folding kickstarter pedal.

Internally mounted footrests, positioned farther to the rear.

Small Competition Lycett saddle, set back, with ample adjustment for height.

Twin throttle and clutch controls are provided and special alloy steel rear wheels. The exhaust is upswept.

The competition engines are exceptionally interesting. A light alloy cylinder head, with cast-in iron valve seatings, is fitted and an aluminium alloy top cover encloses the o.h.v. gear. The light alloy cylinder head casting incorporates wells for the hairpin valve springs. A light alloy cylinder barrel with shrunk-in centrifugally cast liner is secured to the cylinder head by 4 high-tensile steel studs, ⅜" diameter, which, protruding from the crankcase mouth, pass through the cylinder barrel casting, extending nearly to its top face. Sleeve nuts, 3" long, located in the valve gear compartment of the cylinder head secure these studs, leaving both studs and nuts invisible from the exterior.

Optional equipment on these models is a 3 gallon fuel tank, standard rear wheel, standard gear ratios and electric lighting.

A.J.S. MODELS 16MCS and 18CS.

Introduced for the first time in the 1951 range, these are the spring frame versions of the Competition models. They should prove most effective in every type of cross-country competition.

A.J.S. MODEL 20. 498 c.c. o.h.v. vertical twin. Spring frame.

This model, known as the "Springtwin" was introduced at the 1948 Motor Cycle Show and remains substantially unchanged, except for a few detail refinements.

The 498 c.c. engine has a bore of 66 mm. and a 72.8 mm. stroke. Separate light alloy cylinder heads have cast in valve seats, there are separate cast iron cylinders, and the three bearing crankshaft is supported by roller outer bearings and a plain centre main bearing. Light alloy forged connecting rods, twin flywheels, Vandervell big end bearings, wire wound pistons, a rotary crankcase pressure relief valve and dry sump lubrication with positive feed to all moving parts are other salient features of the specification. A Burman 4 speed gearbox, with positive stop foot change and a five spring multi-plate clutch is fitted. Centre front and prop stands are provided and the hinged portion of the rear mudguard allows the rear

A.J.S. Model 18S. 498 c.c., o.h.v.

wheel to be rolled out. A 3 gallon tank, finished in red and chrome, is supplied.

A.M.C. Teledraulic forks and Teledraulic rear suspension are fitted. A Lycett saddle is standard. A gear driven magneto and 45 watt dynamo look after the electrical side.

More is the pity that the greater part of the total production of these fascinating motor cycles for 1951 is, in all probability, destined for export.

A.J.S. MODEL 7R. 348 c.c. o.h.c.

The famous Model 7R, 348 c.c. overhead camshaft racing machine, is again in production for 1951. It provides the enthusiastic private owner with a highly efficient motorcycle conforming to the requirements of International events. The 74 mm. × 81 mm. engine has a light alloy cylinder head and barrel, with totally enclosed valve gear operated by a chain driven camshaft. Duplex hairpin valve springs are fitted and a magnesium alloy crankcase, timing case, rocker box and wheel hubs. The twin gear type oil pumps circulate 26 gallons per hour at 7,000 r.p.m. Teledraulic front and rear suspension is fitted, double leading shoe brakes and light alloy mudguards are other features contributing to stability and low weight.

Pistons for use with 50/50 Petrol Benzol or Alcohol fuels are available if required and all engines are fully bench tested and ready for immediate racing.

SPECIFICATIONS.

A.J.S. MODELS 16M, 16MS, 18 and 18S.

ENGINE. Make. A.J.S. Bore and Stroke, 69 mm. × 93 mm. 347 c.c. (16M, 16MS), 82.5 mm. × 93 mm. 498 c.c. (18, 18S). Single cylinder, o.h.v. air cooled, single port. Totally enclosed push rod operated valves. Triple row Duralumin caged big end bearing and two piece crankpin. Stellite tipped valves, Duplex Hairpin valve springs, wire wound pistons, individually balanced flywheels and lubricated cam type engine shaft shock absorber. Sparking Plug 14 mm.

LUBRICATION. Pressure lubricated by large capacity Duplex rotary reciprocating oil pump. Full dry sump system.

CARBURETTOR. Amal semi-automatic. Twist grip throttle control and air lever.

GEAR BOX. Burman oil lubricated heavyweight, 4 speed with enclosed positive stop foot gear change and kickstarter. Ratios:— 16M, 16MS. 1st 15.57 10.26, 7.47, 5.83 to 1. 18, 18S. 1st 13.35, 8.8, 6.4, 5.0 to 1.

CLUTCH. Multi plate clutch with Bowden operated hand control.

IGNITION. Chain driven Lucas NR1 magneto.

LIGHTING. Separate Lucas dynamo. 6 volt. Constant voltage control. 7" headlamp. Rear lamp, dipper switch and horn button.

PETROL CAPACITY. 3 gallon welded tank with twin filter taps.

OIL CAPACITY. 4 pint welded steel oil tank.

TYRES. Triple Stud Dunlop. 3.25" × 19" front and rear (16M, 16MS). 3.25" × 19" front and 3.50" × 19" rear (18 and 18S).

BRAKES. Quickly adjustable, internal expanding. 7" diameter.

FRAME AND SUSPENSION. Duplex cradle of brazed construction, forged fork ends, integral sidecar and pillion rest lugs. rear front and prop stands. A.M.C. patent Teledraulic forks, 16M, 18. As above but with full Teledraulic rear oil damped suspension. (16MS, 18S).

SADDLE. Fully adjustable. Make Lycett. Height from ground 30".

WHEELBASE. 54".

GROUND CLEARANCE. 5½".

WEIGHT (dry). 344 lb. (16M) 375 lb. (16MS), 354 lb. (18), 368 lb. (18S).

FINISH. Stoved enamel on Bonderised surface. Exhaust system, wheel rims, handlebars etc. chromium plated. Petrol tank and wheel rims hand lined.

EXTRA OR OPTIONAL EQUIPMENT. Detachable luggage carrier, Pillion seat and footrests.

A.J.S. MODELS 16MC and 18C. 16MCS and 18CS.

ENGINE. Make A.J.S. Bore and Stroke, 69 mm. × 93 mm. 347 c.c. (16MC), 82.5 mm. × 93 mm. 498 c.c. (18C). Compression Ratios: With plate 5.88 to 1 (16MC). Less plate 6.35 to 1 (16MC). With plate 5.97 to 1 (18C). Less plate 7.4 to 1 (18C). Single cylinder, o.h.v. air cooled, single port. Totally enclosed push rod operated valves. Light alloy cylinder head and barrel with cast in centrifugally cast iron liner and long retaining bolts. Duplex hairpin valve springs, Stellite tipped valves, wire wound piston, individually balanced flywheels and lubricated cam type engine shaft shock absorber. Sparking plugs 14 m.m.

LUBRICATION. Pressure lubricated by large capacity Duplex Rotary reciprocating oil pump. Full dry sump system.

CARBURETTOR. Amal semi-automatic, with twist grip throttle control and air lever.

GEAR BOX. Burman oil lubricated heavyweight 4 speed enclosed positive stop foot gear change, and folding kickstarter. Ratios, 16MC. 20.94, 14.42, 8.38, 6.56 to 1. 18 C. 18.44, 12.20, 7.47, 5.83 to 1.

CLUTCH. Multi plate clutch with Bowden hand control.

IGNITION. Chain driven Lucas NR1 magneto.

LIGHTING. Optional extra.

PETROL CAPACITY. 2¼ galls. Welded tank with twin filter taps.

OIL CAPACITY. 4 pint oil tank with repositioned filler cap.

TYRES. 3.00" × 21", front 4.00" × 19" (rear).

BRAKES. Quickly adjustable, internal expanding, 7" diameter.

FRAME AND SUSPENSION. Duplex cradle rigid frame. Teledraulic forks. 16MCS and 18CS as above but with full Teledraulic oil damped rear suspension.

SADDLE. Small competition Lycett saddle. Height from ground, 32¼".

WHEELBASE. 52½".

GROUND CLEARANCE. 6⁷⁄₁₆" (16MC), 6¼" (18C).

WEIGHT (dry). 16MC 299 lb. 18C 304 lb.

FINISH. Upswept exhaust system, undershield, light alloy polished mudguards with tubular stays, twin throttle and clutch cables, KE 805 rear spindle, security bolts, Black stove enamel and chromium plate.

EXTRA OR OPTIONAL EQUIPMENT. 3 gallon fuel tank, standard gear ratios, standard rear wheel, electric lighting.

A.J.S. MODEL 20

ENGINE. Make. A.J.S. Bore and Stroke, 66 mm. × 72.8 mm. (498 c.c.). Compression Ratio, 7.25 to 1. Twin cylinder, o.h.v. air cooled, single port. 3 bearing crankshaft with twin flywheels, separate cylinders deeply spigotted into the die cast spherical crankcase. Heavily finned, separate light alloy cylinder heads with the internal rocker posts and eccentric spindle rocker adjustment. Stellite tipped valves, cast-in valve seats, forged light alloy connecting rods, wire wound pistons, roller outer main bearings, with Vandervell centre main and big end bearings. Sparking plugs 14 mm.

LUBRICATION. Full dry sump. High output twin gear pumps.

CARBURETTOR. Amal semi-automatic, with twist grip throttle control and air lever.

GEAR BOX. Burman oil lubricated heavyweight 4 speed with enclosed positive stop foot gear change and kickstarter. Ratios, 1st, 13.35, 8.8., 6.4. 5.0 to 1.

CLUTCH. Multi plate clutch with Bowden operated hand control.

IGNITION. Gear driven Lucas K2F magneto.

LIGHTING. Separate Lucas dynamo, gear driven from timing case. 45 watt, 6 volt, constant voltage control. Head lamp, rear lamp, dipper switch and horn button.

PETROL CAPACITY. 3 gallons. Welded steel tank with twin filter taps.

OIL CAPACITY. ½ gallon welded steel oil tank.

TYRES. Triple stud Dunlop. 3.25" × 19" (front), 3.50" x 19" (rear).

BRAKES. Quickly adjustable, internal expanding, 7" diameter, front and rear.

FRAME AND SUSPENSION. Duplex cradle, with full Teledraulic oil damped rear suspension, A.M.C. patent Teledraulic forks, Centre, front and prop stands. Pillion footrests.

SADDLE. Lycett, fully adjustable Saddle height 30".

WHEELBASE. Length 55¼". Ground clearance 5¼".

WEIGHT (dry). 400 lb.

FINISH. Stoved enamel on Bonderised finish. Exhaust system, wheel rims, handlebars etc. chromium plated. Tank. Black and chrome.

A.J.S.
16 MC 347 c.c. o.h.v.
18 MC 498 c.c. o.h.v.

A.J.S.
MODEL 7R
348 c.c. o.h.c

SPECIFICATION AJS MODEL 7R.

ENGINE. A.J.S. Bore and Stroke, 74 mm × 81 mm. 348 c.c. Compression Ratio, 9 to 1. Single cylinder, o.h.c. air cooled, single port. Chain driven camshaft. Light alloy cylinder head and barrel. Totally enclosed valve gear. Duplex Hairpin valve springs. Sparking Plug 14 mm.
LUBRICATION. Twin gear type oil pumps (26 gall. per hour at 7,000 r.p.m.).
CARBURETTOR. Amal Racing 10 T.T.
GEAR BOX. Burman 4 speed. Positive stop foot gear change. Ratios, 1st 10.14. 2nd, 7.07. 3rd, 5.95. Top 5.24.
CLUTCH. Multi-plate clutch with Bowden hand control.
IGNITION. Lucas NTT 1 magneto. Gear driven.
LIGHTING. Nil.
PETROL CAPACITY. 4¼ gallons.

OIL CAPACITY. 1 gallon.
TYRES. Racing tread. Make Dunlop. Front 3.00" × 21". Ribbed. Rear 3.25" × 20". Triple Stud.
BRAKES. Quickly adjustable, internal expanding, 7". Double leading shoes.
FRAME AND SUSPENSION. Welded steel Duplex cradle frame, Teledraulic front forks, Full Teledraulic rear suspension.
SADDLE. Special racing type. Height from ground 30½".
WHEELBASE. 56". Ground clearance 5½".
WEIGHT (dry) 298 lb.
SPECIAL DETAILS. Magnesium alloy crankcase, timing case, rocker box and wheel hubs. Double leading shoe brakes. Light alloy mudguards, fuel and oil tanks, wheel-rims and straight spoke wheels.
EQUIPMENT. Smith Revolution Counter.

A.B.J.

A. B. JACKSON (CYCLES) LTD.
109-111 POPE STREET · BIRMINGHAM, 1

Amongst the latest additions to an ever growing number of Villiers engined lightweights and auto-cycles are two smart little machines recently put on the market by A. B. Jackson (Cycles) Ltd., of Birmingham.

Two models are being produced, both powered by Villiers 98 c.c. engines, and both are well finished and incorporate many detail refinements.

The auto-cycle is fitted with the Villiers Mark 2F single speed two stroke engine, mounted within a sturdy tubular loop type frame. The single port engine has a light alloy detachable cylinder head, flat top piston and ball bearing mainshaft, with a roller bearing big end.

A spring operated telescopic front fork is fitted to the frame, and weather protection is enhanced by wide section mudguards. The front guard is unusually well valanced, whilst the rear guard is hinged. The wheels are fitted with heavy gauge rims and spokes and Dunlop 2.25" x 21" tyres, front and rear. The specification includes a sturdy tubular rear carrier and a rear spring up stand. 4" diameter hand operated internal expanding brakes are fitted front and rear.

The Villiers carburettor is controlled by twist grip. Lighting is provided by the Villiers flywheel magneto, which supplies current for the 6 volt, 12 watt headlamp, taillamp and a 6 volt electric horn.

Both chains are well protected by top run guards, the handlebars are adjustable and a comfortable large spring seat saddle is supplied. The 1½ gallon tank has a reserve position petrol tap. The final drive ratio is 11.8 to 1. A Smith's lightweight speedometer can be supplied if required, as an extra. The machine weighs 140 lbs. and has a wheelbase of 49¾".

The 98 c.c. lightweight motor cycle has an almost identical specification, but the Villiers Mark 1F two speed engine is supplied, with final drive ratios of 13.04 and 8.47 to 1. Gears are hand controlled. Transmission is by ½" x $\tfrac{3}{16}$" secondary chain, well protected by a top run guard. 4" diameter brakes are again in use, the rear brake however, being foot controlled. Footrests are of course provided on the lightweight machine, and the Villiers flywheel magneto on this model supplies a 6 volt, 6 A.H. capacity battery, which provides current for a 6 volt, 12/12 watt headlamp, a tail lamp, and a 6 volt electric horn.

Other details such as Dunlop tyres, telescopic forks, frame, petrol tank and equipment are as described for the auto-cycle. A toolbag, pump and tools are included in the specification and a Smith's lightweight speedometer is offered at a small additional charge.

A.B.J. Autocycle

SPECIFICATION.
A.B.J. 98 c.c. Auto-Cycle.

Engine. Make, Villiers, Mark 2F.
Bore and Stroke. 47 mm. x 57 mm. 98 c.c.
Compression Ratio. 8 to 1.
B.H.P. 2.1 at 3,800 r.p.m.
Single cylinder, two stroke, air cooled, single port. Light alloy detachable cylinder head, flat top aluminium alloy piston, ball bearing mainshaft, roller bearing big end.
Sparking plugs 14 mm.
Lubrication. Petroil.
Carburettor. Villiers Junior. Twist grip control.
Gearbox. Single speed. Ratio. 11.8 to 1.
Clutch. Two plate, cork insert type, runs in oil.
Transmission. Primary. Chain ¾" x .155".
Secondary. Chain (Driving) ½" x $\tfrac{3}{16}$". Pedalling chain, ½" x ⅛".
Ignition. Villiers Flywheel Magneto.
Lighting. Flywheel magneto. Head 6V. 12 watt. Tail 4V., .3 amp. 6V. electric horn.
Petrol Capacity. 1½ gallons. Reserve petrol tap.
Tyres. Dunlop, 2.25" x 21" front and rear.
Brakes. 4" diameter, internal expanding. Hand operated.
Frame and Suspension. Tubular rigid frame. Telescopic front forks. Hinged rear mudguard.
Saddle. Large spring seat.
Wheelbase. 49¾".
Height from ground. 30".
Ground clearance. 5".
Width over bars. 24".
Weight (dry). 140 lb.
Finish. Black.
Equipment. Carrier. Rear stand. Pump. Toolbag. Toolkit.
Extra or optional equipment. Smith's Lightweight Chronometric Speedometer.
Petrol consumption. 140 m.p.g.

A.B.J. Motor Cycle

SPECIFICATION.
A.B.J. 98 c.c. Lightweight Motor Cycle.

Engine. Make, Villiers, Mark 1F.
    Bore and Stroke. 47 mm. x 57 mm. 98 c.c.
    Compression Ratio. 8 to 1.
    B.H.P. 2.8 at 4,000 r.p.m.
    Single cylinder, two stroke, air cooled, single port, light alloy detachable cylinder head, flat top piston, ball bearing mainshaft, roller bearing big end.
    Sparking plugs. 14 mm.
Lubrication. Petroil system.
Carburettor. Villiers Junior. Twist grip control.
Gearbox. 2 speed, hand controlled.
    Ratios, 13.04 and 8.47 to 1.
Clutch. Cork insert two plate clutch, running in oil.
Transmission. Primary. Chain $\tfrac{3}{8}''$ x .155''.
    Secondary. Chain $\tfrac{1}{2}''$ x $\tfrac{3}{16}''$. Top run guard.

Ignition. Villiers Flywheel Magneto.
Lighting. Head 6V. 12/12 watt. Tail 6V. 3 watt. Stop light 6V. 18 watt. 6V. 6 A.H. capacity battery. 6V. electric horn.
Petroil Capacity. 1½ gallons. Reserve petrol tap.
Tyres. Dunlop, 2.25'' x 21'', front and rear.
Brakes. 4'' diameter, internal expanding, rear foot operated.
Frame and Suspension. Tubular frame. Telescopic front forks.
    Hinged rear mudguard.
Saddle. Large spring seat.   **Height from ground.** 30''.
Wheelbase. 49¾''.   **Ground Clearance.** 5''.
Overall Length. 78''.   **Width over bars.** 24''.
Weight (dry). 140 lb.
Finish. Black.
Equipment. Rear carrier. Rear stand. Pump. Toolbag. Toolkit.
Extra or optional equipment. Smith's Lightweight Chronometric Speedometer
Petrol consumption. 140 m.p.g.

Ambassador

U.S. CONCESSIONAIRES LTD.
PONTIAC WORKS · ASCOT, BERKS.

U.S.A. Distributor:
HAP JONES
237 Valencia St.
San Francisco, Calif.

The latest range of these well-known lightweight machines now includes three models, which should give ample choice to those who are looking for a straightforward and sturdy machine, simple in construction and easy to maintain.

All three models are fitted with the Villiers Mark 6E 197 c.c. engine and the "Popular" or Series Four Model is priced as low as £66 (without purchase tax) and should be an exceptionally attractive proposition for those who need economical and reliable transport. The Series Three machine is to the same general specification, but includes minor refinements of detail and finish, such as a rectified lighting set, electric horn and battery. The series five includes a rectified lighting set, with the addition of newly-designed telescopic front forks-styled the "easy-ride." Ambassadors offer, for the present year, a machine to meet the needs of every type of lightweight user.

Ambassador. Series V.

The Villiers 197 c.c. two stroke engine, fitted to all models has a bore and stroke of 59 mm. x 72 mm., with the usual Villiers features of detachable aluminium alloy cylinder head, single port exhaust, twin transfer ports and flat top piston. The compression ratio is 8 to 1, with an approximate b.h.p. of 8.4 at 4,000 r.p.m. The 3 speed unit construction gearbox is driven by an endless chain enclosed in an oil bath chain case. A 2 plate cork insert type clutch running in oil is fitted and a positive stop foot gear change mechanism is incorporated.

The substantially built tubular frame is of great strength, and gives the machine a "rugged" appearance, unusual for a lightweight. On Models Three and Four, Webb Girder forks, with a hand adjustable shock absorber are fitted—the Ambassador telescopic type on Series Five.

The Villiers Flywheel magneto is fitted to all models, providing direct lighting with a 30 watt beam on the Series Four Machines. A rectifier and accumulator are supplied on the Series Three and Five Machines. All models incorporate Dunlop wheels and 3.00" x 19" tyres and 5" internal expanding brakes front and rear, adjustable handlebars and footrests and a Smith's illuminated speedometer with m.p.h. or k.p.h. dial.

Ambassador 'Popular' Model

A central spring up stand is fitted to all models.

Series Three and Five machines, in addition to the refinements of lighting and forks previously noted, differ in one or two details. Knee grips and rear carriers are for instance fitted to these models, and certain parts such as the hand shock absorber adjustment and rear chain guard are chromium plated.

A variety of attractive finishes is provided. Black, with aircraft grey tanks, is the standard finish for all three models, but alternative finishes for frame, forks and tank of dark red, bright blue or duo-green are available.

Ambassador. Series III.

SPECIFICATION
197 c.c. AMBASSADOR MODELS—SERIES THREE, FOUR AND FIVE.
Engine. Make. Villiers Mark 6E.
    Bore and Stroke. 59 mm. x 72 mm. 197 c.c.
    Compression Ratio. 8 to 1.
    Approximate b.h.p. 8.4 at 4,000 r.p.m.
    Single cylinder, two stroke, air cooled, single port, detachable aluminium alloy cylinder head.
    Sparking plug 14 mm.
Lubrication. Petroil system.
Carburettor. Villiers.
Gearbox. 3 speed unit construction. Positive stop foot change mechanism, Kickstarter. Special oil level dipstick fitted.
    Final drive ratios. 17.33, 9.06, and 5.33 to 1.
Clutch. Two plate cork insert type, running in oil.
Transmission. Primary. Chain ⅝" x .205". Renolds.
    Secondary. Chain ½" x ³⁄₁₆" Renolds.
Ignition. Villiers Flywheel magneto.
Lighting. Series Four. Direct from Villiers Flywheel magneto.
    Series Three and Five. Rectified lighting, with accumulator and electric horn.
Petroil Capacity. 2 gallons. All steel tank.
Oil Capacity. Petroil system.
Tyres. Dunlop 3.00" x 19", front and rear.
Brakes. Fully adjustable, internal expanding, 5" front and rear.
Frame and Suspension. Tubular frame. Webb girder link forks (Series Three and Four). Ambassador Telescopic Forks. (Series Five).
Saddle. Lycett.   **Height from Ground.** 27¼".
Wheelbase. 46".   **Ground Clearance.** 5".
Width over bars. 26".   **Overall length.** 6' 2".
Weight (dry). Series Three 199 lbs. Series Four 184 lbs. Series Five 219 lbs.
Finish. Standard finish, black and grey. Alternative finishes for frame, fork and tanks of dark red, bright blue or duo-green. Bright parts chromium plated Hand adjustment for shock absorber and rear chain guard chromium plated on Series Three and Five. Handlebars chromium plated on all models.
Equipment. Smith's illuminated speedometer. Central spring up stand. Rear carrier and knee grips on Series Three and Five.
Maximum speed in gears 1st 15 m.p.h. 2nd 25 m.p.h. Top 55 m.p.h.

Ariel

ARIEL MOTORS LIMITED
SELLY OAK, BIRMINGHAM, 29

U.S.A. Distributor:
JOHNSON MOTORS, INC.
267 W. Colorado Blvd.
Pasadena, California

Behind the Ariel lies a long and not uneventful history, extending back well into the last century. The amalgamation in 1892 of a number of manufacturers of cycle components led to the production, around 1898 of the first power driven machines—quadracycles and tricycles. The Ariel motor cycle proper emerged about 1902 and was powered by a Kerry engine. Charles Sangster, later joined by his son Jack, were the personalities largely responsible for building up the Ariel business from small beginnings to the leading position in the industry which it now holds. It speaks volumes for the tenacity of the directors, that, despite vicissitudes and several changes of name and reorganisations, the Ariel has been continuously manufactured throughout two wars and the slump period of the early thirties, during which many companies were forced to close down. After the last war came a final reorganisation and the company became part of the B.S.A. group.

Many interesting machines have been produced since the first Ariel machine saw the light of day, including a two-stroke, three speed model in 1915, 6 h.p. and 8 h.p. twins after the first war, and the first of the range of "modern" Ariels in 1926, the famous 500 o.h.v. (with an 80 m.p.h. maximum) and the 550 c.c. side valve machine. Progressive and far reaching changes in design have followed continuously from that day to this—through the popular "Colt" and "Sloper 500" models of 1930, the first 500 c.c. "Square Four," the "Red Hunter" models in 1933, the 600 c.c. "Square Four" and the 1,000 c.c. development of that machine, known affectionately as the "Squariel," to the present range of 9 brilliant machines. Throughout this period the machines have been constantly tested in racing and trials events, such names as Frank Longman and Jock West on the racing side and Harold Perrey in charge of the competition department, increasing the reputation and good name of the machine year by year. Today it is the company's proud boast that it is the only one in the world to produce, in its standard range of machines, four cylinder, twin and single cylinder models.

At the top of the list, and first to capture the enthusiast's imagination is the famous 997 c.c. Ariel Square Four, a smooth and quiet machine with wonderful acceleration and a useful maximum of 95 m.p.h. The latest "Square Four" has an aluminium alloy engine, the alloy cylinders being cast "en bloc" in a square formation, the four vertical cylinders having high expansion iron sleeves to form durable bearing surfaces for the pistons. The pistons in the front and rear pairs of cylinders are operated from normal two-throw crankshafts lying parallel to each other and coupled by large diameter hardened gears having teeth with ground profiles for accuracy and silent running. Each crankshaft carries a centrally disposed flywheel and balance weights are fitted opposite each crank throw to give perfect balance. The crankshafts are carried on roller

**Ariel
Model 4G.
997 c.c. 4 Cyl.**

**Ariel
Model KH.
498 c.c. Twin.**

bearings on the drive side and white metal lined bronze bearings on the timing side. The rear crankshaft carrying the transmission sprocket and shock absorber is supported by an additional roller bearing outside the main coupling gears.

Aluminium alloy pistons each with two compression and one oil scraper ring are carried on light alloy connecting rods by fully floating gudgeon pins. The connecting rods have bronze bushes fitted to the small ends and replaceable white metal lined steel shells fitted to the large ends. The detachable caps are secured to the connecting rods, each by two bolts and nuts, the latter bearing against the connecting rod so that they can be unscrewed from the top opening in the crankcase (after the cylinder block has been removed) and a complete rod and bearing removed without dismantling the crankcase.

Cylinder heads, rocker boxes, inlet and exhaust passages are formed in an aluminium alloy monobloc casting, heavily finned for efficient cooling and securely attached to the cylinder block by twenty studs and nuts. High expansion steel inserts are fitted and formed with an accurate seating for each of the overhead valves. The bronze valve guides are secured in position by the pressure of the valve springs against a collar formed on the guide. The sparking plug holes have threaded bronze bushes as a safeguard against damage when changing sparking plugs. The four push rod tunnels are cast in the cylinder block, and the overhead valves are enclosed and automatically lubricated.

The camshaft and dynamo are driven from the rear crankshaft through a roller chain which makes a conventional triangular drive, and an automatic spring loaded tensioner is provided. At the driven end of the $3\frac{1}{2}''$ diameter dynamo is a pair of spiral gears driving the contact breaker, distributor and automatic ignition gear control.

The lubrication system is of the dry sump type, oil being drawn from a separate oil tank by a plunger pump and circulated throughout the engine, a second pump returning the oil from the crankcase to the oil tank.

Coil ignition and a car type distributor are fitted on Model 4G, and a 70 watt voltage controlled dynamo generates current. The Burman 4 speed gearbox has positive stop foot change.

The latest Model Square Four has now a quickly detachable rear wheel. Other detail improvements added recently are a new speedometer mounting on a bridge between the front fork legs, allowing better reading of the instrument, an improved saddle position and a repositioning of the rear brake to prevent this fouling the exhaust pipe. A neat instrument panel is fitted to the tank top and contains headlamp switch, ammeter, ignition warning light, inspection lamp and oil pressure gauge.

The frame is of the rigid type, with integral sidecar lugs and Ariel Telescopic front forks. A prop stand is included. Ariel coil spring rear suspension can be fitted as an optional extra, and this has been so designed that rear chain tension is constantly maintained. Dunlop tyres are fitted as standard and three attractive finishes are offered, red, black, or green panels with chromium plating.

Next in the Ariel range are the two 498 c.c. o.h.v. vertical twins—the K.G. Model "De Luxe" and K.H. "Red Hunter" Twin. Both engines have a bore of 63 mm., a stroke of 80 mm., with cylinder heads and rocker boxes in one casting. The balanced crankshafts are forged in one piece, and carried on a large roller bearing on the drive side and a plain white metal bearing on the timing side. The light alloy connecting rods have replaceable white metal liners, and light alloy pistons are fitted. The twin camshafts are driven by an automatically adjusted Duplex chain. Oil circulates by a double gear pump, giving a pressure of 25-35 lbs. to the main bearings and rockers. Ignition on these models is by magneto with automatic ignition control and a 56 watt dynamo is fitted. The engine on the Red Hunter K.H., is however specially bench tested and tuned, and has polished ports and cylinder heads, and 7.5 compression ratio pistons can be supplied, for use with 80 octane fuel. (The K.G. has 6.8 ratio pistons). An Amal single lever carburettor is fitted on the K.G., and a large bore Amal with petroflex piping on the K.H. Both models incorporate a 4 speed positive stop foot change gearbox, engine shaft shock absorber and polished aluminium oilbath primary chain cases. A rigid frame, with integral sidecar lugs is supplied, but Ariel rear springing can be fitted as an optional extra to both models. Both machines have Ariel Telescopic forks.

The new speedometer mounting as described above for the "Square Four," is included on the twins, and a similar instrument panel, without, of course, the ignition warning light. A new petrol tank has been designed for these models, with a capacity of $3\frac{3}{4}$ gallons. Tubular front and spring up rear stands and a prop stand are fitted. Model K.G. has 3.50" x 19" rear and 3.25" x 19" front tyres, and Model K.H. 3.50" x 19" rear and 3.00" x 20" ribbed front tyres.

The very popular "Red Hunters" are again in the Ariel range, and are represented by two single cylinder models, the 497 c.c. V.H. and the 347 c.c. N.H. Both models have high efficiency o.h.v. engines, specially bench tested and tuned, and ground and highly polished ports and cylinder head. The forged steel flywheels are polished and light aluminium alloy pistons are fitted— 6.8 compression ratio on the V.H. and 6.2 on the N.H. On the V.H. the large diameter mainshaft is mounted on two heavy duty roller bearings and one ball bearing, and the extra large double roller bearing big end has a duralumin cage. The standard Ariel dry sump lubrication system is employed. The 500 has a single port, low level exhaust pipe, but the 350 is offered with single or double port low level pipes. Both machines have a Lucas 3" dynamo with an output of approximately 60 watts. The usual Ariel features of Telescopic front forks, tubular front, spring up rear and prop stands, polished aluminium chaincases and Dunlop tyres are found on these models. Oil gauges and inspection lamps are fitted to both models and rear springing is an optional extra.

Counterparts to the Red Hunters, but rather more docile, are the two o.h.v. "De luxe" models,—the V.G. 497 c.c. and N.G. 347 c.c. models. Both have high efficiency engines with completely enclosed valve and rocker gear, high tensile steel connecting rods and aluminium alloy pistons. Lubrication is on the Ariel dry sump system. The 500 has the single port low-level exhaust system, the 350 is available with either single or double port low level pipes. The usual features of Ariel telescopic forks, magneto ingition, four speed foot change gear boxes and Dunlop tyres, front and rear stands are fitted, but the prop stand on these two models is an extra. Oil gauges and inspection lamps are fitted to both machines and fully sprung rear frames can be fitted as an optional extra. The approximate maximum speeds are 78 m.p.h for the 500 c.c. and 68 for the 350 c.c. models.

The 598 c.c. Side Valve Model V.B. is a machine that will appeal particularly to the sidecar enthusiast. The engine has a bore of 86.4 mm. and a stroke of 102 mm. totally enclosed valve springs, a double roller bearing big end and aluminium alloy pistons with a 5.0 compression ratio, giving a brake horsepower of 15.5 at 4,400 r.p.m. and a maximum speed of approximately 65 m.p.h. Lubrication is on the dry sump system, and a Burman 4 speed foot change gearbox is fitted. Ariel Telescopic forks are standard and the spring frame can be fitted as an optional extra. The prop stand is also an extra on this model. The frame incorporates integral sidecar lugs, and the standard specification includes Dunlop tyres, Smiths speedometer, oil gauge and inspection lamp.

The latest addition to the Ariel range is the new Competition Model "Red Hunter," the 497 c.c. Model V.C.H., which has been evolved as the result of trials and competition experience by such well known riders as Evans, Ray and Vanhouse. Designed with a view to light weight and ease of handling, the 81.8 mm. x 95 mm. engine is claimed to give a b.h.p. of 25 at 6,000 r.p.m. on a 6.8 to 1 compression ratio. The aluminium alloy cylinder barrel has a nickel iron liner, with a six stud fixing to the magnesium alloy crankcase. The aluminium alloy cylinder head has stainless steel valve inserts, highly polished ports, forged steel flywheels, and large diameter mainshafts mounted on two heavy duty roller bearings and one ball bearing, and a large double roller caged big end bearing. The engine is specially bench tested and tuned. Lubrication is on the dry sump system, with dual plunger pumps, and a half gallon capacity separate oil tank. A racing type B.T.H. magneto is fitted. A four speed wide-ratio foot controlled Burman gear box is standard, with a two-plate neoprene clutch, but close ratio gears and a three plate neoprene clutch can be supplied for scrambles machines. The gear box includes built-in speedometer drive. A 54" short wheel-base frame of fully brazed steel tube construction is employed, with polished duralumin mudguards and a polished aluminium oilbath primary chain case. The single port low-level exhaust system has an upswept silencer. Dunlop universal tyres are fitted but special competition tyres are available on request. A fork mounted speedometer is fitted. The dry weight is given as 300 lbs., with a saddle height of 30" and a ground clearance of 5½". Rear springing cannot be fitted to this model.

All Ariel machines can be fitted with the fully sprung rear frame except the Model V.C.H. The quickly detachable rear wheel, which is standard on the Square Four is available as an extra on machines throughout the range, and air filters are also an optional extra for all machines. Ribbed front tyres are available on all models if desired, and an alternative finish of chrome and Ariel green can be specified in lieu of the usual red and chromium or black and chromium finish. All models incorporate Lucas pre-focused type 7½" headlamps with domed glass.

ARIEL 497 c.c. Model V.C.H. o.h.v. Competition Red Hunter

SPECIFICATION

Engine. Make Ariel
Bore and Stroke 81.8 mm. x 95 mm. 497 c.c.
Compression Ratio 6.8 to 1.
B.H.P. 25 at 6,000 r.p.m.
Single cylinder, air cooled, single port, o.h.v. Aluminium alloy cylinder barrel with nickel iron liner. Magnesium alloy crankcase. Aluminium alloy cylinder head with stainless steel valve inserts. Polished ports.
Sparking plugs 14 mm. Engine bench tested and tuned.
Lubrication. Dry sump. Dual plunger pumps.
Carburettor. Amal.
Gearbox. Burman 4 speed, foot change, wide ratio, (standard).
Ratios 19.1, 12.6, 9.16 and 6.05 to 1. (Wide).
15.3, 9.7, 7.2 and 5.75 to 1. (Close).
Clutch. 2 plate Neoprene. 3 plate Neoprene optional.
Transmission. Primary. Chain ½" pitch x 80 links.
Secondary. Chain ⅝" pitch. 91 links.
Ignition. B.T.H. Racing magneto.
Lighting. Nil.
Petrol Capacity. 2½ gallons.
Oil Capacity. ½ gallon.
Tyres. Dunlop Universal 4.00" x 19" rear. 3.00" x 21" (front).
Competition tyres available.
Brakes. 7" front and rear.
Frame and Suspension. Ariel Telescopic Forks. Rigid frame, short wheelbase. Polished duralumin mudguards.
Saddle. Lycett or Terry. **Height from ground** 30"
Wheelbase. 54". **Ground Clearance** 5½".
Overall Length. 7′ 0". **Width over bars** 27".
Weight (dry). 300 lb.
Finish. Polished aluminium primary chaincase, upswept silencer, Smith's fork mounted 120 m.p.h. speedometer. Machine finished chromium and red lined gold.
Equipment.
Extra or optional equipment. Close ratio gears and 3 plate Neoprene Clutch for scramble machines.

ARIEL 598 c.c. Side Valve. Model V.B.

SPECIFICATION

Engine. Make Ariel.
Bore and Stroke 86.4 mm. x 102 mm.
Compression Ratio 5 to 1.
B.H.P. 15.5 at 4,400 r.p.m.
Single cylinder, air cooled, side valve. Totally enclosed valve springs. Double roller bearing big end. Aluminium alloy piston.
Sparking plugs 14 mm.
Lubrication. Dry sump. Double plunger pumps.
Carburettor. Amal.
Gearbox. Burman 4 speed, foot change.
Ratios 12.6, 8.0, 6.0 and 4.7 to 1. (Solo).
15.3, 9.7, 7.2, and 5.7 to 1. (Sidecar).
Clutch. Multiplate.
Transmission. Primary Chain ½" x .305". 81 links.
Secondary. Chain ⅝" x ⅜". 95 links.
Ignition. Lucas Magdyno.
Lighting. Lucas Magdyno 7½" diameter Lucas headlamp.
Petrol Capacity. 3¼ gallons.
Oil Capacity. 6 pints.
Tyres. Dunlop 3.25" x 19", front and rear.
Brakes. 7" front and rear.
Frame and Suspension. Ariel Telescopic forks. Rigid frame. Rear springing optional extra.
Saddle. Lycett or Terry **Height from ground** 30"
Wheelbase. 56". **Ground Clearance** 5".
Overall Length. 7′ 2". **Width over bars** 27".
Weight (dry) 365 lbs.
Finish. Chrome and black lined gold, or chrome and Ariel green, lined gold.
Equipment. Tubular front and spring up rear stands. Smith's 80 m.p.h. Speedometer. Oil gauge and inspection lamp.
Extra or optional equipment. Quickly detachable rear wheel, air filter, rear springing.
Maximum Speed. 1st 21 m.p.h. 2nd 38 m.p.h. 3rd 49 m.p.h. 4th 61 m.p.h.
Speed at end of quarter mile from rest. 51 m.p.h.
Petrol Consumption 45 m.p.h. 70—75 m.p.g.
Braking (from 30 m.p.h. to rest). 48 ft.

ARIEL 997 c.c. Square Four Model 4G.

SPECIFICATION

Engine Make Ariel.
Bore and Stroke. 65 mm. x 75 mm. 997 c.c. (60.8 cu. ins.)
Compression Ratio 6 to 1. 6.8 optional for 80 octane fuel.
B.H.P. 34.5 at 5,400 r.p.m.
Four cylinder, air cooled o.h.v. Aluminium alloy cylinders cast en bloc in square formation. Aluminium alloy cylinder head with valve seat inserts. Twin alloy steel crankshafts. Aluminium alloy connecting rods.
Sparking plugs 14 mm.
Lubrication. Dry sump with dual plunger pump.
Carburettor. Solex.
Gear Box. Burman 4 speed enclosed positive stop foot change.
Ratios. 12.1, 7.7., 5.7 and 4.5 to 1 (Solo)
13.2, 8.4, 6.2 and 4.9 to 1. (Sidecar).
Clutch. Multiplate.
Transmission. Chain ½" x .305" (72 links) Oil bath chaincase.
Secondary Chain ⅝" x ⅜" (91 links).
Ignition. Lucas coil.
Lighting. Lucas 3½" dynamo 70 watt, voltage controlled. 7½" headlamp with 30 watt bulb.
Petrol Capacity. 3½ gallons.
Oil Capacity. ¾ gallon.
Tyres. Dunlop 3.25" x 19" (front). 4.00" x 18" (rear).
Brakes. 7" front and rear.
Frame and Suspension. Rigid frame with integral sidecar lugs. Ariel telescopic forks. Rear springing optional extra.
Saddle. Lycett or Terry. **Height from ground** 30".
Wheelbase. 56" **Ground Clearance** 5".
Overall Length. 7′ 2. **Width over bars** 27"
Weight (dry) (fully equipped) 412 lbs. Spring frame m/cs. 434 lb.
Finish. Chrome and red, lined gold, chrome and black, lined gold or chrome and green, lined gold.
Equipment. Front rear and prop stands. Smith's trip 120 m.p.h. speedometer, ignition warning light, oil gauge, inspection lamp. Quickly detachable rear wheel.
Extra or optional equipment. Fully sprung rear frame. Air cleaner.
Maximum Speed. 2nd 56 m.p.h. 3rd 74 m.p.h. 4th 92 m.p.h.
Speed at end of quarter mile from rest. 55.3 m.p.h.
Petrol Consumption 65—70 m.p.g. (at 45 m.p.h.)
Braking (from 30 m.p.h. to rest). 32 ft.

ARIEL Model V.G. 500 c.c. De Luxe. ARIEL Model N.G. 350 c.c. De Luxe.

SPECIFICATION

Engine. Make Ariel.
Bore and Stroke. 81.8 mm. x 95 mm. 497 c.c. V.G.
72 mm. x 85 mm. 347 c.c. N.G.
Compression Ratio. 6.8 to 1 (V.G.) 6.2 to 1 (N.G.)
High efficiency o.h.v. push rod engine. Enclosed valve and rocker gear. Aluminium alloy piston. Single port low level exhaust (V.G.) Single or twin port low level exhaust (N.G.)
B.H.P. 22 at 4,600 r.p.m. (V.G.) 14.2 at 4,600 r.p.m. (N.G.)
Sparking plugs 14 mm.
Lubrication. Dry sump system, dual plunger pump.
Carburettor. Amal.
Gearbox. Burman 4 speed, foot change.
Ratios 12.6, 8.0, 6.0 and 4.7 to 1. (Solo V.G.)
15.3, 9.7, 7.2 and 5.7 to 1. (Sidecar V.G.)
15.3, 10.1, 7.3 and 5.7 to 1. (Solo N.G.)
Clutch. Multiplate.
Transmission. Primary. Chain ½" x .305".
Secondary. Chain ⅝" x ⅜".
Ignition. Lucas Magdyno.
Lighting. Lucas Magdyno. Lucas 7½" diam. headlamp.
Petrol Capacity. 2½ gallons (N.G.) 3¼ gallons (V.G.)
Oil Capacity. 4 pints (N.G.) 6 pints (V.G.)
Tyres. Dunlop 3.25" x 19", front and rear.
Brakes. 7" front and rear.
Frame and Suspension. Ariel Telescopic forks. Rigid frame. Rear springing optional extra.
Saddle. Lycett or Terry. **Height from Ground.** 30"
Wheelbase. 56". **Ground Clearance** 5".
Overall Length. 7′ 2". **Width over bars** 27".
Weight (dry. 348 lb. (N.G.) 375 lb. (V.G.). Spring frame 22 lb. heavier.
Finish. Chrome and black, lined gold. Chrome and Ariel green, lined gold.
Equipment. Front and rear stands. Smith's 80 m.p.h. speedometer. Oil gauge and inspection lamp.
Extra or optional equipment. Quickly detachable rear wheel, rear springing, air cleaner.
Maximum Speed. 1st 2nd 3rd 4th 78 (V.G.) 68 (N.G.)
Petrol Consumption (at 45 m.p.h.) 75—80 m.p g

Above **Ariel. Model NH. 347 c.c. o.h.v.**
Right **Ariel. Model VB. 598 c.c. s.v.**

ARIEL Model 347 c.c. N.H. "Red Hunter."
ARIEL Model 497 c.c. V.H. "Red Hunter."
SPECIFICATION
Engine. Make Ariel.
  Bore and Stroke 72 mm. x 85 mm. 347 c.c. N.H.
           81.8 mm. x 95 mm. 497 c.c. V.H.
  Compression Ratio 6.2 N.H. 6.8 to 1 V.H.
  B.H.P. 19.4 at 5,600 r.p.m. (N.H.) 24.6 at 6,000 r.p.m. (V.H.)
  Single cylinder, air cooled o.h.v. push rod operated valves, ground and highly polished ports and cylinder head. Polished forged steel flywheels. Aluminium alloy pistons. Engines specially bench tested and tuned.
  Sparking Plugs 14 mm.
Lubrication. Dry sump, with dual plunger pumps.
Carburettor. Amal.
Gearbox. Burman 4 speed, positive stop foot change.
  Ratios. 15.3, 10.1, 7.3 and 5.7 to 1. (N.H.)
          12.6, 8.0, 6.0 and 4.7 to 1. (V.H. Solo.)
          15.3, 9.7, 7.2, and 5.7 to 1. (V.H. Sidecar.)
Clutch.
Transmission. Primary. Chain ½" x .305".
                 Secondary. Chain ⅝" x ⅜".
Ignition. Lucas Magdyno.
Lighting. Lucas Magdyno. Lucas 7½" headlamp.
Petrol Capacity 2¾ gallons (N.H.) 3¼ gallons (V.H.)
Oil Capacity. 4 pints (N.H.) 6 pints (V.H.)
Tyres. Dunlop 3.00" x 20" ribbed front, 3.25" x 19" studded rear.
Brakes. 7" front and rear.
Frame and Suspension. Ariel Telescopic forks. Rigid frame. Rear springing optional extra.
Saddle. Lycett or Terry.   Height from ground 30".
Wheelbase. 56½".   Ground Clearance 5".
Overall Length. 7' 2".   Width over bars 27".
Weight (dry). 348 lb. (N.H.) 375 lb. (V.H.) Spring frame 22 lbs. heavier.
Finish. Chrome and red, lined gold.
Equipment. Rear, front and prop stands. Smith's 120 (V.H.) or 80 m.p.h. (N.H.) Speedometer, oil gauge and inspection lamp.
Extra or optional equipment. Quickly detachable rear wheel. Spring frame Air cleaner. Twin port, low level exhaust system on N.H. model.
Maximum Speed. N.H. 1st — 2nd 48 m.p.h. 3rd 64 m.p.h. 4th 75 m.p.h.
                   V.H. 1st — 2nd 60 m.p.h. 3rd 76 m.p.h. 4th 86 m.p.h.
Speed at end of quarter mile from rest. 50.2 m.p.h. (V.H.) 47.8 m.p.h. (N.H.)
Petrol Consumption 75—80 m.p.g. at 45 m.p.h.
Braking (from 30 m.p.h. to rest). 29 ft. (V.H.) 31 ft. (N.H.)

ARIEL Models K.H. 498 c.c. "Red Hunter" Twin, and Model K.G. 498 c.c De Luxe Twin.
SPECIFICATION
Engine. Make Ariel.
  Bore and Stroke. 63 mm. x 80 mm. 498 c.c.
  Compression Ratio. 6.8 to 1. 7.5 available at option on V.H.
  B.H.P. 24 at 6,000 r.p.m. (K.G.) 26 at 6,500 r.p.m. (K.H.) Twin cylinder, air cooled, vertical o.h.v. Heads and rocker boxes in one casting. Balanced crankshafts forged in one piece. Twin camshafts driven by duplex chain. Light alloy pistons and connecting rods. K.H. engine has polished ports and cylinder heads and is specially tuned.
  Sparking plugs 14 mm.
Lubrication. Dry sump. Double plunger pumps.
Carburettor. Amal single lever (K.G.) Amal large bore with petroflex tubing (K.H.)
Gearbox. Burman 4 speed, foot change.
  Ratios. 15.40, 10.15, 7.40 and 5.75 to 1. (Sidecar).
          13.85, 9.15, 6.65, and 5.20 to 1. (Solo).
Clutch. Multiplate.
Transmission. Primary. Chain ½" x .305".
                 Secondary. Chain ⅝" x ⅜".
Ignition. Lucas or B.T.H. Magneto.
Lighting. Lucas Dynamo. 7½" headlamp.
Petrol Capacity. 3¼ gallons.
Oil Capacity. 6 pints.
Tyres. K.G. Dunlop 3.25" x 19" front. 3.50" x 19" rear.
          K.H. Dunlop 3.00" x 20" ribbed front. 3.50" x 19" rear.
Brakes. 7" front and rear.
Frame and Suspension. Ariel Telescopic forks. Rigid frame. Rear springing optional extra.
Saddle. Lycett or Terry.   Height from ground 30".
Wheelbase. 56".   Ground Clearance 5".
Overall Length. 7' 2".   Width over bars 27".
Weight (dry). K.G. 384 lb. K.H. 384 lb. Spring frame models 22 lb. heavier.
Finish. Model K.H. Chrome and red, lined gold.
           K.G. Chrome and black or green, lined gold.
Equipment. Front, rear and prop stands. Smith's 120 m.p.h. speedometer, Oil gauge and inspection lamp.
Extra or optional equipment. Quickly detachable rear wheel, air cleaner, spring frame.
Maximum Speed. 85 m.p.h.(K.G.) 90 m.p.h. (K.H.)
Petrol Consumption (at 45 m.p.h.) 75—80 m.p.g.

STOP PRESS

Models NG and VG are not included in the 1951 range, but may be reinstated at a later date.

All models now have ammeter and light switches transferred to headlamp. The tank top instrument panel disappears, increasing petrol capacity by ¼ gallon.

Model 4G. An 8" rear break is now fitted, instead of 7".

A 20 ampere hour battery replaces the previous 12 a.h.

Bond

**BOND AIRCRAFT & ENGINEERING CO. LTD.
TOWNELEY · LONGRIDGE · LANCS.**

The Bond Minibyke, is one of the latest of a growing number of 98 c.c. lightweights to appear on the British market. The design is most unorthodox, not to say revolutionary, nevertheless the appearance of the machine is extremely neat and workmanlike. The manufacturers claim a cruising speed of from 35-40 m.p.h., with a maximum of 45 m.p.h., and a petrol consumption in the region of 200 miles per gallon, and if these figures are borne out in practice, the performance is certainly well above the average for this type of machine.

The frame of the Bond is of exclusive and original design, and is the result of long experience in the aircraft industry, and embodies a number of features which are quite novel to motor cycle design. It is built almost entirely of aluminium alloys, using fabricated sheet panels and alloy castings, scientifically designed and built into a single stressed skin structure of great strength and extraordinary lightness. The engine itself is suspended in a light steel cradle, which is designed to isolate vibration from the rest of the machine. At the same time the frame and fairings ensure very adequate weather protection for the rider, a measure of streamlining, and provide a motor cycle which is exceptionally easy to clean down. Disc pattern pressed steel 8" wheels are fitted, and these are of the split rim type, enabling tyres to be quickly and easily removed without the use of tyre levers. Large fairings cover both the front and rear wheels, and give excellent protection from mud and dirt, at the same time lending a neat appearance to the machine. The rear fairing carries a light metal carrier, on which is suspended the tool bag, and the rear lamp and number plate. It also provides the rear mounting for the sprung saddle. A pair of really efficient looking leg shields add to the weather protection of the rider. The strong and resilient front forks are of tubular construction.

The power unit is the Villiers Mark 1F, with two speed gearbox in unit construction. The 98 c.c. engine has a bore and stroke of 47 mm. x 57 mm., a detachable aluminium alloy cylinder head, flat top aluminium alloy piston, ball bearing crankshaft and roller bearing big end. Transmission is by a primary chain running in an oil bath and a cork insert two plate clutch running in oil. A folding kickstarter is fitted. All gears are constant mesh, with sliding dog operated by a finger-tip control lever mounted on the handlebars.

Ignition and lighting is, of course, by Villiers flywheel magneto and the lighting equipment comprises a 5½" headlamp containing a parking battery. A dipping switch is mounted on the handlebars.

The eight inch wheels carry ultra low pressure 16" x 4.5" tyres, and four inch internal expanding brakes are fitted front and rear. The 1½ gallon capacity tank is built inside the stressed skin backbone of the machine, with the filler cap in an accessible position. The whole machine is attractively finished in polychromatic blue, with chromium plated handlebars, exhaust pipe and silencer.

The future development and performance of this novel little machine, will, without doubt, be watched with interest by a large section of the motor-cycling public.

BOND 98 c.c. MINIBYKE.

SPECIFICATION.

Engine. Make. Villiers. Mark 1F.
  Bore and Stroke. 47 mm. x 57 mm. 98 c.c.
  Compression Ratio. 8 to 1. Approximate b.h.p. 2.8 at 4,000 r.p.m.
  Single cylinder, two stroke, air cooled, single port.
  Flat top aluminium alloy piston, ball bearing crankshaft, roller bearing big end. Detachable aluminium alloy cylinder head.
  Sparking plug. 14 mm.
Lubrication. Petroil system.
Carburettor. Villiers single lever with air cleaner and strangler.
Gearbox. 2 speed unit construction. Constant mesh gears with sliding dog. Folding kickstarter. Handlebar gear lever control.
  Ratios. 1st 7.64 to 1. Top, 4.94 to 1.
Clutch. Cork insert two plate clutch, running in oil.
Transmission. Primary. Chain in oil bath chain case, ¼" pitch.
  Secondary. Chain 96 links x ¼" pitch.
Ignition. Villiers flywheel magneto.
Lighting. Villiers flywheel magneto. 5½" headlamp with parking battery, rear light and dipping switch.
Petroil Capacity. Tank. 1¼ gallons capacity.
Oil Capacity. Petroil system.
Tyres. 4.5 x 16" ultra low pressure, front and rear, Goodyear.
Brakes. Internal expanding 4" front and rear.
Frame and Suspension. Aluminium alloy, with fabricated sheet panels and alloy castings, built into single stressed skin structure. Engine suspended in light steel cradle. Tubular front forks.
Saddle. Soft top mattress type saddle. **Height from ground.** 26"
Wheelbase. 47". **Ground Clearance.** 5".
Width over bars. 23". **Overall length.** 69".
Weight (dry). 91 lbs.
Finish. Whole machine finished in Polychromatic blue, handlebars exhaust pipe and silencer chromium plated.
Equipment. Horn, number plates, electric lighting set, rear carrier, toolbag, legshields.
Maximum speed in gears. 1st 29 m.p.h. Top 45 m.p.h.
Speed at end of ¼ mile from rest 45 m.p.h.
Petrol consumption (at 30 m.p.h.) 200 m.p.g.
Stopping distance in feet (from 30 m.p.h.) (Dry road surface) 45 ft.
An additional model is now on offer:—Bond Minibyke " De Luxe " Model Specification as standard, but telescopic front forks.
Weight. 94 lb.

Bown

BOWN CYCLE COMPANY LTD.
LLWYNYPIA · GLAMORGAN

The name of Bown has a long and honourable record in the Cycle and allied industries, dating back to the latter half of last century. The latest of a long line of thoroughbred machines—this time an Auto-cycle, known as the " Bown Auto-Roadster," was introduced in 1950.

The whole design and layout has obviously been studied carefully to provide safety, stability and simplicity of control, together with a degree of luxury, comfort and accessibility not always associated with the normal auto-cycle.

The engine unit is the Villiers 98 c.c. Mark 2F, with detachable cylinder head and deflectorless piston, the two plate cork insert type clutch being incorporated in the engine unit. A Villiers Junior single lever carburettor is fitted, and the air strangler lever is secured by a bracket at the base of the petrol tank, and can therefore be manipulated with ease. The engine is well silenced.

The Villiers flywheel magneto provides ignition and lighting, a 3½" headlamp being fitted, with an independent parking light and a 6 volt, 12 watt bulb.

The frame, which is hand built throughout, is of the twin-tube cradle type, the angles of the frame being expressly designed to provide light steering and good control under all conditions. This frame gives a 3 point suspension for the Villiers engine. Pressed steel link action forks with a central compression spring give added comfort. Transmission is by heavy roller chain, ½" pitch, with independent adjustment on main and pedal drive. The rear chain is exceptionally well guarded. The internal expanding brakes—3½" front and 4" rear are independently adjustable, and the wheels, built with heavy gauge spokes, have depressed rims and Dunlop 2.25" x 21" tyres. A large well sprung Wrights mattress saddle is fitted.

The all steel welded tank has a capacity of 1¼ gallons and the push type petrol tap is situated in a convenient position. Handlebars and wheel rims are chromium plated. The finish is excellent, all enamel parts being Bonderized, followed by a coat of anti-rust primer, the final finish being in maroon enamel, heavily gold lined. Equipment supplied includes a tubular rear carrier, and clip-up stand, front and rear number plates, a Brooks tool bag with tool kit, licence holder and Bluemels pump. A Smith's lightweight speedometer can be supplied as an optional extra.

The machine weighs approximately 127 lb. with a wheelbase of 48¼" and a ground clearance of 4". Petrol consumption is approximately 150 miles per gallon.

The Bown, with its attractive features of reliability, economy and stability is light to handle and requires little storage space, whilst riding comfort is increased by the oversize tyres, sprung mattress saddle and link action forks. Ease of cleaning has also been thought of, and the engine is protected by efficient shields, and the rear roller chain runs in an oil bath case.

SPECIFICATION. BOWN AUTO-CYCLE.

Engine. Make, Villiers, Mark 2F.
  Bore and Stroke. 47 mm. x. 57 mm. 98 c.c.
  Compression Ratio. 8 to 1.
  B.H.P. Approx. 2.0 at 3,750 r.p.m.
  Single cylinder, two stroke, air cooled. single port, Flat topped piston, aluminium detachable cylinder head.
  Sparking plugs. 14 mm.
Lubrication. Petroil system.
Carburettor. Villiers Junior.
Gearbox. Single speed.
  Ratios. Final drive ratio 10.76 to 1.
Clutch. Two plate cork insert type. Runs in oil.
Transmission. Primary. Chain ⅜" x .225".
  Secondary. Chain, heavy ½" x 3/16". 118 links. Oil bath chain case.
Ignition. Villiers flywheel magneto.
Lighting. Villiers direct lighting from flywheel magneto. 3½" headlamp. 6 volt 12 watt bulb. Independent parking lamp.
Petrol Capacity. 1¼ gallons.
Tyres. Dunlop, 2.25" x 21", front and rear.
Brakes. Internal expanding, 3½" diameter front, 4" diameter, rear.
Frame and Suspension. Twin tube cradle frame, with 3 point engine suspension. Pressed steel link action forks, with central compression spring.
Saddle. Wrights.   **Height from ground.** 32".
Wheelbase. 48¼".   **Ground clearance.** 4".
Overall Length. 6' 5".   **Width over bars.** 22½".
Weight (dry). 120 lb.
Finish. Maroon and gold lines. Frame stove enamelled black. Bright parts chromium plated.
Equipment. Tool kit, pump, engine shields, licence holder, front and rear number plates, tubular rear carrier and stand.
Extra or optional equipment. Smith's Lightweight Speedometer.
Petrol Consumption (at 30 m.p.h.) approx. 150 m.p.g.

B.S.A. Model A7 "Star Twin." 495 c.c. Vertical Twin.

B.S.A.

B.S.A., CYCLES LTD.
SMALL HEATH, BIRMINGHAM, 11.

U.S.A. East Coast Distributor:
RICH CHILD CYCLE CO., INC.
639 Passaic Ave. Nutley, New Jersey

U.S.A. West Coast Distributor:
HAP ALZINA
3074 Broadway Oakland, Calif.

B.S.A. are the world's largest motor cycle manufacturers—hence the slogan which the company adopted in 1922—" One in four is a B.S.A."

The Birmingham Small Arms Company was formed in 1861, from members of the Birmingham Small Arms Trade, as a result of the increasing competition from the Government Arms Factory at Enfield, which had started to produce machine made weapons in 1855. The Birmingham gunsmiths, whose arms were handmade, were therefore forced to co-operate to buy machinery or face extinction.

The new company's first step was to buy its present site at Small Heath, and shortly afterwards it began the production of Enfield rifles. A severe slump in the arms trade in 1878 however, led the company to consider the manufacture of bicycles and, as a result, a cycle invented by a Mr. Otto was produced in 1880, the year in which the company adopted its present well known trademark of the " Piled Arms." A revival of Government contracts, and the outbreak of the Boer War, caused the manufacture of cycles to be discontinued for a considerable period, and production was not begun again until 1908—an interval of 21 years. The first motor cycle was brought out in 1910—the same year that the company took over the firm of Daimler, and shortly afterwards machines were being produced in large numbers for service in the first World War.

Today there are no fewer than 26 companies within the B.S.A. organisation, eleven of these being controlled directly from Small Heath, and including Sunbeam and New Hudson motorcycles.

At the end of the first World War, the production of motorcycles for the civilian market was resumed, and the reputation of B.S.A.'s for reliability and efficiency was so great that in 1934 the company was responsible for 27% of the motor cycle exports of the country. Home sales were stimulated as a result of successes in trials and competitions, and special tests, which included such spectacular feats as a 20,000 mile trip, entailing a crossing of the Andes, and a test over a complete circuit of the coastline of England and Wales, resulted in large contracts from the Post Office, the Automobile Association, Scotland Yard and other official bodies. Collaboration between the War Office and the company resulted in 1932 in the introduction of a special 500 c.c. twin.

In 1939 the company was once again called upon to supply machines to the armed forces in great numbers, and despite severe bomb damage to the chief B.S.A. works at Small Heath, produced no less than 126,000 of the 425,000 machines supplied to the War Office by British manufacturers. In addition, astronomical numbers of rifles, machine and cannon guns, anti-tank guns and rocket projectiles were produced under conditions of the utmost difficulty.

B.S.A.'s have always been notable for their clean and efficient design, and their range has consistently been a very wide one, incorporating machines of every size and type to appeal to all grades of rider. The current range, with alternative specifications on various machines, includes no fewer than 20 models, the largest of any British manufacturer.

Smallest in the range, and probably one of the most popular, is the B.S.A. "Bantam" 123 c.c. two stroke lightweight, which is available in standard, de luxe or competition forms. This little machine has an engine of 52mm. bore x 58 mm. stroke, with 3 speed gear in unit. The engine has a roller bearing big end, ball bearings support the mainshaft, and a domed aluminium alloy piston is fitted and the aluminium alloy cylinder head is detachable. The cork insert clutch runs in oil. A Wico-Pacey flywheel magneto supplies the lighting set, Dunlop 2.75" x 19" tyres are fitted front and rear and telescopic front forks, with a single helical spring in each leg. 5" internal expanding brakes are fitted front and rear. The machine has a maximum speed of approximately 47 m.p.h., with a petrol consumption, (at 30 m.p.h.) in the region of 160 m.p.g. It is attractively finished in pastel green, cream and chromium. A foot gear change and well valanced mudguards are other desirable features. The De Luxe version of the Bantam incorporates plunger type rear springing, Lucas rectified current lighting set and battery, and coil ignition. The Competition "Bantam" has plain blade mudguards, a 3.25" x 19" rear tyre, a saddle position 2" higher than standard, upswept exhaust system, lower gear ratios, folding kickstarter, decompressor and adjustable footrests.

The Model C10, which is the only 250 c.c. side valve machine on the British market, is of clean and straightforward design. The engine has a cast iron cylinder barrel, with aluminium alloy detachable head, and roller bearing big end. Lubrication is by dry sump and double gear pump, and a 3 speed foot change gearbox is fitted.

Ignition is by Lucas coil, while a Lucas dynamo looks after the lighting requirements. Dunlop 3.00" x 19" tyres, and 5½" internal expanding brakes are fitted, front and rear, and the rigid frame is equipped with B.S.A. Telescopic hydraulic forks. Legshields, pillion seat and rests and a prop stand can be supplied as extras on this machine, which weighs, in standard form, 270 lb.

Two further side valve machines are included in the B.S.A. range—Models M 20 and M 21, both to the same general specification and eminently suitable for sidecar work. The M 20 has a bore and stroke of 82 mm. x 94 mm (496 c.c.), whilst in the M 21 the stroke is increased to 112 mm., giving a total capacity of 591 c.c. Both models are available with either solo or sidecar ratios. The single port, side valve engines have cast iron cylinder barrels and heads, high tensile steel connecting rods and roller bearing big ends. The dry sump lubrication system follows standard B.S.A. practice, and 4 speed foot change gearboxes are fitted. A Lucas 6 volt, 60 watt Magdyno is supplied. The M 20 has Dunlop 3.25" x 19" tyres front and rear, but the M 21 has a 3.50" x 19" rear tyre. Both models have 7" internal expanding brakes, and B.S.A. telescopic forks and rigid frames. The standard finish is a silver tank and black wheels, but an alternative matt silver and chromium finish can be supplied.

Turning now to the o.h.v. models, the smallest in the range are the 249 c.c. o.h.v. C11 and C11 de Luxe machines. These have a cast iron cylinder head and barrel, high tensile steel connecting rod and roller bearing big end. Like the C10 side valve machine, coil ignition is used. Specification includes a 3 speed foot change gearbox, B.S.A. Telescopic hydraulic Forks, rigid frame and 3.00" x 20" tyres.

Three "350"s are listed. Firstly the 348 c.c. o.h.v. Model B31, with an engine of 71 mm. bore x 88 mm. stroke. This machine has a cast iron cylinder barrel and head, high tensile steel connecting rod, roller bearing

B.S.A. Model D1. "Bantam De Luxe."

big end and a compression ratio of 6.5 to 1, and develops approximately 17 b.h.p. at 5,500 r.p.m. A 4 speed foot change box is fitted, and ignition is by Lucas magdyno. Telescopic hydraulic forks and a rigid frame are standard specification, but a fully sprung rear frame can be supplied as an optional extra. 7" brakes are provided and the machine is well finished in green and chromium.

A competition version of the B31 should make an immediate appeal to trials and scrambles riders, and is based on actual B.S.A. machines which have gained a most impressive list of premier awards in these events. Bascially the same as Model B 31, the B 32 has an upswept exhaust system, but the standard downswept pipes can be supplied if required. Gear ratios of 21.1, 14.5, 9.3 and 7.1 to 1 have been selected for trials work, and the machine is offered with magneto and bulb horn, or with madgyno. The magneto is a Lucas waterproof. Tyres are 2.75" x 21" front and 4.00" x 19" rear. Telescopic forks and rigid frame are standard, but a fully sprung rear frame can be supplied as an extra on machines with the downswept exhaust system only. The ground clearance is increased to 6¼", as against 5" for the B 31. An alloy cylinder head and barrel can be supplied on this machine for an extra £10. Close ratio gears are also available. The model is finished in green and chromium, with chromium plated guards.

A larger counterpart of this machine, the B 34 Competition model, follows the same specification, but has an engine of 85 mm. x 88 mm., giving a capacity of 499 c.c. The alloy engine and head and spring frame are again optional extras, but the "500" is finished in red and chromium.

The 350 B 32 "Gold Star," which was introduced for the 1949 season, and has proved exceptionally popular, is again in production, accompanied by a larger 500 c.c. edition. Based on the B 31 "350" design, the engines have an aluminium alloy cylinder head and barrel, and are specially tuned and bench tested. The specification is elastic, since port sizes, valve springs, cams, compression and gear ratios can be supplied to suit trials, scrambles, road racing or touring work. For road racing purposes the foot gear change pedal can be fitted in the rearward position with the mechanism inside the box modified to give the normal movement—i.e. the pedal raised to engage a lower gear and conversely. An internal expanding front brake of 8" diameter is now fitted—a feature that will be appreciated by racing men—the rear brake is 7" diameter. Telescopic hydraulic forks are fitted, and plunger type rear suspension, with a quickly detachable rear wheel is a standard fitment on both models. A Lucas magneto or Lucas magdyno can be supplied as required. Tyres sizes are 2.75" x 21" front and 4.00" x 19" rear, and ground clearance is 6¼".

Two 499 c.c. o.h.v. machines complete the range of singles. These are the B33 and M33 models, the M33 being provided with sidecar lugs in the frame and also has the choice of sidecar ratios. This machine is also fitted with a rear stand. A fully sprung rear frame can be fitted on the B33 as an extra, but not on model M33. The o.h.v. engines have a cast iron cylinder barrel and head and 4 speed foot change gear box, with the standard B.S.A. dry sump system of lubrication. Ignition and lighting is by Lucas magdyno, tyres are 3.25" x 19" front and 3.50" x 19" rear, both Dunlop. 7" diameter brakes front and rear and B.S.A. Telescopic hydraulic forks and 3 gallon petrol tanks are fitted to both models. These two "500"s are finished with a silver and chromium tank, but the B33 can be supplied with a Devon Red and chromium finish at a small extra charge.

B.S.A. Twins have already proved exceptionally popular, and a third model of 650 c.c. has been added to the two "500"s. The 495 c.c. o.h.v. vertical twin A7 has a cast iron cylinder barrel and head, and a twin port exhaust system. The big end is an indium-lead-bronze plain bearing. The tappets are operated by a single camshaft at the rear of the engine. The duralumin

B.S.A.
Model C 10
249 c.c. S.V.

B.S.A.
Model B 32
348 c.c. o.h.v.

push rods have specially shaped steel ends and an adequate oil supply is fed to the two overhead rocker spindles. The Amal carburettor is fitted with a built-in air cleaner, and a separate Lucas magneto is fitted, with an automatic advance mechanism. Compression ratio is 6.6 to 1, with a b.h.p. of approximately 25 at 5,800 r.p.m. The 4 speed positive stop foot change gearbox can be supplied with either solo or sidecar ratios, and the frame incorporates sidecar lugs. On the A7 Telescopic hydraulic front forks are fitted, and a rigid rear frame. Plunger type suspension is optional. Front and rear brakes are 7″ diameter. A quickly detachable rear wheel is a standard fitting. Petrol tank capacity is 3½ gallons.

The 495 c.c. A7 " Star Twin " is basically the same as the A7, but has a specially modified engine with high compression pistons (compression ratio 7 to 1) and twin Amal carburettors with flame traps. Plunger type rear suspension, which employs rebound and compression springs is a part of the standard specification for Star Twins however. Tyres (as on the A7) are 3.25″ x 19″ front and 3.50″ x 19″ rear. B.h.p. of the Star Twin is given as 29 at 6,000 r.p.m.

The latest twin, the 650 c.c. o.h.v. " Golden Flash " has an engine of 70 mm. bore x 84 mm. stroke—a total capacity of 646 c.c.

The two cylinders are placed side by side, and the two light alloy connecting rods operate on a one-piece forged steel crankshaft with a central flywheel and bobweight. Indium lead-bronze plain bearings are fitted to the big end as in the A7 models. The main bearing on the drive side is of the roller type. The cylinder head, which has been redesigned for this model is adequately finned. A single aluminium alloy rocker box is fitted in lieu of the twin boxes on the A7 models. A single camshaft at the rear operates the valves, which are set at 85°, through rockers and push rods. The camshafts are not interchangeable with the A7 models however, since the cams in the 650 c.c. model are wider, giving more surface area. Barrel type tappets are fitted, and these have chilled rubbing surfaces. Alumiuium alloy plates allow of easy access to adjust the tappets. The tappet system is copiously lubricated. The engine, which has a maximum b.h.p. of 35, has been developed with an eye to flexibility and slogging at low revolutions, and on solo work is fully equal to pulling a high gear.

Gear box and clutch are identical with the A7 models, but the front brake drum is an 8″ mechanite casting, brake shoes and shoe plates being of aluminium alloy. The duplex cradle frame has Telescopic hydraulic forks. Plunger type rear suspension is an optional fitting. The rear wheel is quickly detachable and sidecar lugs are incorporated in the frame. The Amal carburettor has a built-in air cleaner, and a separate Lucas magneto provides ignition. A Lucas c.v.c. dynamo supplies the lighting set and horn. Several very attractive finishes are offered, including black and chromium, and polychromatic beige and chromium. This machine is so versatile that it provides an unprecedented sidecar performance and should satisfy the most ardent high speed enthusiast.

The motor cyclist who cannot find his requirements in the B.S.A. range must indeed be difficult to please.

B.S.A. 123 c.c. D.1 " Bantam " and D.1 " Bantam " Competition Models. D1 " Bantam De Luxe " Model

SPECIFICATION

Engine. Make B.S.A.
Bore and Stroke. 52 mm. x 58 mm. 123 c.c.
B.H.P. 4.5 at 5,000 r.p.m.
Single cylinder, air cooled two stroke. Detachable aluminium alloy cylinder head.
Sparking plugs 14 mm. Champion L 10.
Lubrication. Petroil.
Carburettor. Amal 261/001D.
Gearbox. 3 speed, foot change.
Ratios. 22.0, 11.7 and 7.0 to 1.
Competition 27.1, 14.50, and 8.65 to 1.
Clutch. Wet, 2 plate, cork inserts.
Transmission. Primary. Chain .375″ pitch x .250″ roller dia.
Secondary. Chain .5″ pitch x .335″ roller dia.
Ignition. F.W. 1005Z Wipac Genimag.
Lighting. F.W. 1005Z Wipac.
Petrol Capacity. 1¾ gallons Petroil.
Tyres. 2.75″ x 19″ front and rear.
Competition 2.75″ x 19″ front. 3.25″ x 19″ rear.
Brakes. 5″ front and rear.
Frame and Suspension. B.S.A. Telescopic forks. Rigid frame.
Saddle. Mansfield/Wrights. **Height from ground.** 27″. Comp. 29″.
Wheelbase. 50″. **Ground Clearance.** Bantam 4¾″. Comp. model 7″.
Overall Length. 77″ **Width over bars.** 26½″
Weight (dry). 153 lb. Comp. Model 167 lb.
Finish. Pastel green and chromium.
Equipment. Competition Model has plain blade mudguards, upswept exhaust system, folding kickstarter, adjustable footrests and decompressor. Speedometer.
Extra or optional equipment. Lucas Battery Lighting Set, electric horn, legshields. Plunger type rear springing.
Maximum Speed. 1st — 2nd 37 m.p.h. 3rd 49 m.p.h.
Speed at end of quarter mile from rest 33.3 m.p.h.
Petrol Consumption (at 30 m.p.h.) 160 m.p.g. (approx.)
Braking (from 30 m.p.h. to rest). 22½ ft.
De Luxe Model as Standard, but with plunger type rear springing, Lucas rectified current lighting set, coil ignition, and modified exhaust system.

B.S.A. 249 c.c. Side Valve. Model C10.

SPECIFICATION

Engine. Make B.S.A.
Bore and Stroke. 63 mm. x 80 mm. 249 c.c.
Compression Ratio 5 to 1.
B.H.P. Approx. 8 at 5,000 r.p.m.
Single cylinder, air cooled, side valve. Cast iron cylinder barrel, aluminium alloy detachable head. Roller bearing big end.
Sparking plugs 14 mm. Champion N 8
Lubrication. Dry Sump. Double gear pump.
Carburettor. Amal 274K/3A.
Gearbox. 3 speed, positive stop foot change.
Ratios. 14.5, 9.8, and 6.6. to 1.
Clutch. Dry, 2 plate, fabric inserts.
Transmission. Primary. Chain ½″ x .305″.
Secondary. Chain ½″ x .305″.
Ignition. Lucas coil. Automatic advance.
Lighting. Lucas Dynamo.
Petrol Capacity. 2½ gallons.
Oil Capacity. 4 pints.
Tyres. 3.00″ x 19″, front and rear. (Dunlop.)
Brakes. 5½″, front and rear.
Frame and Suspension. B.S.A. Telescopic hydraulic forks and rigid frame.
Saddle. Terry. **Height from Ground** 28″.
Wheelbase. 52″. **Ground Clearance.** 4½″.
Overall Length. 80½″ **Width over bars.** 26½″.
Weight (dry). 270 lb.
Finish. Silver and chromium tank. Black wheels.
Equipment. Electric horn, toolkit, pump, licence holder, rear carrier. Speedometer.
Extra or optional equipment. Legshields, pillion seat, pillion rests, prop stand.
Maximum Speed. 1st 26 m.p.h. 2nd 42 m.p.h. 3rd 55 m.p.h.
Speed at end of quarter mile from rest 36 m.p.h.
Petrol Consumption (at 30 m.p.h.) 110 m.p.g.
Braking (from 30 m.p.h. to rest). 34 ft.

B.S.A. 496 c.c. Side Valve. Model M20.
B.S.A. 591 c.c. Side Valve. Model M21.

SPECIFICATION

Engine. Make B.S.A.
Bore and Stroke M20 82 mm. x 94 mm. 496 c.c.
M21 82 mm. x 112 mm. 591 c.c.
Compression Ratio M20 4.9 to 1. M21 5.0 to 1.
B.H.P. M20 Approx. 13 at 4,200 r.p.m.
M21 Approx 15 at 4,000 r.p.m.
Single cylinder, air cooled, side valve, single port. Cast iron cylinder barrel and head, high tensile steel connecting rod, Roller bearing big end.
Sparking plugs 14 mm. Champion L 10
Lubrication. Dry sump and double gear pump.
Carburettor. M20 Amal 276C/1B.
M21 Amal 276BR/1B.
Gearbox. 4 speed positive stop, foot change.
Ratios M20 15.8, 10.9, 7.0 and 5.3 to 1. (Solo)
17.7, 12.2, 7.82 and 5.94 to 1. (Sidecar).
M21 14 15, 9.77, 6.25 and 4.75 to 1. (Solo)
17.7, 12.2, 7.8 and 5.9 to 1. (Sidecar).
Clutch. Dry, 5 plate, fabric inserts.
Transmission. Primary. Chain ½″ x .305″.
Secondary. Chain ⅝″ x ¼″.
Ignition. Lucas Magdyno.
Lighting. Lucas Magdyno 6 volt, 60 watt. Compensated voltage control.
Petrol Capacity. 3 gallons.
Oil Capacity. 5 pints.
Tyres. M20 3.25″ x 19″ front and rear. (Dunlop.)
M21 3.25″ x 19″ front. 3.50″ x 19″ rear. (Dunlop).
Brakes. 7″ Internal expanding, front and rear.
Frame and Suspension. Telescopic Hydraulic forks and rigid frame.
Saddle. Terry. **Height from Ground.** 30½″,
Wheelbase. 54″. **Ground Clearance** 5½″.
Overall Length. 85″. **Width over bars.** 28″.
Weight (dry). M20 369 lb. M21 370 lb.
Finish. Silver tank and black wheels. Frame stove enamelled black. Bright parts chromium plated.
Equipment. Electric horn, tool kit, pump, licence holder. Speedometer.
Extra or optional equipment. Pillion seat, carrier, pillion footrests, prop stand Matt silver and chromium finish extra.
Maximum Speed. M20 62 m.p.h. M21 65 m.p.h.
Petrol Consumption. (at 30 m.p.h.) 70 m.p.g.
Braking (from 30 mp.h. to rest). 32 ft.

B.S.A. 249 c.c. o.h.v. Models C11 and C11 De Luxe.

SPECIFICATION

Engine. Make B.S.A.
Bore and Stroke. 63 mm. x 80 mm. 294 c.c.
Compression Ratio 6.5 to 1.
B.H.P. approx. 11 at 5,400 r.p.m.
Single cylinder, air cooled, o.h.v. Cast iron cylinder head and barrel. High tensile steel connecting rod. Roller bearing big end. Gear driven timing gear.
Sparking plugs 14 mm. Champion L 10s.
Lubrication. Dry sump. Double gear pump.
Carburettor. Amal 274AU/1DA.

Gear Box. 3 speed, positive stop, foot change.
Ratios. 14.5, 9.8 and 6.6 to 1.
Clutch. Dry, 2 plate, fabric inserts.
Transmission. Primary. Chain ½" x .305".
Secondary. Chain ½" x .305".
Ignition. Lucas coil with automatic advance.
Lighting. Lucas dynamo.
Petrol Capacity. 2½ gallons.
Oil Capacity. 4 pints.
Tyres. 3.00" x 20", front and rear (Dunlop).
Brakes. 5½" front and rear.
Frame and Suspension. B.S.A. Telescopic Hydraulic forks and rigid frame.
Saddle. Terry. **Height from ground.** 28½".
Wheelbase. 52". **Ground Clearance.** 5".
Overall Length. 80½". **Width over bars.** 26".
Weight (dry). 284 lbs.
Finish. C11 De Luxe. Tank and wheels blue and chromium.
Equipment. Electric horn, toolkit, pump, licence holder. Speedometer.
Extra or optional equipment. Legshields, pillion seat, carrier, pillion rests, prop stand.
Maximum Speed. 1st 28 m.p.h. 2nd 47 m.p.h. 3rd 65 m.p.h.
Speed at end of quarter mile from rest. 41.3 m.p.h.
Petrol Consumption (at 30 m.p.h.) 120 m.p.g.
Braking (from 30 m.p.h. to rest). 34 ft.

B.S.A. 348 c.c. o.h.v. Model B31.

SPECIFICATION

Engine. Make B.S.A.
Bore and Stroke. 71 mm. x 88 mm. 348 c.c.
Compression Ratio. 6.5 to 1.
B.H.P. approx. 17 at 5,500 r.p.m.
Single cylinder, o.h.v. air cooled, single port. Cast iron cylinder barrel and head. High tensile steel connecting rod. Roller bearing big end.
Sparking plugs 14 mm. Champion L 10 s.
Lubrication. Dry sump and double gear pump.
Carburettor. Amal 276AW/1BB.
Gear Box. 4 speed, positive stop, foot change.
Ratios. 16.7, 11.5, 7.38 and 5.6 to 1.
Clutch. Dry, 4 plate, fabric inserts.
Transmission. Primary. Chain ½" x .305".
Secondary. Chain ⅝" x ¼".
Ignition. Lucas Magdyno.
Lighting. Lucas Magdyno. 6 volt. 60 watt compensated voltage control, sealed beam headlamp, electric horn.
Petrol Capacity. 3 gallons.
Oil Capacity. ½ gallon.
Tyres. 3.25" x 19", front and rear. (Dunlop).
Brakes. 7", expanding front and rear.
Frame and Suspension. B.S.A. Telescopic hydraulic forks and rigid frame. (Spring frame optional extra).
Saddle. Terry/Wrights. **Height from ground.** 30½".
Wheelbase. 54". **Ground Clearance.** 5".
Overall Length. 82". **Width over bars.** 28".
Weight (dry). 343 lbs.
Finish. Green and chromium. Frame stove enamelled black. Bright parts chromium plated.
Equipment. Electric horn, toolkit, pump, licence holder. Speedometer.
Extra or optional equipment. Fully sprung rear frame, pillion seat, pillion rests. prop stand.
Maximum Speed. 1st 32 m.p.h. 2nd 45 m.p.h. 3rd 68 m.p.h. 4th 73 m.p.h.
Speed at end of quarter mile from rest. 41.28 m.p.h.
Petrol Consumption (at 30 m.p.h.) 107 m.p.g.
Braking (from 30 m.p.h. to rest). 33 ft.

B.S.A. 348 c.c. o.h.v. B32 Competition Model.
B.S.A. 499 c.c. o.h.v. B34 Competition Model.

SPECIFICATION

Engine. Make B.S.A.
Bore and Stroke. B32 71 mm. x 88 mm. 348 c.c.
B34 85 mm. x 88 mm. 499 c.c.
Compression Ratio. B32 6.5 to 1. B34 6.8 to 1.
B.H.P. B32 approx. 17 at 5,500 r.p.m. B34 approx. 23 at 5,500 r.pm.
Single cylinder, o.h.v., air cooled, single port. Cast iron cylinder barrel and head. (Alloy cylinder barrel and head available at extra cost). Roller bearing big end. Upswept exhaust system. (Downswept optional).
Sparking plugs 14 mm. Champion L 10 s.
Lubrication. Dry sump and double gear pump.
Carburettor. B32 Amal 276AW/1BB. B34 Amal 289G/1AT.
Gear Box. 4 speed, positive stop, foot change.
Ratios. B32 21.1, 14.5, 9.3 and 7.1 to 1.
B34 16.8, 11.6, 7.4 and 5.6 to 1.
Clutch. Dry, 5 plate, fabric inserts.
Transmission. Primary. Chain ½" x .305".
Secondary. Chain ⅝" x ¼".
Ignition. Lucas waterproof magneto. (Magdyno available at extra charge).
Lighting. Optional extra.
Petrol Capacity. 3 gallons. (2 gallon tank to order).
Oil Capacity. ½ gallon.
Tyres. B32 2.75" x 21", front. 4.00" x 19", rear.
B34 as above.
Brakes. Internal expanding, 7", front and rear.
Frame and Suspension. B.S.A. Telescopic hydraulic forks and rigid frame. Fully sprung rear frame extra (with downswept exhaust system only).
Saddle. Terry/Wrights **Height from ground.** 31½".
Wheelbase. 54". **Ground Clearance.** 6½".
Overall Length. 82". **Width over bars.** 28".
Weight (dry). B32 320 lb. B34 330 lb.
Finish. B32 Green and chromium. B34 Red and chromium. Frame stove enamelled black. Bright parts chromium plated. Chromium mudguards.
Equipment. Toolkit, pump, licence holder. Speedometer.
Extra or optional equipment. Upswept or downswept exhaust system optional. Fully sprung rear frame (with downswept exhaust system only). Alloy engine and head. Magdyno and lighting equipment. Pillion seat, pillion rests and prop stand.
Maximum Speed. B32 60 m.p.h.
B34 70 m.p.h.
Petrol Consumption (at 30 m.p.h.) B32 85 m.p.g. B34 75 m.p.g.
Braking (from 30 m.p.h. to rest). 33 ft.

B.S.A. Model 348 c.c. o.h.v. B32 "Gold Star"
B.S.A. Model 499 c.c. o.h.v. B34 "Gold Star"

SPECIFICATION

Engine. Make B.S.A.
Bore and Stroke. B32 71 mm. x 88 mm. 348 c.c.
B34. 85 mm. x 88 mm. 499 c.c.
Compression Ratio. Optional on both models.
Single cylinder, o.h.v. air cooled, single port. Aluminium alloy cylinder barrel and head. Roller bearing big end. Specially tuned engine.
Sparking plugs 14 mm. Champion N A series
Lubrication. Dry sump and double gear pump.
Carburettor. Amal.

Gear Box. 4 speed, positive stop, foot change.
Ratios. B32 16.7, 11.5, 7.4 and 5.6 to 1. } Alternative ratios
B34 14.9, 10.3, 6.6 and 5.0 to 1. } available.
Clutch. Dry, 5 plate, fabric inserts.
Transmission. Primary. Chain ½" x .305".
Secondary. Chain ⅝" x ¼".
Ignition. Lucas magneto or Lucas magdyno.
Lighting. Optional. Lucas magdyno, 6 volt. 60 watt. compensated voltage control, sealed beam headlamp, electric horn.
Petrol Capacity. 3 gallons (2 gallons to order).
Oil Capacity. ⅝ gallon.
Tyres. 2.75" x 21", front. 4.00" x 19". rear (Dunlop.)
Brakes. Internal expanding. 8" front. 7" rear. 7" front (Trials).
Frame and Suspension. B.S.A. Telescopic hydraulic forks and plunger type rear springing.
Saddle. Terry/Wrights. **Height from ground.** 31½".
Wheelbase. 54¾". **Ground Clearance.** 6½".
Overall Length. 83½" **Width over bars.** 26".
Weight (dry). B32 325 lb. B34 335 lb.
Finish. Silver and chromium tank. Frame stove enamelled black, bright parts chromium plated.
Equipment. Toolkit, pump, licence holder, speedometer. Cams, gear ratios and compression ratios to suit purchaser. Pillion seat, pillion rests, prop stand.
Extra or optional equipment. Racing footchange mechanism in rearward position, rev. counter.
Braking (from 30 m.p.h. to rest). 28 ft.

B.S.A. Model 499 c.c. o.h.v. B33
B.S.A. Model 499 c.c. o.h.v. M33

SPECIFICATION

Engine. Make B.S.A.
Bore and Stroke. 85 mm. x 88 mm. 499 c.c.
Compression Ratio 6.8 to 1.
B.H.P. B33 23 at 5,500 r.p.m. M33 25 at 5,500 r.p.m.
Single cylinder, o.h.v., air cooled, cast iron cylinder barrel and head. High tensile steel connecting rod, roller bearing big end.
Sparking plugs 14 mm. Champion L 10 s.
Lubrication. Dry sump and double gear pump.
Carburettor. Amal 289G/1AT.
Gear Box. 4 speed, positive stop, foot change.
Ratios. B33 14.9, 10.3, 6.6, and 5.0 to 1.
M33 (Solo) 14.2, 9.8, 6.3, and 4.8 to 1.
(Sidecar) 16.72, 11.5, 7.3 and 5.5 to 1.
Clutch. Dry, 5 plate, fabric inserts.
Transmission. Primary. Chain ½" x .305".
Secondary. Chain ⅝" x ¼".
Ignition. Lucas Magdyno.
Lighting. Lucas Magdyno. 6 volt. 60 watt. lighting set, compensated voltage control, sealed beam headlamp. Electric horn.
Petrol Capacity. 3 gallons.
Oil Capacity. B33 ½ gallon. M33 ⅝ gallon.
Tyres. 3.25" x 19" front, 3.50" x 19" rear, (Dunlop).
Brakes. Internal expanding, 7", front and rear.
Frame and Suspension. B.S.A. Telescopic hydraulic forks and rigid frame. Spring frame optional on B33.
Saddle. Terry/Wrights. **Height from ground.** 30½".
Wheelbase. 54". **Ground Clearance.** B33 5".
M33 5½".
Overall Length. 82" and 85". **Width over bars.** 28".
Weight (dry). B33 354 lb. M33 372 lb.
Finish. Silver and chromium tank. Frame stove enamelled black, bright parts chromium plated.
Equipment. Electric horn, toolkit, pump, licence holder, speedometer.
Extra or optional equipment. Fully sprung rear frame (on Model B33), Pillion seat, pillion rests, carrier, prop stand. Devon Red and chromium finish on B33 at extra charge.
Maximum Speed. B33. 2nd 50 m.p.h. 3rd 74 m.p.h. 4th 82 m.p.h.
M33. 45 m.p.h. 66 m.p.h. 80 m.p.h.
Speed at end of quarter mile from rest. 50 m.p.h.
Petrol Consumption (at 30 m.p.h.) 78 m.p.g.
Braking (from 30 m.p.h. to rest). 32ft.

B.S.A. Model A7 495 c.c. o.h.v. Twin, and 495 c.c. Model A7 "Star Twin"

SPECIFICATION

Engine. Make B.S.A.
Bore and Stroke 62 mm. x 82 mm. 495 c.c.
Compression Ratio A7 6.6 to 1. Star Twin 7 to 1.
B.H.P. A7 approx. 25 at 5,800 r.p.m. Star Twin approx. 29 at 6,000 r.p.m.
Vertical twin cylinder o.h.v. air cooled, twin port. Cast iron cylinder barrel and head. Indium lead bronze plain big end bearings. Tappets operated by single camshaft at rear of engine. Star Twin modified engine.
Sparking plugs 14 mm. Champion L 10 s.
Lubrication. Dry sump and double gear pump.
Carburettor. A7 Amal 276DP/1A. Star Twin, Twin Amals 275/AR/1A and 275/AS/1A.
Gear Box. 4 speed, positive stop, foot change.
Ratios. Solo 13.2, 9.0 6.2 and 5.1 to 1.
Sidecar 14.0, 9.5, 6.6, and 5.4 to 1.
Clutch. Dry, 5 plate, fabric inserts.
Transmission. Primary. Chain ⅜" duplex.
Secondary. Chain ⅝" x ⅜".
Ignition. Lucas Magneto.
Lighting. Lucas Dynamo. 6 volt. 60 watt. compensated voltage control, sealed beam headlamp. Electric horn.
Petrol Capacity. 3½ gallons.
Oil Capacity. ½ gallon.
Tyres. 3.25" x 19", front. 3.50" x 19" rear, (Dunlop).
Brakes. 7" front and rear.
Frame and Suspension. A7 Telescopic hydraulic forks and rigid frame. Quickly detachable rear wheel.
Star Twin. Telescopic hydraulic forks and rear suspension. Quickly detachable rear wheel.
Saddle. Terry. **Height from ground.** A7 30".
Star Twin 31½".
Wheelbase. 54⅜". **Ground Clearance.** 4½".
Overall Length. 83" and 84" **Width over bars.** 28".
Weight (dry). A7 369 lb. Star Twin 382 lb.
Finish. Red and chromium or alternative black and chromium. Frame stove enamelled black. Bright parts chromium plated.
Equipment. Electric horn toolkit, pump, speedometer.
Extra or optional equipment. Spring Frame (on Model A7). Pillion seat, pillion rests, propstand.
Maximum Speed. 2nd A7 60 m.p.h. 3rd A7 77 m.p.h. 4th A7 85 m.p.h.
Speed at end of quarter mile from rest. 52.43 m.p.h. [ST 95 m.p.h.]
Petrol Consumption (at 30 m.p.h.) 80 m.p.g.
Braking (from 30 m.p.h. to rest). 30 ft.

B.S.A. 646 c.c. o.h.v. Twin Model A10 " Golden Flash "

SPECIFICATION

Engine. Make B.S.A.
  Bore and Stroke. 70 mm. x 84 mm. 646 c.c.
  Compression Ratio. 6.5 to 1.
  B.H.P. approx. 35.
  Vertical twin cylinder, air cooled, o.h.v. push rod. Cast iron cylinder barrel and head. Light alloy connecting rods. Indium lead-bronze plain bearings to big end. Single camshaft operates tappets.
  Sparking plugs 14 mm. Champion L 10 s.
Lubrication. Dry sump, with double gear pump.
Carburettor. Amal.
Gear Box. 4 speed, positive stop foot change.
  Ratios. 10.7, 7.4, 5.1 and 4.2 to 1.
Clutch. Dry, 5 plate, fabric inserts.
Transmission. Primary. ⅜" duplex chain.
  Secondary. Chain ⅝" x ⅜".
Ignition. Lucas magneto.
Lighting. Lucas dynamo. Compensated voltage control. Sealed beam headlamp.
  Electric horn.

Petrol Capacity. 3½ gallons.
Oil Capacity. ½ gallon.
Tyres. 3.25" x 19", front. 3.50" x 19" rear, (Dunlop).
Brakes. 8" front, 7" rear.
Frame and Suspension. Duplex cradle frame. Telescopic hydraulically damped front forks. Quickly detachable rear wheel.
Saddle. Terry. Height from ground. 30".
Wheelbase. 54¾". Ground Clearance. 4½".
Overall Length. 84". Width over bars. 28".
Weight (dry). 375 lb.
Finish. Gold and chromium. Frame stove enamelled black. Bright parts chromium plated.
Equipment. Electric horn, toolkit, pump, licence holder, speedometer.
Extra or optional equipment. Plunger type rear springing. Pillion seat, pillion rests, prop stand.
Maximum Speed. 2nd 66 m.p.h. 3rd 89 m.p.h. 4th 105 m.p.h.
Speed at end of quarter mile from rest. 56.9 m.p.h.
Petrol Consumption (at 30 m.p.h.) 89 m.p.g.
Braking (from 30 m.p.h. to rest). 25½ ft.

STOP PRESS

Models C10, C11. Spring frames and 4 speed gearboxes are now optional extras.

Models M20, M21. Light alloy cylinder heads now fitted.
  Spring frames now optional extras.

All twin cylinder models are now fitted with new small-clearance "flexible skirt" pistons.

Model A7. Now fitted with an entirely new engine and gearbox. Bore and stroke 66 m.m. x 72.6 m.m., 495 c.c. Standard c.r. 6.7 to 1, pistons giving c.r. 7.2 to 1 available.
  Majority of parts of new engine interchangeable with Model A10.

Model A7 "Star Twin" A single Amal carburettor is now fitted.

Model A10. Sidecar lugs now standard.

Corgi*

BROCKHOUSE ENGINEERING (SOUTHPORT) LTD.
SOUTHPORT · LANCS.

U.S.A. Distributors:
INDIAN SALES CORPORATION
29 Worthington St.
Springfield, Mass.

* Known as the INDIAN PAPOOSE in U.S.

The Corgi, as is probably well known, was developed from the " Welbike " used by paratroops in the last war. This little machine has become increasingly popular and is now in use in considerable numbers all over the world.

This lightweight runabout made by the Brockhouse Engineering Co. Ltd., is unique in that the machine can be folded up for transport or storage, reducing it to such a small size that it can, for instance, be carried in the boot of a car, stored almost anywhere (even under the bed), or used as a tender to a larger vehicle. The handlebars of the Corgi fold flat, the saddle is lowered and the machine folds into a space of 53" long x 13" wide and only 20" high. This "pocket prodigy" of a machine weighs only 95 lbs., gives a speed of 30 m.p.h. with ease, and a petrol consumption of 120 miles to the gallon.

The Mark II Corgi for 1950 has a 98 c.c. Brockhouse " Spryt" two stroke engine—a lively and reliable unit. The engine, placed horizontally in the frame, has a compression ratio of 6.9 to 1. The cylinder head is of aluminium alloy, the main bearing has ball journals and alternate steel and bronze rollers comprise the big end bearing. The connecting rod is a nickel chrome molybdenum forging. Ignition is by flywheel magneto, incorporating coils for direct lighting. A single plate clutch is employed, and the standard model is a single gear machine. The tank carries petrol for a range of 150 miles at one filling. The 1950 machine retains the free engine and kick starter fitting introduced last year. A rigid frame is used, transmission is by chain, and the disc pattern wheels are fitted with $12\frac{1}{2}$" x $2\frac{1}{4}$" tyres, front and rear.

To increase the scope of this little machine, a number of refinements and accessories have been introduced for 1950. Chief amongst these is a 2 speed gearbox, which is available for both Mark I and Mark II types. The gear boxes are an Albion product and are operated by a foot change lever incorporating a neutral position and kick start mechanism. The ratios are 8.5 and 4.8 to 1 for the two speeds. A special silencer, particularly designed for the above conversion is also available.

A further desirable additional modification relates to the forks,—the standard front forks can now be converted to the telescopic pattern.

The universal appeal of the Corgi is well realised by the manufacturers and distributors, and a number of varied accessories give an even greater degree of usefulness to this machine. A selection of well designed front and rear carrier baskets, a seat cover, driving mirror and a large type Terry saddle are optional extras, together with a rear metal carrier, a handlebar screen and a small Smith's speedometer (also available with a kilometre reading).

Of the greatest interest and utility however, are the two Corgi sidecars. A rigid sidecar chassis is produced by the Brockhouse Co., and this supports a detachable tray type box, fitted with a removable canvas cover. This is a very neat and practical job, and is exceptionally useful for carrying parcels or for commercial use. The detachable tray will be much appreciated as an aid to easy loading.

An even more interesting development is the introduction this year of a banking sidecar, which is detachable in a matter of minutes, and allows the Corgi to be ridden and manoeuvred as easily as a solo machine. Manufactured by Feridax Ltd., this sidecar weighs approximately 30 lb. and will carry up to half a hundredweight. The body is of aluminium. Specially designed swivel fittings allow for movement in a vertical plane. A larger wheel sprocket for use with this outfit lowers the gear ratio from 5.82 to 1 to 6.82 to 1. Practical tests have shown that this banking sidecar is most efficient in action. The outfit can be driven in exactly the same manner as a solo motor cycle, without the necessity of mastering a "sidecar technique".

The universal usefulness and performance of the Corgi and its world wide appeal amply justify the makers slogan—" The pocket prodigy of Great Britain".

SPECIFICATION.
CORGI Mark II.

Engine. Make. Brockhouse "Spryt."
Bore and Stroke. 50 mm. x 50 mm. 98 c.c.
Compression Ratio. 6.9 to 1.
Single cylinder, two stroke, air cooled, single port.
Aluminium alloy cylinder head. Dome top piston. Nickel chrome molybdenum forged connecting rod. Roller big end bearing.
Sparking Plug. 14 mm.
Lubrication. Petroil system.
Carburettor. Amal No. 259/001. Jet size, 55. Twist grip throttle control.
Gearbox. Standard machine—single speed.
Final drive ratios:—Single speed, 5.82.
Sidecar ratio, 6.82 to 1.
Clutch. Single plate. Cork inserts.
Transmission. Primary. Chain ⅜" pitch. 56 links.
Secondary. Chain ½" pitch. 82 links.
Ignition. Wico-Pacy Flywheel Generator.
Lighting. Wico-Pacy A.C.
Petrol Capacity. 1¼ gallons.
Oil Capacity. Petroil system.
Tyres. Dunlop 12½" x 2¼", front and rear.
Brakes. 4" front and rear.
Frame and Suspension. Unsprung rigid frame.
Saddle. Lycett or Brooks.   **Height from ground.** 24½" to 26½".
Wheelbase. 39".   **Ground clearance.** 3¾".
Weight (dry). Standard model. 95 lb.
Finish. Tank stove enamelled red. Wheels black.
Extra equipment. Albion 2 speed gearbox. Telescopic forks, Special silencer. Metal carrier, handlebar screen, Smith's speedometer.
Manufacturers Brockhouse, Engineering (Southport) Ltd., Crossens, Southport. Lancs.
Distributors Jack Olding and Co. Ltd., Audley House, North Audley Street, London, W.1.

STOP PRESS

BROCKHOUSE BRAVE. A new machine to meet U.S. demand for small capacity "American styled" model. 248 c.c. s.v. engine, with detachable alloy head. C.R. 6.3 to 1. 3 speed box, 5.7, 9.0 and 16.2 to 1. Telescopic forks. Wheelbase 52". Overall length 79". Overall width 24½". Weight 230 lbs.

Cotton

**THE COTTON MOTOR COMPANY
GLOUCESTER**

The Cotton has always been notable as an outstanding machine for stability at speed, and although produced on a comparatively small scale, the marque was well known before the war and had an established reputation.

Cotton's have won three I.O.M., T.T. races and have taken second or third places in seven others and gained 25 T.T. Replicas in the past, so that there is racing experience behind the breed and many other events and cups have been won from time to time.

One of the most notable features of the machine is the well known Cotton frame design which gives a low, comfortable riding position coupled with remarkable stability and ease of control. The secret lies in its triangulated construction, particularly the vertical and lateral triangulation of the all important points between steering head and rear axle. Druid central spring front forks are fitted, but Teleforks are available on all models as an extra.

Cottons are now planning their 1951 production programme which is to include 10 models, and all machines are individually built. The latest addition to the range will be a new 500 c.c. vertical twin, which will have a Burman 4 speed positive stop footchange, Druid or Teleforks, the Cotton triangulated frame and full mag-dynamo lighting.

A 500 c.c. o.h.v. high camshaft model (known as the 25/Special) is also in production, and the range will include the 30/Special, a 250 c.c. o.h.v. high camshaft machine and the 9/Special, a 350 c.c. o.h.v. high camshaft model. All these machines have vertically mounted J.A.P. engines.

A 500 c.c. o.h.v. and a 600 c.c. side valve with the latest J.A.P. engines are also listed. The o.h.v. machines have totally enclosed, but quickly accessible rocker gear with tappets which are instantly adjustable externally and a new design of shock absorber which gives exceptionally smooth running. The specification includes an Amal or Bowden carburettor and a 4-speed Burman foot change gearbox.

The programme will be completed by a Villiers engined two-stroke lightweight and a 250 c.c. side valve J.A.P. engined model. Speedometers, pillion footrests, carriers and legshields can be supplied as extras to most models in the range, and Cottons are prepared to supply machines with specially polished, tuned and fitted engines or to build machines to special order for T.T. or other racing events.

Cyc-Auto

CYC-AUTO LTD.
BRUNEL ROAD . EAST ACTON · LONDON, W.3.

The makers of the Cyc-Auto can justly claim to be the pioneers of Auto-Cycles, for the Cyc-Auto was introduced at the British Industries Fair as long ago as 1930.

Several interesting features distinguish it from other machines in its category. The power unit is not the ubiquitous Villiers, but a Scott two stroke, redesigned for 1950. This engine is mounted across the frame and drives through a short shaft to helical gears, which are located in the bottom bracket of the frame. A dog clutch is provided and a lateral movement of the crank axle disconnects the engine from the drive, thus eliminating unnecessary drag when pedalling. In addition to the usual internal expanding brakes front and rear, there is an additional safety factor in the powerful transmission brake, which is operated by the clutch lever.

The Scott Simplex 98 c.c. engine has a bore of 50 mm. x 50 mm. stroke.

The cylinder is of patented design and has transfer ports directed towards the semi-spherical detachable aluminium cylinder head. The cylinder itself is of chromidium cast iron, with ample finning to ensure efficient cooling. A decompressor valve is provided for easy starting. A special heat treated aluminium alloy piston has Aero type tapered rings.

The connecting rod is made from a heat-treated steel stamping and the large end is ground to form the outer race of the crank pin bearing, which has roller bearings, the small end having a bush of special bronze. The big end bearing is slotted for lubrication and both bearings are lubricated by contact with Petroil vapour. The Amal adjustable needle type carburettor is controlled by a single throttle lever. A knife type strangler is fitted for easy starting and a large size air filter is fitted.

The drive is through a bronze worm wheel, hardened steel worm shaft and chain to the rear wheel. Twin chrome plated exhaust pipes are fitted with twin tubular silencers, contributing to quiet running.

A Wico flywheel magneto, Lucas 6 watt headlamp, front spring forks and 4″ mudguards are other features contributing to the comfort and efficiency of this little machine, which is truly economical, giving a petrol consumption in the order of 160 m.p.g. with speeds of from 5 to 30 m.p.h. at a running cost of approximately 4 miles for a penny. The machine has a centre of gravity 3″ lower than that of the normal pedal cycle and consequently, excellent stability.

CYC-AUTO AUTOCYCLE.

SPECIFICATION.

Engine. Make. Scott Simplex.
 Bore and Stroke. 50 mm. x 50 mm. 98 c.c.
 Compression Ratio. 5.1 to 1.
 Approximate b.h.p. 2.5.
 Single cylinder, two stroke, air cooled, twin port.
 Detachable aluminium cylinder head.
 Sparking plug. 14 mm.
Lubrication. Petroil system.
Carburettor. Amal adjustable needle type.
Gear Ratio. 11.1 to 1.
Clutch. 5 plate, single spring loaded. Hand operated.
Transmission. Chain and shaft. Power transmission ⅝″ x ¼″ chain.
 Pedal transmission ½″ x ⅛″ chain. Helical shaft primary drive.
Ignition. Wico-Pacy A.C. flywheel generator.
Lighting. Flywheel generator. Lucas 6 watt headlamp. 0.04 watt tail lamp.
Petrol Capacity. 1¼ gallons.
Tyres. Dunlop 26″ x 2″, front and rear.
Brakes. Internal expanding, 4″, front and rear. Transmission brake.
Frame and Suspension. 19″ open type frame. Webb sprung forks. Rear clip up stand.
Saddle. Dunlop Auto-Cycle type.
Wheelbase. 48″.   **Ground clearance.** 5¾″.
Weight (dry). 110 lb.
Finish. Chromium plated handlebars and wheels. Tank finished cream, lined red.
Equipment. Licence holder, bell, tool and tool bag, tyre pump, number plates, 4″ mudguards. 2¼″ rear carrier. (Speedometer extra).

Dot

DOT CYCLE & MOTOR
MANUFACTURING CO. LTD.
MANCHESTER, 15

The first Dot motorcycle was produced as long ago as 1903, and the marque will be remembered as an individually built machine of superb quality and finish. The Dot also took part in the T.T. and the racing experience thus obtained has contributed to the present day machines' road holding, steering accuracy and safety.

The machine has not been in production for a good many years, but was reintroduced in the spring of 1949. The present range consist of two models. Model 200/DST is powered by the Villiers Mark 6E engine of 197 c.c., with 3 speed gearbox. The engine has a bore of 59 mm. and a stroke of 72 mm., with a flat top piston and a compression ratio of 8 to 1, giving an approximate b.h.p. of 8.4 at 4,000 r.p.m. Twin transfer ports, a single large exhaust port, a detachable alloy cylinder head and flywheel magneto ignition are features of the design. A compression release valve is fitted.

The 3 speed gearbox is bolted to the engine in unit construction and driven by an endless chain fully enclosed in an oil bath chain case. The 2 plate cork insert type clutch runs in oil and the foot gear change is operated by a positive stop ratchet mechanism, adjustable for position.

The frame is of cradle loop type, of welded carbon steel tubing, brazed into a one-piece steering head. The 3 point engine mounting is of aluminium alloy and the Webb link action girder spring forks have a hand operated adjustable shock absorber. The 6 pole flywheel magneto is fitted with lighting coils giving an output of approximately 30 watts at 6 volts.

Model 200/RST is similar to Model 200/DST described above. Rectifier accumulator lighting however, is fitted, comprising rectifier, Varley accumulator, accumulator holder and a larger headlamp fitted with an ammeter. Both models include electric horn, central stand, Smith's 80 m.p.h. illuminated speedometer, tools and tyre inflator.

Interesting features which point to the care in design are the use of Simmonds locknuts on a generous scale, Petroflex tubing, and the provision of an alternative set of final gear ratios. The central stand allows either wheel to be removed with ease. The machines are attractively finished in black, with a chromium tank and cerise mudguards.

SPECIFICATION.
DOT. MODEL 200/DST. and 200/RST.

Engine. Make, Villiers Mark 6E.
    Bore and Stroke. 59 mm. x 72 mm. 197 c.c.
    Compression Ratio. 8 to 1.
    Single cylinder, two stroke, air cooled, single port, flat top piston, twin transfer ports, single large exhaust port. detachable alloy cylinder head. Sparking plug. 14 mm.
Lubrication. Petroil system.
Carburettor. Villiers type 4/5 with adjustable taper needle and air filter.
Gearbox. 3 speed unit construction. Positive stop foot change mechanism. Kickstarter.
    Final drive ratios. 1st. 19.1, 2nd 9.98, 3rd. 5.87 to 1.
    Alternative ratios. 18.2   9.52   5.6 to 1.
Clutch. 2 plate cork insert type running in oil.
Transmission. Primary. Chain ⅝" x ¼" Reynolds 110044 Endless pre-stretched. Secondary. ⅝" x ¼", Reynolds 110044, 117 rollers.
Ignition. Villiers Flywheel magneto.
Lighting. Model 200/DST. Direct lighting by flywheel electrical generator, auxiliary stand-by parking battery.
    Model 200/RST. Rectified dynamo lighting, with 6 volt accumulator and larger headlamp.
Petrol Capacity. 2¾ gallon welded tank.
Oil Capacity. Petroil System.
Tyres. Goodyear. 3.00" x 19", front and rear.
Brakes. Quickly adjustable internal expanding, 5" front, 6" rear.
Frame and Suspension. Cradle loop frame of weldless carbon steel tubing, brazed into one piece steering head. Webb girder front forks. Rigid frame.
Saddle. Spring top.   Height from ground. 27".
Wheelbase. 52¾".   Ground clearance. 2¼".
Weight (dry). Model 200/DST. 200 lb. Model 200/RST. 210 lb.
Finish. Stove enamelled black, ivory mudguards. Petrol tank, chain guard, wheels, handlebars, exhaust pipes chromium plated.
Equipment. Electric horn, dipper switch, central spring up stand, headlamps, rear lamp, knee grips, Smith's 80 m.p.h. illuminated speedometer. Pillion seat and footrest equipment extra.
An additional model now in production:—

DOT. "200 Scrambler"
Gear ratios. 24.0, 12.7 and 7.47 to 1.
Tank capacity. 1¼ gallons.
Tyres. Front, 3.00 x 19. Rear 3.25 x 19.

STOP PRESS

Telescopic forks are now fitted, together with new flaired headlamp and speedometer mounting.

Douglas

**DOUGLAS (SALES & SERVICE) LTD.
KINGSWOOD · BRISTOL**

The Douglas is one of our oldest and best known motor cycles and the story of its development is an interesting and eventful one.

The Douglas concern originally established itself in Kingswood, Bristol, in 1882 as a foundry, and although the principal work undertaken was for the boot and shoe trade, the company began to produce cylinders and pistons for an early twin cylinder machine, called the "Fairy" which was marketed by a company called "Light Motors Ltd.," of Orchard St. Bristol. In 1905 two "Fairy" machines were being produced, a single speed 2½ h.p. lightweight with chain and belt drive and a larger 6 h.p. machine—a flat twin. The driving force behind the Fairy machine lay in the hands of Walter Moore and a Mr. Joseph Barter, who had earlier produced a single cylinder engine of his own design. The Douglas brothers began to produce more and more parts for the Fairy concern, and eventually Barter joined the Kingswood company, with a view to producing the first Douglas machine, which emerged in 1907. Two models were manufactured—a 2¾ h.p. flat twin, and a two speed, 6 h.p. four cylinder machine. Neither of these machines was a commercial success.

By this time, Walter Moore had joined the company, and the next few years were to bring developments and improvements into the Douglas range, and many of these design changes—the adoption of a redesigned cylinder head and magneto ignition amongst others, resulted in a greatly improved standard of performance. By 1910, the Douglas, now a 340 c.c. machine, was selling well, and a 5 h.p. machine was introduced, to be followed by three versions of the 2¾ h.p. machine in 1911, amongst which was a sports machine and a open framed model designed for the lady rider.

In the years immediately preceding the first World War, the Douglas machine had definitely "arrived." Competition and racing work had been taken up seriously, and in 1912, a year during which 2,000 Douglas machines were turned out, the marque took first and second in the Junior T.T. in the hands of Harry Bashall and Eric Kickham.

The first World War brought the Douglas company a W.D. contract which, possibly more than anything else, made the machine's reputation, for more than 25,000 flat twin machines saw service in all quarters of the globe.

Post war developments were the conversion of the 340 c.c. machine to all chain drive, the development of the W.D. type and 600 c.c. side valve machines and the the introduction of o.h.v. "R.A." machines in 1921. This period was the hey-day for the Douglas, the machine winning the Senior and Sidecar T.T.'s in 1923, whilst everywhere Douglas' were making the running in road and track racing, trials and competition events, and such names as Freddie Dixon, Alec Bennet, Rex Judd, Cyril Pullin, Vic Anstice, Len Parker and many others will for long be associated with the machine. In 1925 Cyril Pullin designed the famous Douglas "E.W." model, over 20,000 of which were produced, and this was followed in 1928 by modernised versions designed by Freddie Dixon, of 350 c.c. and 600 c.c. A T.T. replica model was also manufactured and it was about this time that the famous speedway machines appeared.

Fortune was now to change however, for in the next decade, the world trade depression caused the company, which had been a private one until then, to reorganise, and in 1932 a new company was formed called Douglas (1932) Ltd. The flotation of this company was not successfull however, and the business returned to the Douglas family in 1933, becoming William Douglas (Bristol) Ltd. Despite the introduction of new Villiers engined and twin cylinder models, the firm was unable to continue in the motor cycle industry, and ceased their manufacture in 1935, in which year a new company —Aero Engines Ltd. was formed to produce industrial trucks, stationary engines and the like, although a few motor cycles were produced until the outbreak of the second World War.

From the outbreak of war the company concentrated on munitions and changed its name again in 1941 to become Douglas (Kingswood) Ltd. producing the Douglas machine again in 1945. Since then the company's title has once again been changed to Douglas (Sales and Service) Ltd.

Douglas' have always been original and progressive, and it is in accordance with the traditions and past history of the concern, that further new developments were announced to coincide with the opening of the Motor Cycle Show in 1949. Augmenting the existing range were two new sports and racing mounts, known as the "80 Plus" and "90 Plus" Models, whilst at the same time it was announced that Douglas was to produce in this country, under licence, the Italian designed and produced Vespa scooter. The Douglas stand at the show was therefore a centre of particular interest.

In all, the present range comprises 5 models. All the motor cycles are powered with the famous Douglas horizontally opposed twin cylinder engine, of 348 c.c. capacity, with overhead valves and set transversely in the frame. First there is the Mark V De Luxe Model, followed by the super sports "80 Plus," with a maximum of over 80 m.p.h. and partnered by the "90 Plus," an even faster machine, and the motorcycle range is completed by the 348 c.c. special competition model. Finally there is the Douglas Vespa scooter.

The reliability of the Douglas engine has been proved over a long period. The 180° opposed power unit is in unit construction with the gear box, a combination of great strength and lightness, which obviates primary chain adjustment. The very strong, but light Duplex cradle frame enables the engine to be mounted with a very low centre of gravity, resulting in increased stability and good road holding qualities. The frames on all machines (except the Competition Model) are fully sprung by a system of torsion bar rear springing. A torsion bar is housed within each of the horizontal frame members which run beneath the engine, and these are connected by short links to the swinging rear fork. Road shocks and rebounds are absorbed by the twisting action of the torsion bars. "Radiadraulic" front forks are fitted to all machines. Of the bottom link type, these have a total movement of approximately 6". One of the characteristics of these forks is the progressive action which is achieved by the variable rate springs which take the impact load, whilst the rebound is absorbed by piston type shock absorbers.

Douglas Mark V.
348 c.c. H.O., o.h.v.
Twin

Douglas "90 Plus"
348 c.c. H.O., o.h.v.
twin

All Douglas engines incidentally have a car type oiling system, which eliminates all external pipes, with a consequent absence of oil leakage. Each cylinder has its own carburettor, which ensures easy starting and a lively performance.

The Mark V twin engine has a bore of 60.8 mm. and a stroke of 60 mm., with a compression ratio of 7.25 to 1. Transversely set across the frame, the cylinder heads project into the air stream and are well cooled. The built up crankshaft is mounted at the flywheel end in double row ball bearings and in a large plain bearing at the timing gear end. The high tensile steel connecting rods are fitted with a plain bearing in the small end and double row roller bearings at the crankpin. Flat topped aluminium alloy pistons are fitted. Twin camshafts located below the crankshaft actuate the push rods. The valve mechanism is totally enclosed, the rockers being mounted in long plain bearings. Twin Amal carburettors are mounted directly on to the cylinders. The valves are set at 60° and a downdraught inlet port is provided. A Lucas magdyno, gear-driven from the crankshaft, and with an ignition button is mounted on top of the crankcase. The oil sump is cast integrally with the crankcase, and a vane type oil pump feeds oil directly to the crankshaft. The sump capacity is half a gallon. A single plate dry clutch, 6¾" diameter has Ferodo linings and is easily adjustable through an inspection cover.

The four speed gearbox is in unit construction with the engine, and is operated by totally enclosed foot change. The gearbox mainshaft is in line with the crankshaft, bevel gearing transfers the drive from the mainshaft to the final drive chain sprocket through a shock absorber. Although the crankshaft and gear box shafts are in line with the frame, the kick starter is designed to work in the normal way, and the engine can be started with light foot pressure. No decompressor is fitted. Transmission to the rear wheel is by chain with deep section guards over the top run.

The frame is the Douglas duplex cradle type, with Radiadraulic forks and torsion bar rear springing. A cast aluminium centre stand enables the machine to be raised by foot pressure. Rubber knee grips, are fitted to the welded steel saddle tank which is adjustable for height.

Firestone 3.25" x 19" tyres are fitted front and rear, and the 7" diameter brakes have light alloy backplates. The rear brake pedal is adjustable. A Lucas 6 volt A.V.C. lighting set is fitted, with a 7" headlamp and an electric horn. The handlebars are fully adjustable for height and reach, a twist grip control and a manual ignition control are fitted. Equipment includes a Smiths' illuminated 120 m.p.h. trip speedometer, twin rear mounted tool boxes with a full tool kit, and extras available are an air filter for the carburettors, crash bars, pillion seat and pillion footrests. Machines are finished with a chromium tank with blue and silver panels and black enamelled frame, but a "Bluebird" finish in polychromatic blue is offered without extra cost. All crankcases and gearboxes are highly polished. On test the machine has given a maximum speed of approximately 80 m.p.h., with a petrol consumption in the region of 85 m.p.g. at 30 m.p.h.

Douglas's new competition machine has been developed from this basic design, but has a rigid cradle duplex frame, but with Radiadraulic front forks. The engine unit has been developed to provide high torque at low speeds and is mounted high in the frame to allow ample ground clearance. Special attention has been given to provide a wide steering lock. Engine details are similar to the Mark V, but the compression ratio on the Competition model is 6.5 to 1. Twin Amal carburettors are mounted on upswept induction pipes to give adequate protection. A gear driven Lucas magdyno with ignition cut-out button or a separate magneto can be fitted. There is handlebar ignition control. The gear box, which is similar to the Mark V, has a folding kickstarter, and the standard trials gear ratios of 6.6, 8.35, 14.3, and 21.7

can be varied through a wide range by optional extra final drive and rear wheel sprockets. A prop stand is fitted to the near side of the machine. The tank has been reduced in width at the rear to assist the rider's control when out of the saddle, and the bottom link forks are of special design for competition work giving adequate steering and a wide steering lock. 4.00" x 19" rear and 3.00" x 21" front tyres are fitted and the " D " section polished aluminium mudguards give ample tyre clear-clearance. A rear lifting handle is fitted. The trials pattern saddle and upswept handlebars are adjustable, and the exhaust system is upswept, both pipes leading into a common expansion chamber mounted high on the offside of the machine. Finish is black stove enamel, with chromium plating for the bright parts, and equipment comprises a single toolbox mounted on the offside, complete with tool kit, a pump, a solid skid pan undershield, a sports type bulb horn, front trials number plate, and speedometer. The model weighs approximately 300 lb. (or 320 lb. with madgyno lighting set), ground clearance is 8" and wheelbase 54".

The most outstanding machines in the Douglas range are the super sports " 80 Plus " and the racing " 90 Plus." Based on the Douglas flat twin engine, the " 80 Plus" has a maximum speed in excess of 80 m.p.h. and the " 90 Plus " is still faster. The " 80 " however is smooth and docile in traffic and provides a road model for normal service with an exceptionally good perfornamce.

The engines are individually assembled and bench tested, and each engine carries a bench record card. The compression ratio for the " 80 Plus " is 7.25 to 1, and for the " 90 Plus " 8.25 to 1. The cylinder heads, of special heat treated alloy are of new design, highly developed to provide maximum efficiency. The heads are heavily finned and the cylinder barrels are honed and polished to fine limits. The carefully balanced crankshaft is carried in a double row ball bearing at the flywheel end and a large plain bearing at the timing gear end. Continuous oil feed through the crankshaft lubricates the double row roller big end bearing of the high tensile connecting rods. High duty Specialloid pistons with two compression and one oil control ring with fully floating $\frac{5}{8}$" diameter gudgeon pin are fitted. The twin camshafts, located below the crankshaft are of special design, giving high performance with economy. The valve operating mechanism is totally enclosed, the rockers being mounted in long plain bearings. Twin Amal carburettors and a gear driven Lucas magneto are fitted.

Lubrication is pressure fed by a vane type oil pump submerged in the sump, which is cast integrally with the crankcase. Four speed, positive stop foot change gearboxes are in unit with the engine, a similar bevel gearing to the standard machines transferring the drive from the mainshaft to the final drive sprocket. A folding kick start pedal is fitted. The " 80 Plus " has standard gear ratios, alternative ratios being available for the " 90 Plus." Transmission is by $\frac{5}{8}$" x $\frac{1}{4}$" chain to the rear wheel. Radiadraulic forks, torsion bar rear suspension, and an aluminium centre stand are fitted. Tyres are 3.00" x 19" front and 3.25" x 19" rear, racing tyres being optional on the " 90 Plus."

Both machines have a 9" diameter front brake and a 7" rear brake. A Lucas 6 volt A.V.C. magdyno with a large headlamp and electric horn are supplied, but a racing magneto is optional on the " 90 Plus." Lightweight mudguards are fitted, the front mudguard being carried on the front fork links. A quick action twist grip and ignition cut-out button are other features of these machines, which are finished in gold, purple and chromium. A Smith's 120 m.p.h. speedometer and twin tool boxes are included in the specification.

A comprehensive list of extras is available, including alternative exhaust systems, racing magnetos, alloy wheelrims, special camshafts, pistons for various compression ratios, T.T. Carburettors, alternative gear ratios and sprockets, alternative capacity petrol tanks and light alloy mudguards. Additional fittings available include a revolution counter, steering damper, air filter, crash bars, " Feridax " Dual seat, pillion seat and pillion footrests. It is emphasised that these extras enable the " 80 Plus " to be converted to the " 90 Plus," thus providing one basic machine for everyday use and for sporting events.

The Douglas Company are now manufacturing in this country, under licence, the Italian " Vespa " Scooter and the " Ape " three wheeled goods vehicle. The Vespa—to be known as the " Douglas Vespa," is built on scooter lines, with an open frame, all-enclosed engine, over which is mounted the saddle and the machine has oil damped rear springing. The machine has particularly good weather protection. The fan cooled 125 c.c. two stroke engine, three speed gear box and rear wheel are all in one unit. The main frame is of pressed steel welded monocoque construction. Front suspension is provided by a tubular fork with bottom trailing links and helical springs. The rear wheels are fully sprung by helical springing suitably damped with an oleo type damper. The 125 c.c. engine has a power output of 4 b.h.p. at 4,500 r.p.m. The carburettor is totally enclosed and accessible through a spring loaded cover. Ignition is by flywheel magneto, an engine cut out button being provided, which is located on the frame under the saddle. The engine and gearbox, forming a single unit with the rear wheel, is carried by the rear suspension on a swinging arm anchored to the main frame. The engine is completely protected and accessible through a hinged cover. It is cooled at all speeds by forced draught from a centrifugal fan which is integral with the flywheel and suitably cowled.

A starting pedal is fitted at the rear wheel and the gearbox had three speed silent mesh gears. There is direct shaft drive to the rear wheel from the gear box shaft. The petrol tank, which is totally enclosed, has an accessible filler cap and holds 1¼ gallons, including a reserve supply for 25 miles. Internal expanding brakes, with detachable brake drums are fitted on each wheel. The wheels themselves are of pressed steel, with 4 stud attachment and are quickly detachable and interchangeable. They are fitted with low pressure 3.5" x 8" tyres, and a spare wheel is supplied as an extra.

Lighting is of course, direct, the headlamp being incorporated in the front mudguard, and providing main and dipped beams. A dry battery provides parking lights. An electric horn is mounted above the front wheel. The handlebars carry a right hand twist grip throttle control and front brake lever, a light switch and horn button, and a left hand twist grip remote gear change control combined with the clutch lever. A rear foot brake pedal is placed at the front end of the scooter frame. The petrol tap and choke control are conveniently located at the rear of the frame, near the saddle. A thief proof lock is fitted to the handlebars. The machine weighs 155 lbs. is finished in polychromatic enamel, and maximum speeds of 45/50 m.p.h. are claimed, with a fuel consumption of 130 m.p.g. at 30 m.p.h. and the ability to climb a hill of 1 in 4 in low gear.

DOUGLAS 348 c.c. Mark V De Luxe Model

SPECIFICATION

Engine. Make Douglas.
Bore and Stroke. 60.8 mm. x 60 mm. 348 c.c.
Compression Ratio. 7.25 to 1.
B.H.P. 21 at 6,000.
Horizontally opposed o.h.v. twin, air cooled, set transversely in frame. Aluminium alloy pistons. Twin camshafts located below the crankshaft. Totally enclosed valve mechanism.
Sparking plugs 14 mm.
Lubrication. Car type sump lubrication with vane type oil pump.
Carburettor. Twin Amals 27/4.
Gear Box. Unit construction, 4 speed, foot change.
Ratios. 16.3, 10.1, 7.42 and 5.86 to 1.
Clutch. Single plate dry clutch, 6¾" diameter.
Transmission. Primary. To gearbox by bevel drive.
Secondary. Chain ⅝" x ¼".
Ignition. Gear driven Lucas magdyno.
Lighting. Lucas 6 volt. A.V.C. Magdyno lighting set, 7" headlamp.
Petrol Capacity. 3⅝ gallons.
Oil Capacity. ½ gallon.
Tyres. Firestone, 3.25" x 19", front and rear. Ribbed front tyre.
Brakes. 7" diameter, front and rear.
Frame and Suspension. Douglas " Radiadraulic " bottom link forks. Duplex cradle type frame. Swinging fork torsion bar rear springing.
Saddle. Terry mattress. **Height from ground.** 28½" (loaded).
Wheelbase. 54½". **Ground Clearance** 5½".
Overall Length. 84½". **Width over bars.** 29¼".
Weight (dry). 350 lb.
Finish. Black enamel on " Bonderised " surface. Bright parts chromium plated. Chromium tank with blue and silver panels. Alternative finish-Polychromatic blue.
Equipment. Centre stand, knee grips, twin tool boxes and tool kit, pump, electric horn. Smith's 120 m.p.h. speedometer.
Extra or optional equipment. Air filter, crash bars, Pillion seat and footrests.

DOUGLAS 348 c.c. " 80 Plus " and " 90 Plus " Models.

SPECIFICATION

Engine. Make Douglas.
Bore and Stroke. 60.8 mm. x 60 mm. 348 c.c.
Compression Ratio. 80 Plus 7.25 to 1. 90 Plus 8.25 to 1.
B.H.P. 80 Plus 25. 90 Plus 28.
Horizontally opposed o.h.v. twin, air cooled, set transversely in frame. Special heat treated alloy cylinder heads. High duty Specialloid pistons. Special design twin camshafts located below the crankshaft. Engine individually assembled and bench tested.
Sparking plugs 14 mm.
Lubrication. Pressure fed by vane type oil pump.
Carburettor. Twin Amals.
Gear Box. Unit construction. 4 speed. foot change. Folding kick starter.
Ratios. 80 Plus 16.3, 10.1, 7.42, 5.86 to 1.
90 Plus. Alternative ratios available.
Clutch. Single plate dry clutch, 6¾" diameter.
Transmission. Primary. To gearbox by bevel drive.
Secondary. Chain ⅝" x ¼".
Ignition. Gear driven Lucas magdyno. Racing magneto optional on 90 Plus.
Lighting. Lucas 6 volt. A.V.C. Magdyno.
Petrol Capacity. 3⅝ gallons.
Oil Capacity. ½ gallon.
Tyres. 80 Plus 3.00" x 19", ribbed front. 3.25" x 19" rear.
90 Plus 3.00" x 19" racing ribbed, front 3.25" x 19" racing rear.
Brakes. Front 9" diameter. Rear 7" diameter.
Frame and Suspension. Douglas " Radiadraulic " Bottom link forks. Special Duplex cradle frame with swinging fork type torsion bar suspension.
Saddle. Terry mattress. **Height from ground.** 28½".
Wheelbase. 54½". **Ground Clearance.** 6¼".
Overall Length. 84½". **Width over bars.** 29¼".
Weight (dry). 320 lb.
Finish. Chromium petrol tank, with purple and gold. Bright parts chromium plated. Light alloy parts highly polished.
Equipment. Smith's 120 m.p.h. speedometer. Twin tool boxes, tool kit, pump. Centre stand, electric horn.
Extra or optional equipment. Racing magneto alloy wheel rims; special camshafts; Pistons for various compression ratios; T.T. Carburettors, gear ratios and alternative sprockets. Light alloy mudguards; revolution counter; steering damper; air filter; crash bars; Feridax dualseat, pillion seat and rests; alternative capacity petrol tanks. Bulb horn optional on 90 Plus.

DOUGLAS 348 c.c. o.h.v. Twin Competition Model.

SPECIFICATION

Engine. Make Douglas.
Bore and Stroke. 60.8 mm. x 60 mm. 348 c.c.
Compression Ratio. 6.5 to 1.
B.H.P. 19.0
Horizontally opposed o.h.v. twin, air cooled. Set transversely in frame. Aluminium alloy pistons. Twin camshafts located below the crankshaft.
Sparking plugs 14 mm.
Lubrication. Car type sump lubrication, with vane type oil pump.
Carburettor. Twin Amals.
Gear Box. Unit construction, 4 speed, foot change. Folding kick starter.
Ratios. 21.7, 14.3, 8.35 and 6.6 to 1. (Alternative ratios available).
Clutch. Single plate dry clutch, 6¾" diameter.
Transmission. Primary. To gearbox by bevel drive.
Secondary. Chain.
Ignition. Gear driven Lucas magdyno or separate Lucas magneto.
Lighting. Gear driven Lucas magdyno.
Petrol Capacity. 2½ gallons. (3 gallon alternative).
Oil Capacity. ½ gallon.
Tyres. Front 3.00" x 21". Rear 4.00" x 19".
Brakes. 7" diameter, front and rear.
Frame and Suspension. Douglas " Radiadraulic " bottom link forks, specially designed for competition work and wide steering lock. Special rigid Duple cradle competition frame.
Saddle. Trials pattern 49/150 Dunlop. **Height from ground.** Adjustable
Wheelbase. 54". **Ground Clearance.** 8"
Overall Length. **Width over bars.**
Weight (dry). 300 lb. 320 lb. with magdyno lighting set.
Finish. Black stove enamel on Bonderised surface. Bright parts chromium plated.
Equipment. Prop stand, polished aluminium mudguards, upswept exhaust system tool box, tools, pump, " skid pan " undershield, Bulb horn, speedometer.
Extra or optional equipment. Magdyno lighting.

The Douglas " Vespa "
125 c.c. Two-stroke

DOUGLAS " VESPA "

SPECIFICATION

Engine. Make Douglas Vespa.
Bore and Stroke. 125 c.c. (7.63 cu. ins.)
Compression Ratio.
B.H.P. 4 at 4,500 r.p.m.
Single cylinder fan cooled two stroke, in unit construction with gear box.
Sparking plugs 14 mm.
Lubrication. Petroil system.
Carburettor. Totally enclosed.
Gear Box. Vespa, 3 speed silent mesh gears. Kickstarter.
Clutch. Multiplate.
Transmission. Direct shaft drive to rear wheel from gearbox shaft.
Ignition. Flywheel magneto, with engine cut out button.
Lighting. Direct. Headlamp in front mudguard provides main and dipped beams. Battery for parking light.
Petrol Capacity. 1½ gallons. (Includes reserve supply)
Tyres. Low pressure 3.5" x 8".
Brakes. Internal expanding, with detachable brake drums.
Frame and Suspension. Welded monocoque construction of pressed steel sheet, front and rear wheels fully sprung by helical springs, rear suspension damped with oleo type damper.
Saddle. **Height from ground.** 30"
Wheelbase. 44½". **Ground Clearance.** 6"
Overall Length. 65½". **Width over bars.** 28¾"
Weight (dry). 155 lbs.
Finish. Polychromatic enamel.
Equipment. Electric lighting set and horn.
Extra or optional equipment. Spare wheel.
Maximum Speed. 45—50 m.p.h.
Petrol Consumption (at 30 m.p.h.) approx. 130 m.p.g.

D.M.W.

D.M.W. MOTOR CYCLES (WOLVERHAMPTON) LTD.
SEDGLEY · DUDLEY, WORCS.

The range of British Villiers engined lightweights has recently received some notable additions from the factory of D.M.W. Motor Cycles of Dudley.

The 1951 programme includes three models, 98 c.c,, 122 c.c. and 197 c.c. machines.

The specification of the 122 c.c. and 197 c.c. models are unusually complete and both machines can be offered in a de luxe edition, with rear springing, suitable for solo and pillion riding, rectifier and battery lighting, a Lucas 6½" diameter headlamp, electric horn, Vokes air filter and foam rubber twin seat.

Both machines are powered by the latest Villiers engines, the Model 125 by the Villiers Mark 10D of 122 c.c., and the Model 200 by the Mark 6E, 197 c.c., engine gear unit. Both machines have D.M.W. design frames of the full-loop tubular type with welded joints, and as all frame tubes are welded directly to each other, malleable lugs have been dispensed with. This frame provides exceptional lightness (the rigid frame weighs only 13 lb.) coupled with great rigidity. Front suspension is by the Metal Profiles telescopic front fork.

A most interesting innovation in frame construction was seen in three machines entered by D.M.W. in the 1950 International Six Days Trial. These had square section frames of 1⅛", 16 gauge material, welded at junctions and to the steering head. It is claimed that the new frame gives increased lateral rigidity, especially to the rear suspension assembly. The de luxe 122 c.c. and 197 c.c. models will be available with this new square tube frame.

A good deal of attention has obviously been given to the rider's comfort, for the "clean" type handlebars are adjustable for angle and the footrest position can also be varied to a large degree. Saddles, too, are adjustable for height and angle. Wide section ribbed mudguards are fitted and the machines have 5" internal expanding brakes front and rear. Tyres are 3.00" x 19" on the 200 Model and 2.75" x 19" on the 125. Both models have a 7" ground clearance. A steel toolbox is fitted on the right hand side at the rear, between the chain and seat stays, a similar box on the left hand side containing the Lucas battery. On the de luxe models the toolbox is located beneath the twin seat. The Villiers flywheel magneto provides ignition and lighting on the standard models. Rectifier lighting is fitted on the de luxe models and the steering head web accommodates a terminal block and rectifier mounting.

Rear suspension on the de luxe models is again a Metal Profiles design, employing compression and rebound springs and plain, oil-impregnated bronze bearings. A shorter spring (inside the main compression spring) comes into action when the weight of a pillion passenger is added, or in abnormally rough conditions. The top end of the spring unit contains a rubber buffer.

A central stand is provided, with an extension on one side to allow of operation from the side of the machine. Tank capacity of both models is 2½ gallons, the 125 having a range of 270 miles with a maximum speed of 48 m.p.h., while the 200 has a range of 210 miles with a maximum of 56 m.p.h. An attractive finish of turquoise blue and chromium plate with gold lining is provided.

These D.M.W.'s are, at the time of writing, for export only, and such features as the robust construction, easy maintenance, good ground clearance, adjustable saddles, footrests and handlebars, and large capacity tanks will obviously be appreciated by the overseas rider.

The 98 c.c. machine will be powered by the Villiers Mk 1F unit.

D.M.W. Model 200

D.M.W. Models 125 and 200. 122 c.c. and 197 c.c.

SPECIFICATION

Engine. Make Villiers. (125-Mark 10D). (200-Mark 6E).
Bore and Stroke 125. 50 mm. x 62 mm. (122 c.c.).
200. 59 mm. x 72 mm. (197 c.c.).
Compression Ratio 8 to 1.
B.H.P. 122 c.c. 4.8 at 4,400 r.p.m.
197 c.c. 8.4 at 4,000 r.pm.
Single cylinder, two stroke, air cooled, single port, flat top deflectorless piston, detachable alloy cylinder head.
Sparking plugs 14 mm.

Lubrication. Petroil.

Carburettor. Villiers.

Gear Box. Villiers 3 speed. Unit construction, Foot change, kickstarter.
Ratios. 20.1, 10.6 and 7.6 to 1 (Model 125).
15.6, 8.2 and 5.9 to 1 (Model 200).

Clutch. 2 plate cork insert type, running in oil.

Transmission. Model 125. Primary chain. ⅜-in. x .225-in. } Secondary-chain
Model 200. Primary chain. ½-in. x .205-in. } ½-in. x .205-in.

Ignition. Villiers Flywheel Magneto.

Lighting. Villiers Flywheel Magneto. 5½-in. diameter headlamp, twin filament and dip switch. Rectifier, battery and 6½-in. headlamp on de luxe models.

Petrol Capacity. 2½ gallons.

Tyres. 2.75-in. x 19-in. (Model 125). 3.00-in. x 19-in. (Model 200)).

Brakes. 5-in. (127 mm.) diam., front and rear.

Frame and Suspension. Tubular D.M.W. welded frame. MP. telescopic front forks. MP. spring rear suspension on de luxe models.

Height from Ground 28½-ins.—32-ins.

Wheelbase. 47-ins. (1200 mm.). **Ground Clearance** 7-ins. (178 mm.).

Overall Length. 75-ins. (1910 mm.). Width over bars 26-ins. (660 mm.).

Weight (dry). 182 lbs. (83 kilos.)—Model 125. 195 lbs. (89 kilos.)—Model 200.

Finish. Turquoise blue and chromium plate. Tank gold lined.

Equipment. Toolkit, bulb horn, inflator, central stand, speedometer.

Extra or optional Equipment. (De luxe models) Spring frame, rectifier and battery lighting, 6½-in. headlamp, electric horn and Vokes air filter.

Maximum Speed. (125) 48 m.p.h. (77 k.p.h.)
(200) 56 m.p.h. (90 k.p.h.)

Range. 125, 270 miles (430 kilometres). 200, 210 miles (335 kilometres).

Excelsior

THE EXCELSIOR MOTOR COMPANY LTD.
KINGS ROAD · BIRMINGHAM, 11

U.S.A. Distributor:
INDIAN SALES CORPORATION
29 Worthington St.
Springfield, Mass.

Excelsiors can proudly claim that 75 years experience lies behind their present day range of machines, for the company has been engaged in the engineering industry since 1874. Although of late years they have established a very high reputation in the lightweight field, there is a background of racing and trials experience in the long history of the company. Almost certainly the first company to be engaged solely in the manufacture of bicycles in this country, they were also first to market a motorcycle, as distinct from a tricycle. As long ago as 1903 Harry Martin, riding an Excelsior, was the first rider officially to exceed a mile a minute.

Excelsiors sprung a double surprise at the 1949 Motor Cycle Show at Earls Court, for the company had introduced a few days before the show, an entirely new vertical twin two stroke machine in the 250 c.c. class, which created a very great deal of interest, and also announced that all their motor cycles (as distinct from Auto Cycles) for the current season would be equipped with fully sprung rear frames. Naturally enough the Excelsior stand was one of the main centres of attraction.

All the latest models in the range, of which there are seven, are in the lightweight or auto-cycle class. There are two 98 c.c. Auto-Cycles, one with the single speed and one with a two speed gearbox, styled the "De-Luxe Autobyk," and the "Super Autobyk," respectively. The 122 c.c. "Universal" Model, with Villiers engine is available with either direct or rectified lighting, and the 197 c.c. "Roadmaster" is also offered in these two forms. Finally there is the 244 c.c. Model TT1, "Talisman" twin cylinder machine.

Dealing first with the 98 c.c. "De Luxe Autobyk," Model S1, the engine unit of this machine is the Excelsior "Spryt" two stroke engine of 50 mm. bore by 50 mm. stroke. The engine has an alloy piston, a detachable cylinder head, ball bearing mainshaft and roller bearing big end. Oil retaining seals are provided in the crankcase and the Amal carburettor has a single lever handlebar control. A weldless steel tube frame, with a patented bottom bracket allows of separate adjustment for the cycle chain. The engine is mounted at approximately 45° in the frame. The newly designed Excelsior front fork is of tubular design and is made from Reynolds 531 steel tube, incorporating rubber suspension. A Wico-Pacey flywheel magneto supplies the 21 watt lighting circuit, including the Miller 6" headlamp with independent parking light. The all steel tank holds 11 pints and 4" internal expanding hub brakes are fitted to both wheels. Dunlop 26" x 2" heavy Carrier tyres are fitted. A special large soft topped saddle and raised adjustable handlebars with chromium plated finish and rubber grips are other features of the specification.

The 98 c.c. "Super Autobyk," Model G2, is very similar in general design and details, but in this case, an Excelsior 98 c.c. "Goblin" two stroke engine is fitted, with unit construction two speed gear operated by lever. The engine has a detachable cylinder head, alloy piston and a ball bearing mainshaft. Rubber sprung parallel-ruler action tubular front forks are similar to the "De Luxe Model" and frame details are to the same specification. A Wico-Pacey flywheel magneto supplies the 6" headlamp, which however includes a dipper switch. The saddle on the G2 has an Aero cord elastic mattress top covered with weatherproof leathercloth. Dunlop 21" x 2.25" tyres are fitted in lieu of the 26" x 2" on the S1 model, and the silencer on Model G2 is chromium plated.

The smallest model in the motor cycle range is the 122 c.c. "Universal," Model U1. The Villiers two stroke Mark 10D engine gear unit is used for this machine, with a three-speed foot operated box. The engine has a flat top deflectorless piston and an aluminium detachable cylinder head. The frame has coil spring suspension at the rear and the telescopic front forks are of alloy steel tubing. Dual double action coil springs absorb the road shocks and deep phosphor bronze bushes support the sliding fork members protected by oil seals. A Villiers high tension magneto supplies the ignition and lighting. The 24 watt headlamp has an independent parking light and dipper switch, 5" internal expanding brakes are fitted front and rear and Dunlop 19" x 2.75" tyres and a spring up central stand are supplied. Model U2 is fitted with rectified lighting, accumulator and electric horn.

The 197 c.c. Villiers engined Roadmaster follows the same general design as the Universal. The power unit in this case however, is the Villiers Mark 6E (59 mm. x 72 mm.) engine, with single port detachable head, ball bearing mainshaft and roller bearing big end. This unit incorporates the 3 speed foot-operated box. Ignition and lighting are similar to the Universal, and the engine is fitted in a three-point engine mounting to a fully sprung frame with the Excelsior telescopic front forks. Brakes are 5" internal expanding and tyres are Dunlop 19" x 3". A neat triangular tool box is supplied on both this and the U series models and Smith's Chronometric Speedometers are fitted to these lightweight models. Model R2 is fitted with rectified lighting, battery, and electric horn.

The most interesting machine is undoubtedly the new "Talisman" Twin two stroke, of 244 c.c. The 50 mm. x 62 mm. bore and stroke engine has entirely separate parallel vertical cylinders and separate heads. The crank throws are at 180° to each other, each piston has its own crankcase and the mainshaft has 5 bearings. The 4 speed unit construction foot change gearbox is bolted to the rear of the crankcase. The engine, which is Petroil lubricated, is mounted vertically in the frame and secured by two pairs of engine plates—a pair at the front and a pair at the rear. The ball bearing crankshaft drives a Wico-Pacey generator. The connecting rods are of nickel chrome steel. The aluminium alloy pistons are flat topped and are fitted with two rings. Each cylinder has the induction port at the rear and an exhaust port at the front and an aluminium alloy manifold connects the induction ports and carries an Amal carburettor. The manifold is designed to give a downswept action to the gases. The transfer ports are so designed that the gases flow to the rear of the combustion chamber, where the plugs are located. The cylinder barrels are spigotted to a depth of $\frac{9}{16}$" into the crankcase. The cylinder heads are of aluminium alloy. The small end carries a phosphor-bronze bush and the big end bearings are alternate steel and bronze rollers. The two exhaust pipes join and run into a common silencer situated on the left hand side of the machine.

The 4 speed positive stop foot change gearbox drives through a 2 plate cork insert clutch running in oil.

The frame and suspension are similar to the Roadmaster, Excelsior Telescopic front forks being fitted, with the new plunger type rear suspension, which allows a movement of 1¾". A steel housing contains two springs—a short rebound coil spring and a double coiled compression spring, which is slightly longer. A phosphor bronze bush at top and bottom of the housing form bearings for the housing to slide up and down. The housing carries the wheel spindle, and is packed with grease and provided with suitable sealing glands. The spring unit can be swivelled round for easy wheel detachment by removal of a chain adjuster. Rubber buffers fitted at top and bottom of the assembly cushion the movement.

3.00" x 19" Dunlop tyres and internal expanding brakes (the front 5", the rear 6") a triangular tool box and central spring up stand are also features of the specification. The flywheel magneto supplies a 30 watt electric lighting set, battery and electric horn. A Smith's hub-driven speedometer is also supplied.

SPECIFICATION.
EXCELSIOR 98 c.c. Auto-Cycle. Model S1 De Luxe.

Engine. Make, Excelsior Spryt.
Bore and Stroke. 50 mm. x 50 mm. 98 c.c.
Compression Ratio. 8 to 1.
B.H.P. 2.5.
Single cylinder, air cooled two stroke, single port. Alloy piston. Detachable cylinder head.
Sparking plugs 14 mm.
Lubrication. Petroil.
Carburettor. Amal.
Gear box. Final drive ratio. 11.29 to 1.
Clutch. Single Plate.
Transmission. Primary. Chain ¾" x 7/32".
Secondary. Chain ½" x 3/16".
Ignition. Flywheel Magneto.
Lighting. Flywheel magneto. 21 watt electric lighting. Miller 6" headlamp with independent parking light.
Petrol Capacity. Petroil, 1¾ gallons.
Oil Capacity. Petroil system.
Tyres. Dunlop, 26" x 2", front and rear.
Brakes. 4" diameter, internal expanding, front and rear.
Frame and Suspension. Weldless steel tube rigid frame, with patent bottom bracket with separate adjustment for cycle chain. Excelsior steel tubular forks.
Saddle. Large soft top saddle. **Height from ground.** 3' 3".
Wheelbase. 50". **Ground Clearance.** 5".
Overall Length. 6' 6". **Width over bars.** 23¼".
Weight (dry) 118 lb.
Finish. Tank stove enamelled black, with cream panels. Bright parts chromium plated.
Equipment. Tool box, tools, pump, horn and licence holder.
Extra or optional equipment. Lightweight speedometer (extra).
Maximum Speed. 35 m.p.h.
Petrol consumption (at 30 m.p.h.) 150—180 m.p.g.

EXCELSIOR 98 c.c. Auto-Cycle. Model G2. " Super."

SPECIFICATION.

Engine. Make, Excelsior," Goblin."
Bore and Stroke. 50 mm. x 50 mm. 98 c.c.
Compression Ratio. 8.0 to 1.
B.H.P. 2.6.
Single cylinder, air cooled two stroke, single port. Alloy piston, detachable cylinder head.
Sparking plugs. 14 mm.
Lubrication. Petroil.
Carburettor. Amal.
Gearbox. Unit construction, two speed, hand change.
Ratios. 17.12 and 8.87 to 1.
Clutch. Single plate.
Transmission. Primary. Chain ¾" x 7/32".
Secondary. Chain ½" x 3/16".
Ignition. Flywheel Magneto.
Lighting. Flywheel magneto. 21 watt electric lighting. Miller 6" headlamp, with independent parking light.
Petrol Capacity. 1⅞ gallons.
Oil Capacity. Petroil system.
Tyres. Dunlop, 21" x 2.25" front and rear.
Brakes. 4" internal expanding, front and rear.
Frame and Suspension. Weldless steel tube rigid frame, with patent bottom bracket with separate adjustment for cycle chain. Excelsior steel tubular forks.
Saddle. Large soft top saddle. **Height from ground.** 3' 3".
Wheelbase. 50". **Ground clearance.** 5".
Overall Length. 6' 6". **Width over bars.** 23¾".
Weight (dry) 120 lb.
Finish. Tank stove enamelled black, with cream panels. Bright parts chromium plated.
Equipment. Tool box, tools, pump, horn and licence holder.
Extra, or optional equipment. Lightweight speedometer (extra).
Maximum Speed. 35 m.p.h.
Petrol Consumption (at 30 m.p.h.) 150—180 m.p.g.

EXCELSIOR 122 c.c. Models U1 and U2 "Universal."

SPECIFICATION.

Engine. Make, Villiers, Mark 10D.
　　Bore and Stroke. 50 mm. x 62 mm. 122 c.c.
　　Compression Ratio. 8.0 to 1.
　　B.H.P. Approx. 3.25.
　　Single cylinder, air cooled two stroke, single port. Flat top piston, aluminium alloy detachable cylinder head.
　　Sparking plugs. 14 mm.
Lubrication. Petroil.
Carburettor. Villiers Automatic.
Gearbox. 3 speed, foot change, integral with engine unit.
　　Ratios. 23.27, 12.2, and 7.17 to 1.
Clutch. 2 plate cork insert type running in oil.
Transmission. Primary. Chain ⅜" x .225".
　　Secondary. Chain ½" x ³⁄₁₆".
Ignition. Villiers Flywheel Magneto.
Lighting. 24 watt direct lighting from flywheel dynamo. 6" headlamp. U2 model has accumulator and rectified lighting.

Petroil Capacity. 2¾ gallons.
Oil Capacity. Petroil system.
Tyres. Dunlop, 2.75" x 19", front and rear.
Brakes. 5" internal expanding, front and rear.
Frame and Suspension. Sprung frame with rear coil spring suspension. Excelsior type telescopic forks.
Saddle. Large supple top type.　　**Height from ground.**　3' 4"
Wheelbase. 49".　　**Ground clearance.**　6"
Overall Length. 6' 4".　　**Width over bars.**　25"
Weight (dry). 145 lb.
Finish. Tank finished maroon with cream side panels. Bright parts chromium plated.
Equipment. Tool box, tools, horn, licence holder and pump. Spring up central stand. Smith's Chronometric Speedometer.
Extra or optional equipment.
Maximum Speed. 48 m.p.h.
Petrol Consumption (at 30 m.p.h.) 115 m.p.g.

EXCELSIOR 197 c.c. Models R1 and R2 "Roadmaster."

Engine. Make, Villiers, Mark 6E.
　　Bore and Stroke. 59 mm. x 72 mm. 197 c.c.
　　Compression Ratio. 8 to 1.
　　B.H.P. Approximately 6.8.
　　Single cylinder, air cooled two stroke, single port. Flat topped piston, aluminium alloy detachable cylinder head.
　　Sparking plugs. 14 mm.
Lubrication. Petroil.
Carburettor. Villiers.
Gearbox. 3 speed, foot change, integral with engine unit.
　　Ratios. 19.08, 9.97 and 5.86 to 1.
Clutch. 2 plate cork insert type running in oil.
Transmission. Primary. Chain ½" x .205". Oil bath chaincase.
　　Secondary. Chain ½" x ³⁄₁₆".
Ignition. Villiers Flywheel Magneto.
Lighting. Flywheel magneto, with 30 watt direct lighting and 6" headlamp. Rectified lighting and accumulator on Model R2.

Petroil Capacity. 2¾ gallons.
Oil Capacity. Petroil system.
Tyres. Dunlop, 19" x 3", front and rear.
Brakes. 5" internal expanding, front and rear.
Frame and Suspension. Sprung frame with rear coil spring suspension. Excelsior type telescopic forks.
Saddle. Large supple top type.　　**Height from ground.**　3' 6"
Wheelbase. 49".　　**Ground clearance.**　6"
Overall Length. 6' 4".　　**Width over bars.**　25"
Weight (dry). 160 lb.
Finish. Tank finished in maroon enamel with cream side panels. Bright parts chromium plated.
Equipment. Tool box, horn, licence holder, pump, central spring up stand, Smith's chronometric speedometer.
Extra or optional equipment. Rear carrier and pillion equipment.
Maximum Speed. 58 m.p.h.
Petrol Consumption (at 30 m.p.h.) 100 m.p.g.

EXCELSIOR
TWIN CYLINDER
244 c.c. TT1
"Talisman" Model.

Engine. Make. Excelsior.   Bore and Stroke. 50 mm. x 62 mm. 244 c.c.
Compression Ratio. 8 to 1.
Twin cylinder, air cooled, two stroke, separate vertical cylinders, flat topped aluminium alloy pistons. Detachable alloy cylinder head, ball bearing mainshaft, roller bearing big end.   Sparking plugs. 14 mm.
Lubrication. Petroil system.   **Carburettor.** Amal.
Gearbox. 4 speed footchange, unit construction gearbox.
Ratios. 16.1, 9.9, 7.42, and 5.5. to 1.
Clutch. 2 plate cork insert type, running in oil.
Transmission. Primary. Chain ⅜" x $\frac{7}{32}$". Oil bath chaincase.
Ignition. Wico-Pacey High Tension flywheel magneto.
Lighting. Flywheel magneto supplies 30 watt electric lighting set. Accumulator. 6" headlamp, with independent parking light and dipper switch.

Petroil Capacity. 2¾ gallons.
Tyres. Dunlop Universal, 19" x 3", front and rear.
Brakes. Internal expanding, 5" front, 6" rear.
Frame and Suspension. Fully sprung frame with rear coil spring suspension. Excelsior type telescopic forks.
Wheelbase. 49".   **Ground clearance.** 5".
Overall Length. 6' 8".   **Width over bars.** 3' 8".
Weight (dry). 200 lb.
Finish. Frame parts rust-proofed and stove enamelled maroon. Tank finished maroon enamel with cream side panels. Bright parts chromium plated.
Equipment. Tool box, tools, electric horn, pump, Smith's Chronometric 65 m.p.h. speedometer.
Maximum Speed. 65 m.p.h.   Petrol Consumption (at 30 m.p.h.) 90 m.p.g.

Francis-Barnett

FRANCIS AND BARNETT LTD.
LOWER FORD STREET · COVENTRY

The firm of Francis and Barnett was founded by Gordon Francis and the late Arthur Barnett in 1919, the first motor cycle produced being a 293 c.c. J.A.P. engined machine. Since 1923, the main concentration has been on lightweight two-stroke machines in what may be termed the "utility" class.

As long ago as 1928, the Francis-Barnett Pullman was produced, with a twin cylinder two-stroke engine with unit construction gearbox. The well known 250 c.c. "Cruiser," manufactured from 1934 to 1941 was an interesting departure—an attempt to produce a really weatherproof and enclosed motorcycle, and one which, unlike some other attempts, was very successful, the model becoming exceedingly popular.

Many competition successes were gained by Francis-Barnett machines between 1922 and 1936, which regularly took part in all the important reliability trials. In the years before the last war, however, the firm concentrated more on the purely utility side of motorcycling, and it can be fairly claimed that the marque has had a considerable influence on the development of the small class utility machine in this country.

Present day Francis-Barnett machines comprise a 98 c.c. Auto-cycle—the "Powerbike," and 122 c.c. and 197 c.c. Villiers engined models. The little auto-cycle has been almost entirely redesigned and now incorporates the latest Villiers 2F single speed engine. The 122 c.c. Merlin Model 52 is powered by the latest Villiers 10D two-stroke engine, the 53 Merlin having the same specification with the addition of rectified lighting and battery. The range is completed by the 197 c.c. Model 54 "Falcon," fitted with Villiers 6E two stroke engine, and the model 55 "Falcon," a similar machine but again fitted with rectified lighting and battery.

Model 54 Falcon and 55 Falcon. 197 c.c.

These two machines conform to the same general specification as the Merlin Models, but are fitted with the Villiers Mark 6E, 197 c.c. (59 mm. bore x 72 mm. stroke) 2 stroke engine, with gear ratios altered to suit the more powerful engine. Model 55 has a battery lighting set and electric horn, Model 54, direct lighting from the Villiers flywheel dynamo magneto.

Model 52 "Merlin" and 53 "Merlin". 122 c.c.

Both models are powered by the latest Villiers Mark 10D engine of 122 c.c. (50 mm. bore x 62 mm. stroke), with deflectorless piston, and 3 speed unit-construction gearbox. There are several very practical features on this machine—foot change is standard, a telescopic fork with 20" 3 rate springs allows a movement of over 5" for the inner slider tubes, the rear mudguard is designed for easy wheel removal without disturbing the rear "built-in" tail lamp. Larger saddles with a 1" range of adjustment and ribbed front tyres which help to provide good steering are new 1950 features. 5" diameter internal expanding front and rear brakes are fitted, the rear brakes having a finger adjustment. A separate oil tank to carry up to 3 pints of oil is fitted to the machine, a feature which will appeal to overseas riders. The handlebar layout is exceptionally clean, a combined headlight dipper switch and push button for the electric horn being provided on both Merlin 53 and Falcon 55 models. The Merlin 53 model is to the same specification as the Merlin 52, but with the addition of Battery lighting set and electric horn.

Model "56" Powerbike. 98 c.c.

The 56 Powerbike has a new loop type welded frame, the Villiers engine being fixed at three points. The Villiers Mark 2F engine has a bore and stroke of 47 mm. x 57 mm. Ignition is by Villiers flywheel magneto. The lighting output has been increased on the latest models, so that a 12 watt headlamp bulb can now be used.

$2\frac{1}{4}$" section Dunlop tyres assure riding comfort, a large spring top saddle and a link action front fork, with rubber suspension gives added comfort over rough roads. A powerful rear brake is provided on the Powerbike and this is operated motor-cycle fashion by foot pedal, with the obvious advantage of leaving the rider's hands free to use clutch and front brake levers. A tubular carrier is supplied, and there is provision in the front hub for a worm drive, should the owner wish to fit a speedometer to the machine.

**Francis-Barnett
Model 52
122 c.c. Two-stroke**

SPECIFICATIONS.
FRANCIS-BARNETT.
Models 52 and 53 Merlin 122 c.c.
Models 54 and 55 Falcon 197 c.c.

Engine. Make, Villiers. Merlin 52 and 53. Mark 10D. Falcon 54, 55 Mark 6E.
Bore and Stroke. Merlin 52 and 53. 50 mm. x 62 mm. 122 c.c.
Falcon 54 and 55. 59 mm. x 72 mm. 197 c.c.
Compression Ratio. 8 to 1.
B.H.P. Approximate Merlins 4.8 at 4,400 r.p.m.
Falcons. 8.4 at 4,000 r.p.m.
Single cylinder, two stroke, air cooled, single port, flat top deflectorless piston, detachable alloy cylinder head.
Sparking plug. 14 mm.
Lubrication. Petroil system.
Carburettor. Merlin 52, 53, Villiers Lightweight.
Falcon, 54, 55, Villiers Mediumweight.
Gearbox. 3 speed, unit construction. Foot gear change, kickstarter.
Ratios. Merlin 52, 53, 19.1, 10 to 1, 7.2 to 1.
Falcon, 54. 55, 15.6 to 1, 8.2 to 1. 5.9 to 1.
Clutch. 2 plate cork insert type, running in oil.
Transmission. Merlin 52, 53. Primary. Chain ⅜″ x .225″.
Falcon 54, 55. Primary. Chain ½″ x .205″.
Secondary. Renold chain ½″ x .205″.
Ignition. Villiers Flywheel Magneto.
Lighting. Merlin 52, Falcon 54, Direct lighting from Villiers flywheel magneto.
Merlin 53, Falcon 55, Villiers rectified D.C. battery lighting set and electric horn.
Petrol Capacity. Welded steel tank. 2¼ gallons capacity. Two level tap fitted.
Oil Capacity. Petroil system. Separate oil tank to carry 3 pints.
Tyres. Front. Dunlop. 3.00″ x 19″, Ribbed.
Rear, Dunlop. 3.00″ x 19″, Universal pattern.
Brakes. Internal expanding, 5″ diameter, front and rear. Finger adjustment for rear brakes.
Frame and Suspension. Francis Barnett Telescopic forks, with 20″, 3 rate springs.
Tubular rigid frame, welded and brazed.
Saddle. Lycett spring top. **Height from ground.** 27¾″ to 29″.
Wheelbase. 49″. **Ground clearance.** 5″.
Overall Length. 78¼″. **Width.** 26½″.
Weight (dry). Merlin 52, 181 lb. Merlin 53, 193 lb. Falcon 54, 187 lbs.
Falcon 55, 199 lbs.
Finish. Best quality black enamel. Tank-gold lined. Handlebars, exhaust system and other bright parts chromium plated.
Equipment. Bulb horn (on Merlin 52 and Falcon 54). Front and rear stands. Smith's Lightweight Speedometer (Merlin models) Smith's Trip Speedometer (Falcon Models). Legshields extra, available on all models.

**Francis-Barnett
Model 55
197 c.c. Two-stroke**

FRANCIS-BARNETT, Model 56, 98 c.c. "Powerbike."

SPECIFICATION.

Engine. Make, Villiers Mark 2F.
  Bore and Stroke. 47 mm. x 57 mm. 98 c.c.
  Compression Ratio. 8 to 1.
  B.H.P. Approximately 2.0 at 3,750 r.p.m.
  Single cylinder, two stroke, air cooled, single port. Flat top piston, aluminium detachable cylinder head.
  Sparking plug. 14 mm.
Lubrication. Petroil system.
Carburettor. Villiers Junior.
Gearbox. Single speed. Ratio. 11.8 to 1.
Clutch. Two plate cork insert type. Runs in oil.
Transmission. Primary. Chain $\frac{3}{8}''$ x .225".
  Secondary (Power) Renold Chain $\frac{1}{2}''$ x .92".
  Pedal. Renold Chain $\frac{1}{2}''$ x .130".
  Independent adjustment for pedalling and transmission chains.
Ignition. Villiers Flywheel Magneto.
Lighting. Villiers direct lighting from flywheel magneto. Parking battery in headlamp.
Petroil Capacity. Steel welded tank. Capacity 1¼ gallons. Two level petrol tap fitted.
Oil Capacity. Petroil system.
Tyres. 2.25" x 21" Dunlop, front and rear.
Brakes. Internal expanding, 4" diameter, front and rear. Rear brake foot operated, front by handlebar lever.
Frame and Suspension. Tubular loop frame, welded construction. Tubular link action forks, with rubber suspension. Rigid frame.
Saddle. Lycett spring top.   Height from ground.   31¼".
Wheelbase. 48¼".   Ground clearance.   5".
Weight (dry). 125 lb.
Finish. Best quality black enamel. Tank and engine shields gold lined. Handlebars, wheel rims, exhaust system and other bright parts chromium plated.
Equipment. Large silencer. Rear, clip up stand. Bulb horn, licence holder, Tubular carrier, with metal tool box and tools.
  Speedometer (extra).

STOP PRESS
Alternative finish now available—azure blue.

James

**THE JAMES CYCLE COMPANY LTD.
GREET · BIRMINGHAM, 11.**

The James Company are famous for their range of modern lightweights, but it is not generally realised that a machine was first produced as long ago as 1901, which incorporated a Minerva engine. This was followed in 1903 by further models using British engines. 1908 saw the introduction of the first James model proper, manufactured in the company's works. Improvements followed quickly, and in 1911 the James machine was fitted with all-chain drive, a final drive oil bath chain case, kick starter, 2 speed gear box and multi-plate clutch.

The 1950 programme comprises six lightweight motor cycles and an autocycle. In addition the 122 c.c. and 197 c.c. machines are offered in competition form. All models are fitted with the latest type of Villiers engines and the 197 c.c. de luxe machine has a fully sprung rear frame.

The 98 c.c. "Superlux" autocycle is fitted with the Villiers Mark 2F engine of 47 mm. x 57 mm. An engine shield is fitted which can be detached quickly by unscrewing three wing nuts, and an aperture in the shield allows of access to the petroil tap. Link action girder forks with a central compression spring are fitted and the specification includes 4" internal expanding brakes front and rear, a heavy-duty carrier and rear stand and 2.25" x 21" tyres.

The 98 c.c. Comet Motor cycles have the two-speed Villiers 1F two-stroke engine incorporating the Villiers flywheel magneto. The de luxe model "Comet" is fitted with battery and rectifier lighting and an electric horn, and a larger petrol tank of 2½ gallons capacity, and a rear carrier. 2.50" x 19" tyres are fitted to both Comet models. The forks are of the brazed-up, weldless steel tapered tube parallel link type. The engine is built in unit with the two-speed gearbox, and the cast iron deeply finned cylinder has one exhaust and two transfer ports of the latest Villiers design. The petrol consumption for this machine is given as 160-180 miles per gallon.

Next in the range are the 122 c.c. "Cadet" and "Cadet de Luxe" models, powered by Villiers Mark 10D engines with 3 speed positive stop foot change gear box and Villiers flywheel generator. The frame on this machine, which was previously similar to that on the 197 c.c. model, has been lowered for 1950, resulting in an improved appearance. A new design of James telescopic fork is fitted to the 122 c.c. machine. An outer static tube contains an inner sliding member operating in two phosphor bronze bushes. Three rubber springs are fitted to a central rod inside the sliding tube and provide the suspension medium. 5" internal expanding brakes are fitted front and rear. On the "De Luxe" model, rectifier lighting, battery and electric horn and a rear carrier are fitted. Rear suspension can also be supplied as an optional extra on these "Cadet" 122 c.c. models. Approximate figures are a top speed of 45 m.p.h. with a petrol consumption of 120 miles per gallon.

The Captain De Luxe Model, the largest machine in the range, is fitted with the 197 c.c. Mark 6E Villiers engine, with flywheel generator, 3.00" x 19" tyres, heavier gauge wheel spokes, 5" brakes, a rear carrier, and larger tool boxes. James telescopic front forks and rectifier lighting are standard fittings, but plunger rear suspension of the spring type is available on this model if required. This machine has a "Man-size" riding position, with speeds in the neighbourhood of 58 m.p.h., and a petrol consumption of about 100 miles per gallon, and is powerful enough to carry an occasional pillion passenger.

The 122 c.c. and 197 c.c models are offered in competition form, based on the machines used in the International Six Days Trial. These models are fitted with light alloy wide clearance mudguards, Dunlop tyres, 2.75" x 19" front and 3.25" x 19" rear. The handlebars are slightly raised and a high-level exhaust system is fitted. Alternative gear ratios can be supplied, and direct lighting is fitted, with a smaller headlamp.

A combined legshield and crashbar can be fitted as an extra to all models. A Smith's non-trip speedometer is fitted to Cadet and Captain Models but speedometers can be supplied as an extra to the Auto-Cycle and Comet machines. Girder forks can be fitted in place of the telescopic type on Cadet and Captain models at a reduction in price.

SPECIFICATION.
JAMES 98 c.c. " Superlux " Autocycle.
Engine. Make. Villiers Mark 2F.
Bore and Stroke. 47 mm. x 57 mm. 98 c.c.
Compression Ratio. 8 to 1.
B.H.P. 2.0 at 3,750 r.p.m.
Single cylinder, air cooled two stroke, single port.
Flat top piston, aluminium detachable cylinder head.
Sparking plugs. 14 mm.
Lubrication. Petroil system.
Carburettor. Villiers Junior.
Gearbox. Single speed. Ratio. 10.78.
Clutch. Two plate cork insert type. Runs in oil.
Transmission. Primary. Chain ⅜" pitch.
Secondary. Chain ½" x .305".
Ignition. Villiers Flywheel Magneto.
Lighting. Villiers A.C. direct.
Petrol Capacity. 1½ gallons petroil
Tyres. 2.25" x 21" front and rear.
Brakes. 4" internal expanding, front and rear.
Frame and Suspension. Rigid frame. Girder type centre spring forks.
Wheelbase. 49¾". **Height from ground.** 31¼" —35¼".
Overall Length. 6' 7" **Ground Clearance.** 5¼".
Weight (dry) 134 lbs. **Width over bars.** 23".
Finish. Maroon enamel. Bright parts chromium plated.
Equipment. Rear carrier, rear stand, tool kit.
Extra or optional equipment. Smith's Non-trip speedometer.
Maximum Speed. approximately 35 m.p.h.
Petrol consumption (at 30 m.p.h.) Approximately 150 m.p.g.

SPECIFICATION.

JAMES 98 c.c. "Comet" and "Comet de Luxe" Motor cycles.

Engine. Make. Villiers Mark 1F.
Bore and Stroke. 47 mm. x 57 mm. 98 c.c.
Compression Ratio. 8 to 1.
B.H.P. 2.8 at 4,000 r.p.m.
Single cylinder, two stroke, air cooled, single port, flat top piston, light alloy detachable cylinder head. Ball bearing mainshaft, roller bearing big end.
Sparking plugs. 14 mm.
Lubrication. Petroil.
Carburettor. Villiers Junior.
Gearbox. 2 speed, hand control.
Ratios. 13.04 and 8.47 to 1.
Clutch. Cork insert, two plate clutch, running in oil.
Transmission. Primary. Chain ⅜" pitch.
Secondary. Chain ½" x .305".
Ignition. Villiers Flywheel Magneto.
Lighting. Comet. Villiers A.C. Direct.
Comet de Luxe. Villiers D.C. Rectifier and battery. Electric horn and stoplight.
Petrol Capacity. 2¼ gallons. Petroil.
Tyres. 2.50" x 19". front and rear. Dunlop.
Brakes. 4" internal expanding, front and rear.
Frame and Suspension. Rigid frame, girder type, centre spring forks.
Wheelbase. 46½". **Height from ground.** 28" (Comet). 29" (Comet de Luxe).
Overall Length. 6' 1¾". **Ground Clearance** 5½" (Comet). 4½" (Comet de Luxe).
Width over bars. 25½".
Weight (dry) 128 lb. (Comet) 148 lb. (Comet de Luxe).
Finish. Comet. Maroon enamel, with blue tank panels.
Comet de Luxe. Maroon enamel. Silencer, tank top strip and other parts chrome plated.
Equipment. Central stand. Rear carrier and electric horn on "De Luxe" Model.
Extra or optional equipment. Comet. Rear carrier, Smith's Non-trip Speedometer, Crash-bar leg shields.
Comet de Luxe. Smith's Non-trip Speedometer, Crashbar-legshields.
Maximum Speed. 40 m.p.h.
Petrol Consumption (at 30 m.p.h.) app. 150 m.p.g.

SPECIFICATION.

JAMES 122 c.c. "Cadet" and "Cadet de Luxe" Models.

Engine. Make. Villiers Mark 10D.
Bore and Stroke. 50 mm. x 62 mm. 122 c.c.
Compression Ratio. 8 to 1.
B.H.P. 4.8 at 4,400 r.p.m.
Single cylinder, two stroke, air cooled, single port. Flat top, deflectorless piston. Detachable alloy cylinder head.
Sparking plugs. 14 mm.
Lubrication. Petroil system.
Carburettor. Villiers Lightweight.
Gearbox. 3 speed, unit construction, foot change. Kickstarter.
Ratios. 23.35, 12.2, and 7.185 to 1.
Clutch. 2 plate, cork insert type, running in oil.
Transmission. Primary. Chain ⅜" pitch.
Secondary. Chain ½" x .335".
Ignition. Villiers Flywheel Magneto.
Lighting. Cadet. Villiers A.C. Direct Lighting.
Cadet de Luxe. Villiers D.C. rectifier and battery. Electric horn and stop light.
Petrol Capacity. 2¼ gallons Petroil.
Tyres. Dunlop 3.00" x 19", front and rear.
Brakes. 5" internal expanding, front and rear.
Frame and Suspension. James Telescopic forks and rigid frame. Girder forks available at reduced price.
Wheelbase. 48½". **Height from ground.** 28¾".
Overall Length. 6' 7". **Ground clearance.** 5".
Width over bars. 25½".
Weight (dry) Cadet 170 lb. Cadet de Luxe. 189 lb.
Finish. Maroon enamel. (Silencer, tank top strip and other parts chromium plated on de luxe model).
Equipment. Central spring-up stand. Rear carrier on "De Luxe Model." Smith's Non-trip Speedometer.
Extra or optional equipment. Rear carrier (Cadet Model), crashbar-legshields (both models).
Maximum Speed. 1st 15 m.p.h. 2nd 24 m.p.h. 3rd 45 m.p.h.
Speed at end of quarter mile from rest. 40 m.p.h.
Petrol Consumption (at 30 m.p.h.) 120 m.p.g. (approx.)
Braking (from 30 m.p.h. to rest). 31 ft.
Cadet Competition Model to above specification, but with light alloy wide clearance mudguards. Dunlop tyres, 2.75" x 19", front and 3.25" x 19", rear. Raised handlebars, high-level exhaust system alternative gear ratios and direct lighting with smaller headlamp.

SPECIFICATION.

JAMES 197 c.c. "Captain" Model.

Engine. Make, Villiers Mark 6E.
Bore and Stroke. 59 mm. x 72 mm. 197 c.c.
Compression Ratio. 8 to 1.
B.H.P. 8.4 at 4,000 r.p.m.
Single cylinder, two stroke, air cooled, single port, flat top, deflectorless piston, detachable alloy cylinder head.
Sparking plugs. 14 mm.
Lubrication. Petroil.
Carburettor. Villiers Middleweight.
Gearbox. 3 speed, unit construction, foot change. Kickstarter.
Ratios. 19.0, 9.96, and 5.86 to 1.
Clutch. 2 plate, cork insert type, running in oil.
Transmission. Primary. Chain ⅜" pitch.
Secondary. Chain ½" x .335".
Ignition. Villiers Flywheel Magneto.
Lighting. Villiers D.C. Rectifier and battery.
Petrol Capacity. 2¼ gallons, Petroil.
Tyres. 3.00" x 19", front and rear, Dunlop.
Brakes. Internal expanding, 5" front and rear.
Frame and Suspension. James Telescopic Forks. Rigid frame.
Fully sprung, plunger type rear springing on "De Luxe"
Wheelbase. 48½". **Height from ground** 30½"
Overall Length. 6' 7". **Ground clearance.** 6½".
Width over bars. 25½".
Weight (dry) 200 lb. (De luxe Model 215 lb.)
Finish. De Luxe maroon enamel, bright parts chromium plated.
Equipment. Central spring-up stand. Rear carrier. Smith's Non-trip speedometer.
Extra or optional equipment. Crashbar-legshields. Girder forks in place of telescopic type at reduced price.
Maximum Speed. 1st 21 m.p.h. 2nd 37 m.p.h. 3rd 58 m.p.h.
Speed at end of quarter mile from rest. 43 m.p.h.
Petrol Consumption (at 30 m.p.h.) 100 m.p.g. approx.
Braking (from 30 m.p.h. to rest). 31 ft.
Captain Competition Model to above specification, but with light alloy, wide clearance mudguards, Dunlop tyres, 2.75" x 19" front, and 3.25" x 19", rear. Raised handlebars, high-level exhaust system, alternative gear ratios and direct lighting with smaller headlamp.

Matchless

ASSOCIATED MOTOR CYCLES LTD.
PLUMSTEAD ROAD · LONDON · S.E. 18

U.S.A. Distributor (Except California):
INDIAN SALES CORPORATION
29 Worthington St.
Springfield, Mass.

California Distributor:
COOPER MOTORS
4401 S. Figueroa St.
Los Angeles, Calif.

Associated Motor Cycles Ltd., the makers of Matchless machines, occupy a leading place in the British motor cycle industry. Formerly H. Collier and Sons Ltd, the firm has made the famous Matchless machine continuously since 1899, when Charles and Harry Collier, sons of the founder of the company, produced the first model. In the early nineteen-hundreds the Matchless rapidly established a racing reputation, and C. R. Collier won the first Isle of Man Tourist Trophy Race in 1907 at 38.23 m.p.h., his brother, H. A. Collier repeating the feat in 1909.

Since those days the name of Matchless has been constantly in the forefront of motor cycling sport, and many enthusiasts will remember with affection such well-known machines as the Model H fully-sprung sidecar outfit of post Great War years, the 1927 998 c.c. Vee twin, and the 500 c.c. Model V2. In 1931 the 400 c.c. Vee twin Silver Arrow was introduced, followed in 1934 by the 600 c.c. Vee 4 cylinder Silver Hawk. Both machines created a great sensation at the time. These are only a few of the machines which have made history.

During the last war, Associated Motor Cycles produced over 80,000 o.h.v. machines for the services and many will remember the faithful service given by the Matchless G3/L in every part of the world.

The company occupies a very high place in the industry so far as exports are concerned, and Matchless machines are maintaining British prestige, and earning much-needed currency all over the world. In 1949, during which year the export market hardened considerably, the export figure was over 70% of the total output.

The Matchless range for 1951 comprises nine models. In both the 350 c.c. and 500 c.c. classes four versions are offered—a standard model with rigid frame, a standard model with swinging arm rear frame and Teledraulic spring units, a Competition model with rigid frame and a similar machine available for the first time with spring frame. The 500 c.c. vertical twin "Super Clubman" completes the range.

This range incorporates the results of a further year's development work. Engine efficiency of the single cylinder models has been increased by the introduction of a light alloy cylinder head of entirely new design.

The rear suspension units of the spring frame models have been redesigned, and further modifications made to the Teledraulic front forks.

MATCHLESS MODEL G3/L. 347 c.c. o.h.v.

These machines are powered by a high efficiency single port, o.h.v. push rod engine (69 mm. bore × 93 mm. stroke) employing duplex overlapping hairpin valve springs and low clearance wire-wound anti-slap pistons with two piece crankpin and three row roller big end bearings. Lubrication is by the dry sump method, employing a duplex rotary reciprocating plunger pump. A Burman 4 speed positive stop foot change gear box is provided, with a four spring clutch. The primary drive and the dynamo drive are contained in an oil bath chaincase. A redesigned Amal carburettor has been fitted.

A Duplex cradle type frame is employed with Teledraulic front forks, with non-bottoming oil damping.

The brake shoes are now provided with adjustable thrust pads and on all machines smoother front wheel braking has been secured with the incorporation of a longer anchor arm. Other detail modifications are: redesigned front and rear mudguard of deep section, with a stiffening rib. The tool box has been repositioned to allow of better mounting for panniers, and exhaust pipes have been provided with greater clearance for cornering. New and wider rear hubs have been fitted with detachable races.

Historic Matchless models (top) 998 c.c. V. twin, 1912, (centre) 347 c.c. O.H.C. single, 1926, and (bottom) the Army G3/L, 1941.

MATCHLESS MODEL G3/L 350 c.c. o.h.v.

MATCHLESS MODEL G3/LS. 347 c.c. o.h.v. spring frame.

These machines are similar to Model G3/L but the Duplex cradle frame incorporates full Teledraulic oil-damped rear suspension, a swinging arm of massive construction pivoting in a self-lubricating bush in a light alloy casting. The range of movement at the wheel spindle is 3″. A valanced rear mudguard is supplied on these models.

MATCHLESS MODEL G 80. 498 c.c. o.h.v.

The 498 c.c. models are counterparts of the 350 c.c. machines, but with an engine of 82.5 mm. bore × 93 mm. stroke. A five spring clutch in place of the four spring on 350 c.c. models, and a 3.50″ × 19″ rear tyre instead of a 3.25″ × 19″ as on the 350, are the only substantial differences.

MATCHLESS MODEL G 80 S. 498 c.c. o.h.v. Spring Frame.

Similar to Model G 80, but with full rear suspension and valanced rear mudguard.

MATCHLESS MODELS G3/LC (347 c.c.) and G80C (498 c.c.) Competition Models.

These competition models have been designed to fill the requirements of the enthusiastic clubman, and the fact that the 1950 Scottish Six Days' Trial, the 1947 and 1949 British Experts' Trial and many other open events have been won on these models is sufficient proof of the success of the design.

The major modifications to the standard single cylinder machines are as follows:—

Special shortened frame with wheelbase of 52½″, and ground clearance of 6¾″. Undershield is fitted.

Narrow section aluminium alloy mudguards.

Front wheel: 10 gauge spokes with 3.00″ × 21″ tyre.

Rear wheel: 6 gauge spokes fitted with 4.00″ × 19″ tyre.

KE 805 rear spindle and security bolts.

Small capacity (2¼ gallon) petrol tank.

4 pint oil tank with repositioned filler neck.

Racing type Lucas waterproof magneto.

Wide ratio gearbox with folding kickstarter pedal.

Internally mounted footrests, positioned farther to the rear.

Small Competition Lycett saddle, set back, with ample adjustment for height.

Twin throttle and clutch controls are provided and special alloy steel rear wheels. The exhaust is upswept.

The competition engines are exceptionally interesting. A light alloy cylinder head, with cast-in iron valve seatings, is fitted and an aluminium alloy top cover encloses the o.h.v. gear. The light alloy cylinder head casting incorporates wells for the hairpin valve springs. A light alloy cylinder barrel with shrunk-in centrifugally cast liner is secured to the cylinder head by 4 high-tensile steel studs, ⅜″ diameter, which, protruding from the crankcase mouth, pass through the cylinder barrel casting, extending nearly to its top face. Sleeve nuts, 3″ long, located in the valve gear compartment of the cylinder head secure these studs, leaving both studs and nuts invisible from the exterior.

Optional equipment on these models is a 3 gallon fuel tank, standard rear wheel standard gear ratios and electric lighting.

MATCHLESS MODELS G3/LCS and G8GCS.

Introduced for the first time in the 1951 range, these are the spring frame versions of the Competition models. They have already been proved very successful in the hands of Works' riders, and will be watched with interest in future sporting events.

MATCHLESS MODEL G9. 498 c.c. o.h.v. vertical twin. Spring frame.

This model, known as the Super Clubman was introduced at the 1948 Motor Cycle Show and remains substantially unchanged, except for a few detail refinements.

The 498 c.c. engine has a bore of 66 mm. and a 72.8 mm. stroke. Separate light alloy cylinder heads have cast in valve seats, there are separate cast iron cylinders, and the three bearing crankshaft is supported by roller outer bearings and a plain centre main bearing. Light alloy forged connecting rods, twin flywheels, Vandervell big end bearings, wire wound pistons, a rotary crankcase pressure relief valve and dry sump lubrication with positive feed to all moving parts are other salient features of the specification. A Burman 4 speed gearbox, with positive stop foot change and a five spring multi-plate clutch is fitted. Centre front and prop stands are provided and the hinged portion of the rear mudguard allows the rear wheel to be rolled out. A 3 gallon tank, finished in red and chrome, is supplied.

A.M.C. Teledraulic forks and Teledraulic rear suspension are fitted. A wide tandem integral Dunlopillo seat is standard. A gear driven magneto and 45 watt dynamo look after the electrical side.

More is the pity that the greater part of the total production of these fascinating motor cycles for 1951 is, in all probability, destined for export.

MATCHLESS MODEL G9
498 c.c. Super Clubman

MATCHLESS G3/L, G3/LS, G 80 and G 80S.
ENGINE. Make. Matchless. Bore and Stroke, 69 mm. × 93 mm. 347 c.c. (G3/L, G3/LS), 82.5 mm. × 93 mm. 498 c.c. (G80, G80S). Single cylinder, o.h.v. air cooled, single port. Totally enclosed push rod operated valves. Triple row Duralumin caged big end bearing and two piece crankpin. Stellite tipped valves, Duplex Hairpin valve springs, wire wound pistons, individually balanced flywheels and lubricated cam type engine shaft shock absorber. Sparking Plug 14 mm.
LUBRICATION. Pressure lubricated by large capacity Duplex rotary reciprocating oil pump. Full dry sump system.
CARBURETTOR. Amal semi-automatic. Twist grip throttle control and air lever.
GEAR BOX. Burman oil lubricated heavyweight, 4 speed with enclosed positive stop foot gear change and kickstarter. Ratios:— G3/L, G3/LS. 1st 15.57 10.26, 7.47, 5.83 to 1. G80, G80S. 1st 13.35, 8.8, 6.4, 5.0 to 1.
CLUTCH. Multi plate clutch with Bowden operated hand control.
IGNITION. Chain driven Lucas NR1 magneto.
LIGHTING. Separate Lucas dynamo. 6 volt. Constant voltage control. 7" headlamp. Rear lamp. dipper switch and horn button.
PETROL CAPACITY. 3 gallon welded tank with twin filter taps.
OIL CAPACITY. 4 pint welded steel oil tank.
TYRES. Triple Stud Dunlop. 3.25" × 19" front and rear (G3/L, G3/LS). 3.25" × 19" front and 3.50" × 19" rear (G80, G80S).
BRAKES. Quickly adjustable, internal expanding. 7" diameter.
FRAME AND SUSPENSION. Duplex cradle of brazed construction, forged fork ends, integral sidecar and pillion rest lugs. rear front and prop stands. A.M.C. patent Teledraulic forks, G3/L, G80. As above but with full Teledraulic rear oil damped suspension. (G3/LS, G80S).
SADDLE. Fully adjustable. Make Lycett. Height from ground 30".
WHEELBASE. 54".
GROUND CLEARANCE. 5½".
WEIGHT (dry). 344 lb. (G3/L) 375 lb. (G3/LS), 354 lb. (G80), 368 lb. (G80S).
FINISH. Stoved enamel on Bonderised surface. Exhaust system, wheel rims, handlebars etc. chromium plated. Petrol tank and wheel rims hand lined.
EXTRA OR OPTIONAL EQUIPMENT. Detachable luggage carrier, Pillion seat and footrests.

MATCHLESS G3/LC & G 80C. G3/LCS & G 80CS.
ENGINE. Make. Matchless. Bore and Stroke, 69 mm. × 93 mm. 347 c.c. (G3/LC), 82.5 mm. × 93 mm. 498 c.c. (G80C). Compression Ratios: With plate 5.88 to 1 (G3/LC). Less plate 6.35 to 1 (G3/LC). With plate 5.97 to 1 (G80C). Less plate 7.4 to 1 (G80C). Single cylinder, o.h.v. air cooled, single port. Totally enclosed push rod operated valves. Light alloy cylinder head and barrel with cast in centrifugally cast iron liner and long retaining bolts. Duplex hairpin valve springs, Stellite tipped valves, wire wound piston, individually balanced flywheels and lubricated cam type engine shaft shock absorber. Sparking plugs 14 m.m.
LUBRICATION. Pressure lubricated by large capacity Duplex Rotary reciprocating oil pump. Full dry sump system.
CARBURETTOR. Amal semi-automatic, with twist grip throttle control and air lever.
GEAR BOX. Burman oil lubricated heavyweight 4 speed enclosed positive stop foot gear change, and folding kickstarter. Ratios, G3/LC. 20.94. 14.42, 8.38, 6.56 to 1. G 80 C. 18.44, 12.20, 7.47, 5.83 to 1.
CLUTCH. Multi plate clutch with Bowden hand control.
IGNITION. Chain driven Lucas NR1 magneto.
LIGHTING. Optional extra.
PETROL CAPACITY. 2¼ galls. Welded tank with twin filter taps. 2¼ galls.
OIL CAPACITY. 4 pint oil tank with repositioned filler cap.
TYRES. 3.00" × 21", front 4.00" × 19" (rear).
BRAKES. Quickly adjustable, internal expanding, 7" diameter.
FRAME AND SUSPENSION. Duplex cradle rigid frame. Teledraulic forks. G3/LCS and G80CS as above but with full Teledraulic oil damped rear suspension.
SADDLE. Small competition Lycett saddle. Height from ground, 32¼".
WHEELBASE. 52½".
GROUND CLEARANCE. 6⁷/₁₆" (G3/LC), 6⅛" (G80C).
WEIGHT (dry). G3/LC 299 lb. G80C 304 lb.
FINISH. Upswept exhaust system, undershield, light alloy polished mudguards with tubular stays, twin throttle and clutch cables, KE 805 rear spindle, security bolts, Black stove enamel and chromium plate.
EXTRA OR OPTIONAL EQUIPMENT. 3 gallon fuel tank. standard gear ratios, standard rear wheel, electric lighting.

MATCHLESS MODEL G 9.
ENGINE. Make. Matchless. Bore and Stroke, 66 mm. × 72.8 mm. (498 c.c.). Compression Ratio, 7.25 to 1. Twin cylinder, o.h.v. air cooled, single port. 3 bearing crankshaft with twin flywheels, separate cylinders deeply spigotted into the die cast spherical crankcase. Heavily finned, separate light alloy cylinder heads with the internal rocker posts and eccentric spindle rocker adjustment. Stellite tipped valves, cast-in valve seats, forged light alloy connecting rods, wire wound pistons, roller outer main bearings, with Vandervell centre main and big end bearings. Sparking plugs 14 mm.
LUBRICATION. Full dry sump. High output twin gear pumps.
CARBURETTOR. Amal semi-automatic, with twist grip throttle control and air lever.
GEAR BOX. Burman oil lubricated heavyweight 4 speed with enclosed positive stop foot gear change and kickstarter. Ratios, 1st, 13.35, 8.8, 6.4, 5.0 to 1.
CLUTCH. Multi plate clutch with Bowden operated hand control.
IGNITION. Gear driven Lucas K2F magneto.
LIGHTING. Separate Lucas dynamo, gear driven from timing case. 45 watt, 6 volt, constant voltage control. Head lamp, rear lamp, dipper switch and horn button.
PETROL CAPACITY. 3 gallons. Welded steel tank with twin filter taps.
OIL CAPACITY. ½ gallon welded steel oil tank.
TYRES. Triple stud Dunlop. 3.25" × 19" (front), 3.50" x 19" (rear).
BRAKES. Quickly adjustable, internal expanding, 7" diameter, front and rear.
FRAME AND SUSPENSION. Duplex cradle, with full Teledraulic oil damped rear suspension, A.M.C. patent Teledraulic forks, Centre, front and prop stands. Pillion footrests.
SADDLE. Dunlopillo integral leather (for rider and pillion passenger). Saddle height 30".
WHEELBASE. Length 55¼". Ground clearance 5½".
WEIGHT (dry). G 9 400 lb.
FINISH. Stoved enamel on Bonderised finish. Exhaust system, wheel rims, handlebars etc. chromium plated. Tank. Red and chrome.

New Hudson

NEW HUDSON LTD.
BIRMINGHAM, 11.

Although the name of New Hudson is an old established one and their motor cycles were well known in the 1920's, production has been concentrated on one model only for 1950—a smart and efficient Autocycle.

Basically the machine follows the 1949 design. The latest model has a modified frame, which improves stability and ease of handling and is fitted with the Villiers 2F power unit of 98 c.c., developing approximately 2 b.h.p. at 3,800 r.p.m.

The single port engine of 47 mm. bore x 57 mm. stroke incorporates a redesigned port layout, giving increased power output. The built-up crankshaft is supported on both sides by journal ball races. The shaft carries the engine sprocket, and, at the taper end, the flywheel magneto. The big end bearing is formed by two rows of 3/16" x 3/16" steel rollers operating direct on the steel connecting rod. A phosphor bronze bush is pressed in the connecting rod at the small end. The flat-crowned aluminium alloy piston has two pegged compression rings. The inlet port is at the rear, the single exhaust port at the front, and the two transfer ports are situated one at each side. The aluminium alloy cylinder head has a hemispherical combustion chamber and incorporates a 14 mm. sparking plug. A direct joint is employed between head and cylinder—a gasket is dispensed with. A ⅜" pitch chain connects engine and clutch sprockets; a ½" pitch chain is used for the final drive, with an overall gear ratio of 10.76 to 1.

A 2 plate cork insert type clutch operates in oil. A Villiers Junior single lever carburettor is fitted, with the latest Villiers wire mesh automatically oil-wetted filter. This filter incorporates a strangler for easy starting. The 6 pole flywheel magneto incorporates lighting coils and gives an output of over 12 watts at 6 volts. The well known Villiers system of revolving magneto and stationary coils is employed. The weight of the 2F engine unit, less lighting set, is approximately 31 lb.

A redesigned tubular cradle type frame with solid drop out fork ends supports the engine at three points. A pressed steel motor cycle type front fork with a central compression spring, internal expanding brakes, motor cycle type exhaust system, Dunlop tyres, a central stand, large spring seat saddle and efficient engine shields are other attractive features of this model, which, it is claimed, has a petrol consumption of approximately 180 miles to the gallon, at a speed of 20–25 m.p.h.

NEW HUDSON AUTOCYCLE

SPECIFICATION

Engine. Make. Villiers Mark 2F.
  Bore and Stroke. 47 mm. x 57 mm. 98 c.c.
  Single cylinder, two stroke, air cooled, single port.
  Flat top piston, aluminium detachable cylinder head.
  Sparking plug. 14 mm.
Lubrication. Petroil system.
Carburettor. Villiers Junior single lever.
Gear Ratio. 10.76 to 1.
Clutch. 2 plate cork insert type. Runs in oil.
Transmission. Driving Chain. Renolds ⅜-in. x 3/16-in. Pedalling chain. ½-in. x 1/8-in. with independent adjustment. Both protected by pressed steel guards.
Ignition. Villiers Flywheel Magneto.
Lighting. Villiers Flywheel electrical unit, with parking battery in headlamp.
Petrol Capacity. Petrol tank. 1 5/8 gallons.
Tyres. Dunlop 21-in. x 2.25-in. front and rear.
Brakes. Internal expanding, 4-in. diameter, front and rear, operated by inverted type handlebar levers.
Frame and Suspension. Tubular cradle type, low built, fully brazed-up, with taper chain and seat stays, and solid drop-out fork ends. Lightweight pressed steel motor cycle type front fork.
Saddle. Large spring seat saddle. Height from ground. 32¼-ins.
Wheelbase. 50". Ground clearance. 5¼-ins.
Weight (dry) 120 lb.
Finish. All frame parts rust-proofed and enamelled. Tank finished in black with red and gold transfer panels, gold lined. All bright parts chromium plated.
Equipment. Central stand. Tubular carrier. Engine shields. Motor cycle type tyre inflator, bulb horn, licence holder. Rubber grips. Welded on clutch and decompressor levers on handlebars.

Norman

NORMAN CYCLES LTD.
BEAVER ROAD · ASHFORD, KENT

Although the Norman concern has not been established as long as some of its competitors, it has rapidly built up a reputation for high quality lightweight machines, which, if one can judge from the numbers to be seen on the road, are rapidly increasing in popularity. A further model was added to this attractive range just before the 1949 Motor Cycle show, a 98 c.c. ultra lightweight motorcycle, as distinct from the already well known 98 c.c. Autocycle.

In all, 4 machines are listed for 1950, three of which are available as de luxe models, fitted with rectifier lighting, accumulators and electric horn, thus following the general trend in the trade to make this equipment an "optional extra" on selected machines.

The four machines are the 98 c.c. Autocycle, and 98 c.c. ultra lightweight motor cycle, the 122 c.c. and 197 c.c. lightweights—all Villiers engined.

The 98 c.c. Autocycle—Model "C," is fitted with the Villiers 2F single speed engine, with the usual features of a light alloy detachable cylinder head, flat top aluminium alloy piston, ballbearing mainshaft and roller bearing big end. Villiers Flywheel magneto ignition also runs the lighting system. A parking light supplied by a dry battery is fitted inside the headlamp. The frame and forks are of Norman design, the forks being of the parallel ruler type, each blade being formed by a single tube. An eccentric bracket for tensioning the pedal chain is fitted, thus dispensing with a jockey sprocket. Adjustment of the driving chain is by the orthodox method of chain adjusters. Dunlop 2.25" x 21" tyres, 4" internal expanding hub brakes operated by handlebar levers and a multi spring, soft top saddle are other details of the specification. Large aluminium alloy shields are fitted to each side of the engine unit. A useful rear carrier is provided.

The new model D, 98 c.c. ultra lightweight employs the Villiers Mark 1F two speed engine unit. The frame is however of a similar design to the two larger motor cycles. An item of interest on this machine is the new Norman telescopic front fork. Two phosphor bronze bushes support each sliding leg in its main tube, the sliding leg itself being slotted to take the wheel spindle. Synthetic rubber blocks hold a single coil spring in place inside each main tube. The block, which is fitted inside the first few coils of the spring, is fitted with a retaining bolt, the tightening of which expands the rubber between the coils, and whilst holding the springs, allows sufficient movement to provide a cushion on depression and recoil.

The two speed gearbox is operated by a handlebar control lever, and transmission is by roller chain throughout, the primary chain running in an oil bath and the driving chain being protected by an efficient chain cover. 4" internal expanding brakes are fitted, the front operated by handlebar lever and the rear by an adjustable brake pedal. Dunlop 2.5" x 19" tyres are fitted, deep section steel mudguards and a tubular central stand with an automatic return to the riding position. This model is available as Model D/DL with rectified lighting, 6 volt accumulator and electric horn.

The two larger models are to the same general specification in most details, the 122 c.c. machine being fitted with the Villiers Mark 10D engine with 3 speed gearbox, the 197 c.c. employing the Mark 6E unit, also with 3 speed box. In each case straight tubes form the frame and these are brazed into malleable iron castings, pressed steel plates link the front down tube and seat tube and form an engine cradle. Special Norman telescopic oil damped forks are fitted on these two machines. A piston is attached to the wheel spindle clamp by a central rod. This piston, as it rises, forces oil into a damper unit joining the main fork legs. The inner cylinder of this damper is drilled with a series of small holes, $\frac{1}{8}$" diameter. The restriction on the flow of oil as it passes these holes provides a compensated damping effect on both fork legs. Similarly rebound damping is effected by restricting the oil return from the main cylinder as it passes the inner cylinder holes on its way back to the reservoir provided. Steel pressings form the fork head lug and steering column.

The three speed gear box is in unit construction with the engine, and is operated by a positive stop foot change lever. The drive is taken by a cork plate clutch running in oil. The Villiers flywheel magneto provides ignition and L.T. current for lighting. The output is 6 volt, 35 watt. This is used with a $5\frac{1}{2}$" headlamp and provides for a 6 volt, 30 watt headlamp and a 6 volt, 3 watt tail lamp. Transmission is by chain throughout, the primary chain running in an oil bath chain case.

There are several interesting detail points on these two machines. Handlebars are fully adjustable, the footrests have a positive adjustment allowing of four positions, and the rear brake pedal is adjustable to correspond with each of these positions. The mudguards are deep D section, heavily ribbed down the centre, and a pressed steel toolbox and rear carrier are fitted to the rear mudguard. A tubular central spring-up stand with semi-ball feet is fitted. The exhaust pipe has been increased in diameter on the curve of the pipe near the cylinder port, and this forms an expansion chamber. The cylindrical silencer has detachable fishtails and baffles.

Other points are the fitting of well designed knee grips and the provision of air cleaners for the carburettor and the use of Petroflex tubing for the petrol supply.

Both these machines are available as de luxe models, with rectified lighting, $6\frac{1}{2}$" headlamps, accumulator and electric horn at an extra basic cost of £5. Smith's lightweight motor cycle speedometers are also an optional extra on all models. Standard finishes for all models are black and maroon with chromium plated rims, handlebars, exhaust pipes and silencers, but the 122 c.c. and 197 c.c. models are offered with the petrol tank finished in chromium plate, with maroon and gold panels, at an extra charge.

Norman Model C. Autocycle

Norman Model B2. 197 c.c. Two Stroke

SPECIFICATION

NORMAN AUTO-CYCLE. Model C. 98 cc.

Engine Make Villiers. Mark 2F.
Bore and Stroke. 47 mm. x 57 mm. 98 c.c.
Compression Ratio. 8 to 1.
Approximate b.h.p. 2.0 at 3,750 r.p.m.
Single cylinder, two stroke, air cooled, single port. Light alloy detachable cylinder head, flat top aluminium alloy piston, ball bearing mainshaft, roller bearing big end.
Lubrication. Petroil system.
Carburettor. Villiers Junior.
Gearbox. Single speed. Ratio 10 .75 to 1.
Clutch. Two plate, cork insert type. Runs in oil.
Transmission. Primary Chain $\frac{3}{8}$" x .155".
Secondary. Chain $\frac{1}{2}$" x $\frac{3}{16}$".
Pedal. chain. $\frac{1}{2}$" x $\frac{1}{8}$".
Ignition. Villiers flywheel magneto.
Lighting. Villiers direct lighting from flywheel magneto. Dry battery runs parking light in headlamp.
Petroil Capacity. 1$\frac{1}{4}$ gallons Petroil.
Oil Capacity. Petroil system.
Tyres. Dunlop 2.25" x 21" front and rear.
Brakes. Internal expanding, 4" front and rear.
Frame and Suspension. Norman design, Rigid frame. Single tube, fully sprung girder forks.
Saddle. Multi spring, soft top.
Wheelbase. 50$\frac{1}{4}$".   **Height from ground.** 31".
Width over bars. 27$\frac{1}{2}$".   **Ground clearance.** 4$\frac{1}{2}$".
                                       Overall length. 76".
Weight (dry). 128 lb.
Finish. Finished in black, maroon tank and engine shields, gold lined chromium plated rims, handlebars, exhaust pipe and silencer.
Equipment. Bulb horn, rear carrier tubular central stand. Smith's Lightweight speedometer extra.
Maximum speed. 35 m.p.h.
Petrol consumption (at 20 m.p.h.) 150 m.p.g.

NORMAN MODEL D. 98 c.c. MOTORCYCLE.

Engine. Make. Villiers Mark 1F.
Bore and Stroke. 47 mm. x 57 mm. 98 c.c.
Compression Ratio. 8 to 1.
Approximate b.h.p. 2.8 at 4,000 r.p.m.
Single cylinder, two stroke, air cooled, single-port, light alloy detachable cylinder head. Flat top piston, ball bearing mainshaft, roller bearing big end.
Sparking plug. 14 mm.
Lubrication. Petroil system.
Carburettor. Villiers Junior.
Gearbox. 2 speed. Ratios 12.5 and 8.125 to 1.
Clutch. Cork insert, two plate clutch, running in oil.
Transmission. Primary Chain $\frac{3}{8}$" x .155". Oil bath chain case.
Secondary. Chain $\frac{1}{2}$" x $\frac{3}{16}$".
Ignition. Villiers Flywheel magneto.
Lighting. Villiers direct A.C. lighting. D.C. lighting and rectifier on D/DL.
Petroil Capacity. 1$\frac{1}{4}$ gallons.
Oil Capacity. Petroil system.
Tyres. Dunlop 2.5" x 19", front and rear.
Brakes. 4" internal expanding, front and rear, Front by lever, rear by pedal

Frame and Suspension. Rigid frame. Norman telescopic rubber damped forks.
Saddle. Mattress type, 3 point suspension   **Height from ground.** 28".
Wheelbase. 48".   **Ground clearance.** 4$\frac{1}{2}$".
Width over bars. 27$\frac{1}{2}$".   **Overall length.** 72".
Weight (dry). 143 lb.
Finish. Black, maroon tank, gold lined, chromium plated rims, handlebars, exhaust pipes and silencer.
Equipment. Rear carrier, tubular central stand. Smith's lightweight speedometer. extra. Rectified lighting, accumulator and horn on Model D/DL.
Maximum speed 40 m.p.h.
Petrol consumption at 30 m.p.h. 120—130 m.p.g.

NORMAN MODELS B1 and B2. 122 c.c. and 197 c.c. MOTORCYCLES.

Engine. B1. Villiers Mark 10D.
B2. Villiers 6E.
Bore and Stroke. B1. 50 mm. x 62 mm. 122 c.c.
B2. 59 mm. x 72 mm. 197 c.c.
Compression Ratio. 8 to 1 both models.
Approximate b.h.p. B1. 4.8 at 4,400 r.p.m.
B2. 8.4 at 4,000 r.p.m.
Single cylinder, two stroke, air cooled, single port, aluminium alloy detachable cylinder head, flat top aluminium piston, ball bearing mainshaft, roller bearing big end.
Sparking plug. 14 mm.
Lubrication. Petroil system.
Carburettor. B1. Villiers lightweight.
B2. Villiers mediumweight.
Gearbox. Unit construction, 3 speed. Positive stop foot change.
Ratios. B1. 22.75, 11.9 and 7.0 to 1.
B2. 19.0, 9.9, and 5.86 to 1.
Clutch. Cork insert, type, 2 plate, running in oil.
Transmission. Primary. Chain $\frac{3}{8}$" x .225". Oilbath chain case.
Secondary. Chain $\frac{1}{2}$" x $\frac{3}{16}$".
Ignition. Villiers Flywheel magneto.
Lighting. Villiers A. C. Direct lighting. 5$\frac{1}{2}$" headlamp.
Rectified lighting and accumulator on de luxe models.
Petrol Capacity. 2$\frac{3}{4}$ gallons.
Oil Capacity. Petroil system.
Tyres. Dunlop 3.00 x 19" front and rear.
Brakes. 5" internal expanding, front and rear.
Frame and Suspension. Norman patent telescopic oil damped forks, Rigid frame.
Saddle. Mattress type 3 point suspension   **Height from ground.** 27$\frac{1}{2}$".
Wheelbase. 51".   **Ground clearance.** 6$\frac{1}{2}$".
Width over bars. 27$\frac{1}{2}$".   **Overall length.** 76".
Weight (dry). B1. 172 lb. B2. 206 lb.
Finish. Black and maroon with chromium plated rims, handlebars, exhaust pipes and silencer.
Optional finish. Petrol tank in chromium plate with maroon and gold panels (Extra).
Equipment. Tubular central stand, steel tool box, lifting handle, knee grips. Rectified lighting and accumulator extra, standard on Models B1/DL and B2/DL.
Smith's Lightweight speedometer extra.
Maximum speed in gears. B1. 50 m.p.h. B2. 55 m.p.h.
Petrol consumption at 30 m.p.h. B1. 120 m.p.g. B2. 110 m.p.g.

Norton

NORTON MOTORS LIMITED
BRACEBRIDGE ST., BIRMINGHAM, 6.

U.S.A. Distributor:
INDIAN SALES CORPORATION
29 Worthington St.
Springfield, Mass.

To tell the full story of the "Unapproachable Norton" and the history of its racing successes would take a complete volume to itself. In the 1950 Tourist Trophy races Nortons gained a sweeping success. The first three places in both the Senior and Junior races were taken by Norton riders, and new records established. It is sufficient to say, perhaps, that Nortons have built themselves a reputation which must be the pride of this country and the envy of the world.

The story of the Norton motor cycle concern and its famous products begins in 1898, when the late Mr. James L. Norton, who was one of the founder members of the Institute of Automobile Engineers, established a firm known as the Norton Manufacturing Company. The first motor cycle he produced was the Norton "Energette." It is still recalled as a pioneer of the motor cycle era, and it embodied many of the principles of design that are standardised throughout the industry today. From this original machine have evolved all the famous Nortons that have since made motor cycling history throughout the world.

In the early 1890s Mr. Norton introduced into motor cycle design the present type of low frame and rational riding position. Though this was very soon universally adopted, at its first appearance it was greeted with ridicule and the Norton machine was nicknamed "the ferret," because of its long, low build, as opposed to the usual high, upright type of frame. The late Mr. Norton was, in fact, the doyen of motor cycle designers and is still held in the greatest respect by those who remember him. He died in 1924, his last public appearance being at a Civic Reception given by the Lord Mayor of Birmingham to the Norton riders who had won the Tourist Trophy races that year.

It is, of course, in the world of racing that the Norton marque has achieved its greatest fame. As long ago as 1902, Norton machines were creating new records and winning races of all kinds, and in 1907 a Norton machine won the Twin Cylinder class of the first Tourist Trophy race by a margin of 33 minutes.

Norton Motors Ltd. have won more Tourist Trophy races than any other manufacturer—24 in all, a record of which any company might be proud. In the spectacular Norton victory in the 1950 races, new records were established. In the Senior, Geoffrey Duke won at 92.27 m.p.h., with a fastest lap of 93.33 m.p.h., beating the previous lap record of 91 m.p.h. set up by Harold Daniell in 1938. Artie Bell established a new record speed of 86.327 m.p.h. in the Junior. In addition to the Isle of Man T.T. Races they have a wonderful record of successes in Continental races. Nortons have won the Swiss Grand Prix 11 times and the Belgian Grand Prix 22 times, and on several occasions they have

Norton
497 c.c. o.h.v.
"Dominator"
Vertical Twin

Norton
490 c.c. o.h.v.
Trials Model

been victorious in the South African T.T., the Australian T.T., the Championship of Portugal and the principal Irish road races. At periods in their history Nortons have held more World Speed Records than any other manufacturer, and during 1949 a Norton team secured no fewer than 21 worlds records in the 350 c.c. and 500 c.c. and sidecar classes, all these being broken on the Montlhery track, near Paris.

The present Chairman of the company is Mr. C. A. Vandervell, famous as the originator of the C.A.V. battery and C.A.V. lighting set. The managing director is Mr. C. Gilbert Smith, who vigorously pursues the racing policy introduced by the late Mr. Norton—a policy which has been so successful that the "race bred" Nortons are known and esteemed throughout the world.

Another famous name associated with the Norton racing successes is that of Joe Craig, technical director of the firm, who from the year 1925 onward has been responsible for the development of the wonderful series of racing machines which have made the Norton name supreme. Nortons have also been fortunate in the riders they have chosen to pilot their machines in important events. Many famous names and reputations have been made on Nortons, including those of Stanley Woods, Alec Bennett, Tim Hunt, the late Jim Guthrie, Freddie Frith, Harold Daniell and Artie Bell—and, of course, Geoffrey Duke, the brilliant young 1950 T.T. victor.

As may well be imagined, the current range of Norton machines are especially noted for their lively performance, steering, road-holding and "slogging" characteristics and the ten machines which are being produced at the present time cater for racing, fast solo touring, the sidecar enthusiast and trials. The range consists of two side valve machines, the 490 c.c. Model 16H, and the 596 c.c. " Big 4,' two 490 c.c. o.h.v. push rod operated singles, the Models 18 and ES2 (the latter with a spring frame), the famous 490 c.c. and 348 c.c. overhead camshaft machines, Models 30 and 40, the purely racing machines—the twin overhead camshaft ("double knocker") 499 c.c. and 348 c.c. Model 30 Manx and 40 Manx, a 490 c.c. Competition Model, and the Model 7 497 c.c. " Dominator " Vertical twin. In addition, the Models 30 and 40 are available with light alloy head and barrel and central oil feed to the rocker box at an extra charge.

Basically there have been few changes to Norton machines for the current year. The major new feature is the fitting of the redesigned gearbox, which was introduced for the new vertical twin, to all models with the exception of the International and Manx machines. The foot change mechanism in this box has been modified and will be similar to that fitted to the Dominator, and the change speed lever has a greatly reduced pedal travel giving smoother and easier operation of the gear change mechanism. A side prop stand of great rigidity is now fitted to all models with the exception of the racing machines. This replaces the central stand and hinges from the forward engine plate and can be brought into use with the foot while the rider is astride the machine. On the trials model this prop stand is attached to the near side chain stay. On all machines except the twin, the voltage control is now accommodated in the tool box, which gives it greater protection. Finally on the International machines the method of fixing the petrol and oil tanks has been modified. They are now secured by means of bolts passing through the tanks, similar to the fixing of the tanks on the Manx machines.

Dealing firstly with the side valve machines, both the 16H and " Big 4 " follow the same general specification, but the 16H has a bore and stroke of 79 mm. x 100 mm. (490 c.c.) whilst the " Big 4 " has a bore of 82 mm. and a stroke of 113 mm., giving a capacity of 596 c.c. Compression ratios are 4.9 to 1 for the 16H, with a b.h.p. of 12½, and 4.5 to 1 for the Big 4, with a b.h.p. of 14. Both are single cylinder, side valve, air cooled single port engines, lubrication being by dry sump and Norton gear pump. These machines have the redesigned 4 speed positive stop foot change gearbox, rigid frames and Norton Telescopic " Roadholder" forks. 7" internal expanding brakes are fitted front and rear, Dunlop 3.25" x 19" tyres, and Lucas magnetos and dynamos. A 2¾ gallon tank is fitted, finished in the well known Norton colours, and equipment includes front, rear and centre prop stands and speedometer. Both machines are ideally suited for sidecar work.

Both Model ES2 and Model 18 have 490 c.c. (79 mm. x 100 mm.) push rod operated o.h.v. engines, and the ES2 differs only from the Model 18 in being fitted with rear springing as part of the standard specification. Compression ratio is 6.6 to 1, giving a b.h.p. of 21. The whole of the valve gear is totally enclosed and automatically lubricated. The valve operating mechanism has flat-base tappets bearing directly on the cams and is exceptionally quiet. Ball and roller bearings support the mainshaft, and lubrication is by dry sump and Norton gear pump. A Norton 4 speed positive stop foot change gearbox is fitted and 7" diameter brakes front and rear, which with the Roadholder Telescopic forks and Norton sprung rear frame, give exceptional controlability, roadholding and braking. An Amal carburettor is fitted with a lever operated throttle stop for easy starting. A Lucas magdyno, with manually operated advance and retard mechanism, an 8" diameter headlamp, with domed glass, Dunlop 3.25" x 19" tyres front and rear, centre prop stand, front and rear stands and speedometer complete the specification. These machines, on test, have given a maximum speed of approximately 78 m.p.h. with a petrol consumption in the region of 98 m.p.g. at 30 m.p.h.

A competition version of this machine, styled the 500T has been introduced, and is fitted with Norton Telescopic forks and a rigid frame. Ignition is by B.T.H. magneto, and the gearbox has ratios of 18, 13.15, 8.1 and 5.5 to 1. Dunlop 3.00" x 21" front and 4.00" x 19" rear tyres are fitted, and with a ground clearance of 7¼", a wheelbase of 53", saddle height of 32¼" and a dry weight of 300 lb., the machine should be ideal for trials work.

The famous International Models, the 348 c.c. o.h.c. Model 40, and 490 c.c. o.h.c. Model 30 are retained with little change for the current year. They do not incorporate the redesigned gearbox however, but the new Norton prop stand is fitted, and petrol and oil tanks are now fitted with bolts and are rubber mounted in the same manner as the Manx machines. The Model 40 has an engine of 71 mm. bore x 88 mm. stroke, and a compression ratio of 7.33 to 1, whilst the Model 30 has a bore of 79mm., a stroke of 100mm., compression ratio is 7.12 to 1 and the b.h.p. is given as 29. Both machines can be supplied with a light alloy head and barrel, with central oil feed to the rocker box at an extra charge. Lubrication is by dry sump and Norton gear pump, Amal T.T. type carburettors and Lucas magnetos and dynamos are fitted, Norton Telescopic forks, plunger type rear springing and 7" brakes are standard features. Tyres are 3.00" x 21" front and 3.25" x 20" rear, and both machines have, of course, 4 speed foot change boxes.

The two purely racing models are the 30 Manx and 40 Manx. The former has an engine of 79.62 mm. x 100 mm. bore and stroke, whilst the 40 Manx with dimensions of 71 mm. x 88 mm. has a capacity of 348 c.c. Both machines have the famous twin overhead camshaft engine. An Aluminium alloy head and barrel, and light alloy crankcase, hubs, petrol and oil tanks are part of the standard specification. A B.T.H. magneto is provided and an Amal T.T. remote control carburettor. Compression ratio of the 30M is 7.2 to 1, and of the 40M 7.3 to 1. All engines are specially built and individually tuned. Norton Telescopic forks and fully sprung rear frame, and a foot change racing gearbox without kick-starter and incorporating a special clutch are fitted and the usual racing features of quick lift filler caps, straight through exhausts with megaphone, Dunlop racing tyres, racing handlebar levers, mudguards and chainguards are to be found. The petrol tank capacity is 4½ gallons, and brakes are 8″ front and 7″ rear. It is these machines which have built such a great reputation for themselves in every form of road and track racing.

Norton's new vertical twin—the 497 c.c. Dominator, was introduced in 1948 and remains substantially unchanged. The machine was a great success from its inception. With a bore and stroke of 66 mm. x 72.6 mm., the engine has a b.h.p. of 29 and a compression ratio of 6.7 to 1. Very great care has been taken with the design, particularly in regard to the cooling. The engine is generously finned. The design of cylinder head and barrel allows cooling air to pass between the inlet and exhaust valves in addition to the spaces between the combustion chambers. There is also an air flow between the cylinder barrels and between the bores and the push rod housings. The exhaust ports themselves are widely spaced and positioned to secure excellent ventilation. The cylinder head and valves are totally enclosed and positively lubricated, and the design allows of a very efficient and compact inlet side. The cast iron cylinder head has an integral rocker box and the nearly upright valves, which are placed at an angle of 58° to each other, allow shallow combustion chambers to be used. Access to the exhaust rockers is by two separate covers, one cover being provided for the inlet rockers. Car type cast iron tappets, with chilled rubbing surfaces are fitted. Tappet guides are dispensed with, the tappets operating directly in the cast iron barrel block casting. The barrel block is spigoted into both the cylinder head and the crankcase and is held down to the latter by 9 bolts. The push rods operate inside cast iron cavities and to eliminate leaky joints the rocker gear oil drains are built in. The main bearings are 72 mm. x 30 mm. x 19 mm.—a roller journal on the driving side and a ball journal on the timing side. A cast iron flywheel is fitted to the three piece crankshaft. R.R. 56 light alloy forged connecting rods have steel backed Micro-Babbitt separate shell bearings. The connecting rods have a phosphor bronze small end bush and a fully floating gudgeon pin. Flat topped Lo-Ex aluminium alloy pistons are fitted, and have two compression rings and one scraper ring. There are small valve cutaways in the piston crowns, and the location of these makes it necessary to provide a left hand and a right hand piston. A fixed centre chain drive runs to the single high camshaft, which incorporates a built in well ported mechanical breather.

Lubrication is on the dry sump system, with a separate oil tank, and a Norton gear type double action pump and pressure relief valve eliminate cylinder lubrication bias. The Lucas automatic advance magneto has silent chain drive and a separate 45 watt dynamo is provided. A spring loaded silent fibre gear wheel forms a slipping clutch drive to this dynamo.

An entirely new design of petrol tank, holding 3¾ gallons, and finished in the usual Norton colours has been designed for the twin, and incorporates an oil gauge. The latest design of Norton 4 speed foot change gearbox, which was, of course, designed for this machine, is retained. The Twin also has Norton Teledraulic forks and plunger type rear springing is fitted as standard. Solo Gear ratios are 14, 88, 8.85, 6.05 and 5.0 to 1. Dunlop 3.00 x 21 ribbed front and 3,50 x 19 triple stud rear tyres and 7″ internal expanding brakes, a prop stand, a front stand, detachable rear mudguard and speedometer are other features of the specification of the Dominator, which has proved itself a worthy stable companion to the rest of the famous Norton range.

Norton 596 c.c. s.v. "Big Four"

NORTON 490 c.c. Side Valve Model 16H.
NORTON 596 c.c. Side Valve. "Big Four," (Model 1.)

SPECIFICATION

Engine. Make Norton.
Bore and Stroke. 16H 79 mm. x 100 mm. 490 c.c.
"Big Four" 82 mm. x 113 mm. 596 c.c.
Compression Ratio. 16H 4.9 to 1. "Big Four" 4.5 to 1.
B.H.P. 16H—12½. "Big Four"—14.
Single cylinder, air cooled, side valve.
Sparking plugs 14 mm.
Lubrication. Dry sump and Norton gear pump.
Carburettor. Amal 276/AT.
Gear Box. 4 speed, positive stop, foot change.
Ratios. 16H. 16.2, 9.6, 6.6 and 5.46 to 1.
"Big Four" 14.6, 8.67 5.93 and 4.9 to 1.
Clutch. Multi-plate.
Transmission. Primary. Chain ½″ x .305″.
Secondary. Chain ⅝″ x ¼″.
Ignition. } Lucas Magdyno.
Lighting. }
Petrol Capacity. 2¾ gallons.

Oil Capacity. ½ gallon.
Tyres. 3.25″ x 19″, front and rear.
Brakes. 7″ internal expanding, front and rear.
Frame and Suspension. Rigid frame. Norton Telescopic Roadholder forks.
Saddle. Terry or Lycett — **Height from ground.** 28″.
Wheelbase. 54½″. — **Ground Clearance.** 5½″.
Overall Length. 84″. — **Width over bars** 30″.
Weight (dry). 16H 389 lb. "Big Four" 413 lb.
Finish. Norton silver-grey, chromium and black. Bright parts chromium plated. Frame stove enamelled black.
Equipment. Speedometer, Centre prop stand, front and rear stand. Electric horn, tools and pump.
Extra or optional equipment.
Maximum Speed. 1st 22 m.p.h. 2nd 36 m.p.h. 3rd 53 m.p.h. 4th 65 m.p.h.
Speed at end of quarter mile from rest. 48 m.p.h.
Petrol Consumption (at 30 m.p.h.) 70 m.p.g.
Braking (from 30 m.p.h. to rest). 30 ft.

Norton
490 c.c. o.h.v.
E.S.2

NORTON 490 c.c. o.h.v. Models 18 and ES2.

SPECIFICATION

Engine. Make Norton.
Bore and Stroke. 79 mm. x 100 mm. 490 c.c.
Compression Ratio. 6.6 to 1.
B.H.P. 21.
Single cylinder, o.h.v. air cooled, single port. Totally enclosed valve gear.
Sparking plugs 14 mm.
Lubrication. Dry sump and Norton gear pump.
Carburettor. Amal 276 AU.
Gear Box. 4 speed, positive stop foot change.
Ratios. 13.84, 8.24, 5.64, and 4.66 to 1.
Clutch. Multi-plate
Transmission. Primary. Chain ½" x .305".
Secondary. Chain ⅝" x ¼".
Ignition. } Lucas Magdyno.
Lighting. }
Petrol Capacity. 3¾ gallons.
Oil Capacity. 6 pints.
Tyres. 3.25" x 19", front and rear.
Brakes. 7", front and rear.
Wheel sizes 21" x 3" (front), 20" x 3.50" (rear).
Frame and Suspension. Model 18. Norton "Roadholder" Telescopic forks and rigid frame
Model ES2. Norton "Roadholder" Telescopic forks and plunger type rear springing.
Saddle. Terry or Lycett. **Height from ground.** Model 18 28". Model ES2 30".
Wheelbase. 45½". **Ground Clearance.** Model 18—5½". Model ES2 6½".
Overall Length. 84½". **Width over bars.** 30".
Weight (dry). Model 18 409 lb. Model ES2 413 lb.
Finish. Norton silver-grey, chromium and black. Bright parts chromium plated. Frame stove enamelled black.
Equipment. Speedometer, centre prop stand, front and rear stands, electric horn, tools and pump.
Extra or optional equipment.
Maximum Speed. 1st 28 m.p.h. 2nd 45 m.p.h. 3rd 65 m.p.h. 4th 80 m.p.h.
Speed at end of quarter mile from rest. 68 m.p.h.
Petrol Consumption (at 30 m.p.h.) 90 m.p.g.
Braking (from 30 m.p.h. to rest). 30 ft.

NORTON 497 c.c. o.h.v. "Dominator" Vertical Twin

SPECIFICATION

Engine. Make Norton.
Bore and Stroke 66 mm. x 72.6 mm 497 c.c.
Compression Ratio. 6.7 to 1.
B.H.P. 29 at 6,500.
Twin cylinder, air cooled, twin port, (vertical twin.) Cast iron detachable cylinder head, with integral rocker box. Flat topped aluminium alloy piston.
Sparking plugs 14 mm.
Lubrication. Dry sump and Norton gear pump.
Carburettor. Amal 76/AK/1AT.
Gear Box. 4 speed, positive stop foot change.
Ratios. 14.88, 8.85, 6.05 and 5.0 to 1.
Clutch. Multi-plate.
Transmission. Primary. Chain ½" x .305".
Secondary. Chain ⅝" x ¼".
Ignition. Lucas magneto.
Lighting. Lucas dynamo.
Petrol Capacity. 3¾ gallons.
Oil Capacity. ¾ gallon.
Tyres. 3.00" x 21", front. 3.50" x 19" rear. (Dunlop). Ribbed—front. Studded—rear.
Brakes. Internal expanding, 7", front and rear.
Frame and Suspension. Norton "Roadholder" Telescopic forks and plunger type rear springing.
Saddle. Terry or Lycett. **Height from ground.** 30".
Wheelbase. 54½". **Ground Clearance.** 6½".
Overall Length. 84½". **Width over bars.** 30".
Weight (dry). 440 lb.
Finish. Norton silver grey, chromium and black. Bright parts chromium plated. Frame stove enamelled black.
Equipment. Speedometer, prop, front and centre stands, electric horn, tools and pump. Oil gauge.
Extra or optional equipment.
Maximum Speed 1st 32 m.p.h. 2nd 60 m.p.h. 3rd 80 m.p.h. 4th 90 m.p.h.
Speed at end of quarter mile from rest. 79 m.p.h.
Petrol Consumption (at 30 m.p.h.) 80 m.p.g.
Braking (from 30 m.p.h. to rest). 30 ft.

NORTON 348 c.c. o.h.c. Model 40M.
NORTON 499 c.c. o.h.c. Model 30M.

SPECIFICATION

Engine. Make Norton.
Bore and Stroke. 30M 79.62 mm. x 100 mm. 499 c.c.
40M 71 mm. x 88 mm. 348 c.c.
Compression Ratio. 30M, 7.2 to 1. 40M, 7.3 to 1.
B.H.P. 30M. 35 at 5,500. 40M. 27 at 6,250.
Single cylinder, air cooled, o.h.c. single port. Engines specially built and tuned. Aluminium alloy head and cylinder barrel. Twin overhead camshafts. Light alloy crankcase.
Sparking plugs 14 mm.
Lubrication. Dry sump and Norton gear pump.
Carburettor. Amal R.N.
Gear Box. 4 speed, positive stop, foot change racing gearbox. No kickstarter.
Ratios. 30M 7.82, 5.88, 4.86 and 4.42 to 1.
40M. 9.12, 6.86, 5.67 and 5.16 to 1.
Transmission. Primary Chain ½" x. 305".
Secondary. Chain ⅝" x ¼".
Ignition. B.T.H. racing magneto.
Lighting. Not fitted.
Petrol Capacity. 4½ gallons.
Oil Capacity. 1 gallon.
Tyres. Dunlop, 3.00" x 21", ribbed front. 3.25" x 20" ribbed rear.
Brakes. Internal expanding, 8" front, 7" rear.
Frame and Suspension. Norton Roadholder" Telescopic forks and plunger type rear springing.
Saddle. Terry or Lycett. **Height from ground.** 30".
Wheelbase. 54½". **Ground Clearance.** 5½".
Overall Length. 84½". **Width over bars.** 28½".
Weight (dry). 30M. 430 lb. 40M. 380 lb.
Finish. Norton silver grey, chromium and black. Bright parts chromium plated, frame stove enamelled black.
Equipment. Light alloy hubs, petrol and oil tanks. Quick lift filler caps, straight through exhaust with megaphone, racing handlebar levers, mudguards and chainguards. Special clutch. Revolution counter.

Models 40M and 30M are to be available in 1951 with the T.T. type duplex tube frame, with sprung rear suspension as used on the winning Nortons in the last T.T. races.

NORTON 490 c.c. o.h.v. Model 500T.

Engine. Make Norton.
Bore and Stroke. 79 mm. x 100 mm. 490 c.c.
Compression Ratio. 6 to 1.
B.H.P. 21.
Single cylinder, air cooled, o.h.v. push rod operated.
Sparking plugs 14 mm.
Lubrication. Dry sump and Norton gear pump.
Carburettor. Amal 276/AT.
Gear Box. 4 speed, positive stop foot change.
Ratios. 18, 13.15, 8.1, and 5.5 to 1.
Clutch. Multi-plate.
Transmission. Primary. Chain ½" x .305".
Secondary. Chain ⅝" x ¼".
Ignition. B.T.H. Magneto.
Lighting. Not fitted.
Petrol Capacity. 2½ gallons.
Oil Capacity. ⅜ gallon.
Tyres. Dunlop 3.00" x 21" front. 4.00" x 19" rear.
Brakes. Internal expanding, 7" front and rear.
Frame and Suspension. Norton Telescopic forks. Rigid frame.
Saddle. Dunlop. **Height from ground.** 32¼".
Wheelbase. 53". **Ground Clearance.** 7½".
Overall Length. 82". **Width over bars.** 28".
Weight (dry) 300 lb.
Finish. Norton silver grey, chromium and black. Bright parts chromium plated, frame stove enamelled black.
Equipment. Prop front and rear stands. Speedometer.

Norton 348 c.c. o.h.c. Model 40

NORTON 490 c.c. o.h.c. Model 30.
NORTON 348 c.c. o.h.c. Model 40.
SPECIFICATION

Engine. Make Norton.
    Bore and Stroke. Model 30 79 mm. x 100 mm. 490 c.c.
                           Model 40 71 mm. x 88 mm. 348 c.c.
    Compression Ratio. Model 30 7.12 to 1. Model 40 7.33 to 1.
    B.H.P. Model 40 24 at 6,000. Model 30 29 at 5,500.
    Single cylinder, air cooled, single port, o.h.c.
    Sparking plugs 14 mm.
Lubrication. Dry sump and Norton gear pump.
Carburettor. Amal T.T.
Gear Box. 4 speed, positive stop foot change.
    Ratios. Model 40 10.02, 6.85, 5.67, and 5.16 to 1.
           Model 30 10.8, 6.18, 5.1, and 4.66 to 1.
Clutch. Multi-plate.
Transmission. Primary. Chain ½" x .305".
                 Secondary. Chain ⅝" x ¼".
Ignition. } Lucas Magdyno.
Lighting. }
Petrol Capacity. 3¾ gallons.
Oil Capacity. ¾ gallon.
Tyres. 3.00" x 21" front. 3.25" x 20" rear.
Brakes. Internal expanding, 7", front and rear.
Frame and Suspension. Norton "Roadholder" Telescopic forks. Plunger type rear springing.
Saddle. Terry or Lucas.   **Height from ground.** 30".
Wheelbase. 54½".   **Ground Clearance.** 5¼".
Overall Length. 84½".   **Width over bars.** 30".
Weight (dry). Model 30 415 lb. Model 40 409 lb.
Finish. Norton Silver grey, chromium and black. Bright parts chromium plated. Frame stove enamelled black.
Equipment. Speedometer, prop and front stands, electric horn, tools and pump.
Extra or optional equipment. Light alloy cylinder head and barrel, with central feed to rocker box available at extra charge.
Maximum Speed. 1st 47 m.p.h. 2nd 69 m.p.h. 3rd 80 m.p.h. 4th 90 m.p.h. (30).
                      40 m.p.h.   62 m.p.h.   70 m.p.h.   80 m.p.h. (40).

O.E.C.

O.E.C., LIMITED
STAMSHAW ROAD · PORTSMOUTH

O.E.C. Ltd. have for many years been manufacturing high quality motor cycles, and their machines have always been notable for the originality of their design, and the many interesting features included in their specifications.

Some considerable time before the last war they were producing powerful and efficient machines, in many cases powered by J.A.P. engines, which included the famous O.E.C. Duplex steering, and such modern features as 4 speed footchange boxes and spring frames.

For the current year the company is concentrating on two very efficient looking lightweight machines, which proved themselves in 1949, by winning the Cotswold Scramble and the Blandford Road Races in the 125 c.c. class.

Both machines are powered by the latest Villiers engines, the Mark 10D, 122 c.c. and the Mark 6E 197 c.c. These engines are of the single port type, with deflectorless pistons, and ball and roller bearings throughout. The gear box is in unit construction with the engine, and driven by a chain, totally enclosed in an aluminium oil bath. The three speed gear box is foot controlled, and a kick starter is provided. The standard Villiers single plate clutch is fitted.

Ignition, of course, is by the usual Villiers flywheel magneto, and this, with rectifier lighting and an accumulator, supplies current for the head and tail lamps. The 6½" headlamp includes an ammeter, and a stop light is incorporated in the tail lamp.

The all steel welded loop type frame is of patent O.E.C. design, and has no castings or lugs. This type of frame has given very satisfactory service in O.E.C. machines over many years. The front forks are of O.E.C. telescopic design, the load and rebound being taken by compression springs. 5" wide dome section mudguards are provided front and rear, and the handlebars are of the adjustable sports type, with lever controls and a twist grip throttle control.

A low level exhaust pipe with a large capacity silencer is fitted, and both machines have internal expanding brakes—4" front and 5" rear. Tyres are Dunlop 2.75" x 25 on the 125 c.c. model and 3.00" x 25 on the larger 197 c.c. machine. The Petroil tank holds 2½ gallons.

The machines are well equipped with electric horn, rear stop light, central stand, tool box and kit, pump and licence holder. Both models have a Lycett multi-spring saddle. Speedometers are available as an extra.

The finish is enamelled polychromatic silver, with a blue panel, for the petrol tank, the wheels have chromium plated rims, and the mudguards are enamelled polychromatic silver.

These two lightweights have already proved very popular and are making an excellent reputation for themselves.

SPECIFICATION.
O.E.C. 122 c.c. and 197 c.c. Two Strokes.
Engine. Make, Villiers Mark 10D, 122 c.c. Mark 6E, 197 c.c.
  Bore and Stroke. 50 mm. x 62 mm. 122 c.c. 59 mm. x 72 mm. 197 c.c.
  Compression Ratio. 8 to 1.
  B.H.P. 4.8 at 4,400 r.p.m. 122 c.c. 8.4 at 4,000 r.p.m. 197 c.c.
  Single cylinder, air cooled, single port, two stroke, deflectorless piston.
  Sparking plugs. 14 mm.
Lubrication. Petroil system.
Carburettor. Villiers automatic, with air filter and easy starting device. Twist grip throttle control.
Gearbox. Unit construction, 3 speed, foot change.
  Ratios. 122 c.c. 23.0, 12.0, and 7:1.
  197 c.c. 17.3, 9.0, and 5.33:1.
Clutch. Single plate.
Transmission. Primary. Chain in aluminium oil bath chaincase.
  Secondary. Chain.
Ignition. Villiers flywheel magneto.
Lighting. Rectifier lighting with accumulator. 6½" headlamp with ammeter. Stop light in tail lamp.
Petrol Capacity. 2½ gallons.
Tyres. 122 c.c. Dunlop, 2.75" x 25".
  197 c.c. Dunlop, 3.00" x 25".
Brakes. Internal expanding brakes, 4" front, 5" rear.
Frame and Suspension. All steel loop frame. O.E.C. compression spring telescopic forks.
Saddle. Lycett Multi-spring. **Height from ground.** 28".
Wheelbase. 50". **Ground clearance.** 6".
Overall Length. 80". **Width over bars.** 26".
Weight (dry). 122 c.c. 180 lbs. 197 c.c. 190 lbs.
Finish. Tank enamelled polychromatic silver with blue panel. Mudguards enamelled polychromatic silver. Frame enamelled black and bright parts chromium plated.
Equipment. Electric horn, rear stop light, central stand, tool box, tool kit, pump, licence holder. Speedometer.
Maximum Speed. 122 c.c. 55 m.p.h. 197 c.c. 65 m.p.h.
Petrol consumption (at 30 m.p.h.) 122 c.c. 130 m.p.g. 197 c.c. 110 m.p.g.

Panther

PHELON & MOORE LTD.
CLECKHEATON . YORKS.

Although the name of Panther is a comparatively modern one, many motor cyclists are aware that the manufacturers—Messrs. Phelon and Moore Ltd., have been producing motor cycles for over 40 years.

Those machines, which will be familiar to the older generation as the " P. & M." have always had a first class reputation, and were exceptionally popular and highly thought of in their time. Large numbers of P. & M. machines were in use during the first World War, and did yeoman service everywhere.

1932 saw the introduction of the "Red Panther" 248 c.c. model, meeting the demand that existed for a reasonably priced, medium powered and reliable machine. This model rapidly established itself as a first class seller, and it is perhaps significant that Panthers still cater for the 250 c.c. market.

Shortly after the outbreak of the second World War, the Panther factory at Cleckheaton was switched to precision engineering, but a striking range of Panthers is again in production and they are proving as popular as ever. Six machines comprise the current range, two " 250 "s, the 65 and 65 De Luxe, a 350 c.c., the model 75, and the famous 600 c.c. model. The range is completed by two special competition machines, a 250 c.c. and 350 c.c., known as the " Stroud " models. All have o.h.v. engines.

The two standard 250 c.c. o.h.v. machines have a bore and stroke of 60 mm. x 88 mm. (248 c.c.), with a compression ratio of 6.5 to 1, developing 8.75 b.h.p. at 5,000 r.p.m. On the 250 c.c. and 350 c.c. models the engines are vertically mounted, and are of the single port o.h.v. type with enclosed push rods and detachable cylinder heads. The Hepolite piston is slightly domed and the cylinder barrel is deeply spigotted into the top of the crankcase. The crankshaft main bearings are lead-bronze bushes. Lubrication is by semi-dry sump system with pressure lubrication to the main bearings, the flywheel rims returning surplus oil to the sump. Amal carburettors are fitted, and ignition on the two 250 c.c. models is by Lucas coil with automatic advance and retard mechanism. A gear driven Lucas dynamo is provided with voltage regulator. Burman foot change gear boxes are fitted to both machines, the " 65 " however, having a 3 speed box, with ratios of 15.94, 9.78 and 6.04 to 1., whilst the 65 De Luxe has a 4 speed box with ratios of 15.67, 10.34, 7.53, and 5.88 to 1. The primary chain is enclosed in an oil bath chain case.

The frame is rigid, but Dowty Oleomatic air sprung front forks, with hydraulic damping are fitted to both models, which are fitted with Dunlop 3.25" x 19" tyres—ribbed, front, and studded, rear, and 6" front and 6½" rear brakes. A central stand is fitted to these machines, the rear mudguard hinges for easy wheel removal, and a neat triangular toolbox is fitted at the rear of the machine. Equipment includes Burgess silencers, Smith's Chronometric speedometers and Terry or Lycett saddles. The 65 is finished in royal blue enamel, panelled in egg-shell blue and lined gold. The 65 De Luxe has a chromium tank panelled cream and lined in black and red, chromium rims, centred black and lined red. In addition to the provision of a four speed gearbox, the " De Luxe" Model is distinguished from the standard 65 by chromium plating on the chain case rim and saddle springs.

The 348 c.c. o.h.v. Model 75 has an almost identical specification to the 250 c.c. models. Bore and stroke are 71 mm. x 88 mm., with a compression ratio of 6.5 to 1 and a b.h.p. of 12 at 5,000 r.p.m. Ignition on the 350 is by Lucas magneto however. A separate gear driven Lucas magdyno is mounted at the front of the crankcase. A four speed Burman foot change box has ratios of 14.05, 9.25, 6.73 and 5.26 to 1. Dowty Oleomatic front forks, Dunlop tyres, and 6" front and 6½" rear brakes are fitted. The petrol tank, which holds $2\frac{7}{8}$ gallons is rubber mounted. The " 75 " has a spring-up prop stand and a rear "roll-on" stand. Finish of the " 75 " is chromium tank, cream panelled and lined with red and black, chromium rims, centred black and lined red, with a chromium rim to the oil bath chaincase and chromed saddle springs. Weight is 314 lbs.

The two " Stroud " Competition Models were introduced over a year ago, and have had an exceptionally good reception. As a result of recent trials experience, the engine has been improved in regard to low speed torque characteristics. All Stroud machines are hand built and tested as trials models. Whilst the engine design and main features of the specification follow the standard 248 c.c. and 348 c.c. models, many practical features that will appeal to the trials rider have been incorporated. The headlamp and rear stand are quickly detachable, a crankcase shield is fitted, and the machine has rigid narrow footrests and a folding kickstarter. The 248 c.c. machine has a Burman 4 speed box with ratios of 24.00, 15.50, 9.50 and 7.25 to 1, whilst the larger model has ratios of 21.75, 14.00 8.75 and 6.75 to 1. A manually controlled Lucas magneto and a Lucas 40 watt dynamo are fitted, Petro-flex pipes are fitted to the fuel system, a high saddle position has been achieved and the $\frac{7}{8}$" handlebars are carefully placed to ensure ease of control. Dowty Oleomatic forks are, of course, included, and brakes are 6" front and 8" rear. Tyres are Dunlop Universal 2.75" x 21", front and 4.00" x 19", rear. Buffed aluminium alloy mudguards and a high level exhaust system are other trials features. The machines weigh 273 lbs., with a wheelbase of 54" and a ground clearance of 6".

The 598 c.c. Panther o.h.v. Model 100 is an old and tried favourite, which has gained a fine reputation as a great dual-purpose machine, capable of an effortless and untiring performance when ridden solo, and capable of pulling the heaviest sidecar load. It has also an excellent "top-end" performance and is noted for its fuel economy. The model can be supplied with forks and gear ratios suitable for either solo or sidecar use.

A notable feature of this machine, and one which dates back a very long time indeed, is the incorporation of the engine in the frame structure in place of the front down tube. This has always been a distinguishing feature of Panther and P. & M. machines, but the 598 c.c. machine is the only current model to retain the sloping engine and this form of construction. With a bore and stroke of 87 mm. x 100 mm., the twin port o.h.v. push rod engine develops 23 b.h.p. at 5,000 r.p.m. The compression ratio is 6.5 to 1. Lubrication is on the Panther semi-dry sump system, a Lucas gear driven magneto provides the ignition, and a separate Lucas A.V.C. Dynamo is fitted. The Burman 4 speed box is supplied with either solo or sidecar ratios. The petrol tank holds 3 gallons and brakes are 7" diameter front and 8" rear. The frame is rigid, but Dowty Oleomatic front forks are fitted. Tyres are Dunlop 3.25" x 19" front and rear. A front stand and the Panther cam action rear stand are fitted.

The machine is finished with a chromium tank, panelled cream and lined with red and black, chromium rims and a polished aluminium oil bath chaincase. An alternative finish of green, cream and chromium is available at small extra cost. Equipment includes a Smith's Chronometric speedometer, and extras offered are a pillion seat, pillion rests, luggage carrier, air cleaner for the carburettor, and a 3.50" rear tyre. The machine weighs 385 lb. in standard form.

53

Panther
Model 65
248 c.c. o.h.v.

PANTHER MODELS 65 and 65 De Luxe. 248 c.c. o.h.v.

SPECIFICATION

Engine. Make Panther.
    Bore and Stroke. 60 mm. x 88 mm. 248 c.c.
    Compression Ratio. 6.5 to 1.
    B.H.P. 10.42 at 5,000 r.p.m.
    Single cylinder, air cooled, single port o.h.v. enclosed push rods, detachable cylinder head.
    Sparking plugs 14 mm.
Lubrication. Semi dry sump.
Carburettor. Amal 28"/32" bore.
Gear Box. Burman 3 speed, positive stop, foot change. 65.
    Burman 4 speed, positive stop, foot change. 65 de luxe.
    Ratios. 15.94, 9.78 and 6.04 to 1. 65.
    15.67, 10.34, 7.52 and 5.88 to 1. 65 de luxe.
Clutch. 65, Dry cork. 65 De Luxe, Neoprene in oil.
Transmission. Primary. Chain ⅜" x .305".
    Secondary. Chain ⅜" x .305".

Ignition. Lucas coil.
Lighting. Lucas dynamo, A.V.C.
Petrol Capacity. 2¼ gallons.
Oil Capacity. 2¼ pints.
Tyres. Dunlop 3.25" x 19", ribbed, front. 3.25" x 19" rear.
Brakes. 6" front. 6½" rear, internal expanding.
Frame and Suspension. Dowty Oleomatic forks and rigid frame.
Saddle. Lycett or Terry.   Height from ground 28¼".
Wheelbase. 54".   Ground Clearance. 6".
Overall Length. 83".   Width over bars. 29".
Weight (dry). 65 304 lb. 65 de luxe 306 lbs.
Finish. 65. Tank-royal blue enamel, lined gold. Bright parts chromium plated.
    65 de luxe. Chromium tank, panelled cream, lined black and red. Wheels chromium rims, centred black.
Equipment. Speedometer, centre stand.
Extra or optional equipment. Pillion seat, pillion rests, luggage carrier and air cleaner.

Panther
Model 75
348 c.c. o.h.v.

PANTHER 348 c.c. o.h.v. Model 75.

SPECIFICATION

Engine. Make Panther.
    Bore and Stroke. 71 mm. x 88 mm. 348 c.c.
    Compression Ratio. 6.5 to 1.
    B.H.P. 15.4 at 5,000 r.p.m.
    Single cylinder, air cooled, single port, o.h.v., enclosed push rod operated valves.
    Sparking plugs 14 mm.
Lubrication. Semi dry sump.
Carburettor. Amal ⅞" bore.
Gear Box. Burman 4 speed, positive stop, foot change.
    Ratios. 14.05, 9.25, 6.73 and 5.26 to 1.
Clutch. Neoprene in oil.
Transmission. Primary. Chain ⅜" x .305".
    Secondary. Chain ⅜" x .305".
Ignition. Lucas Magneto.

Lighting. Lucas dynamo, A.V.C.
Petrol Capacity. 2¼ gallons.
Oil Capacity. 2¼ pints.
Tyres. Front, Dunlop ribbed, 3.25" x 19". Rear-Universal 3.25" x 19".
Brakes. Internal expanding, 6" front, 6½" rear.
Frame and Suspension. Dowty oleomatic forks and rigid frame.
Saddle. Lycett or Terry.   Height from ground. 28¼".
Wheelbase. 54".   Ground Clearance. 6".
Overall Length. 83".   Width over bars. 29".
Weight (dry). 314 lbs.
Finish. Chromium tank, cream panelled, lined red and black. Chromium rims centred black and lined red. Frame stove enamelled black.
Equipment. Tools, pump, number plates, prop. and rear stands.
Extra or optional equipment. Pillion seat, pillion rests, luggage carrier and air cleaner.

PANTHER 598 c.c. o.h.v. Model 100.

SPECIFICATION

Engine. Make Panther
  Bore and Stroke 87 mm x 100 mm 598 c c
  Compression Ratio, 6.5 to 1
  B.H.P. 23 at 5,000 r.p.m.
  Single cylinder, air cooled, twin port o.h.v. enclosed push rod operated valves. Inclined engine.
  Sparking plugs 14 mm.
Lubrication. Semi dry sump.
Carburettor. Amal 1¼" bore.
Gear Box. Burman 4 speed, positive stop foot change.
  Ratios. Solo. 11.98, 7.04, 5.65 and 4.49 to 1.
    Sidecar, 13.61, 8.00, 6.42 and 5.10 to 1.
Clutch. Neoprene in oil.
Transmission. Primary. Chain ½" x .305".
  Secondary. Chain ⅝" x ¼".
Ignition. Lucas Magneto.
Lighting. Lucas dynamo. A.V.C.

Petrol Capacity. 3 gallons.
Oil Capacity. 4 pints.
Tyres. Dunlop, 3.25" x 19". Ribbed front. studded rear.
Brakes. Internal expanding. 7" front. 8" rear.
Frame and Suspension. Dowty oleomatic forks. Rigid frame. Optional solo or sidecar rake adjustment.
Saddle. Lycett or Terry.   Height from ground. 28".
Wheelbase. 54".   Ground Clearance. 6".
Overall Length. 83".   Width over bars. 29".
Weight (dry) 385 lbs.
Finish. Chromium tank. panelled cream, lined red and black. Chromium rims, centred black, lined red, black mudguards, lined gold. Frame stove enamelled black.
Equipment. Horn, tools, pump, number plates, front and rear stands, speedometer.
Extra or optional equipment. Pillion seat pillion rests. luggage carrier, air cleaner 3.50" rear tyre.

PANTHER 248 c.c. and 348 c.c. "Stroud" Competition Models.

SPECIFICATION

Engine. Make Panther.
  Bore and Stroke. 60 mm. x 88 mm. 248 c.c.
                   71 mm. x 88 mm. 348 c.c.
  Compression Ratio. 6.5 to 1.
  B.H.P. 248 c.c. 11.2 at 5,000 r.p.m. 348 c.c. 16, at 5,000 r.p.m.
  Single cylinder, air cooled single port. o.h.v. enclosed push rod operated valves.
  Sparking plugs 14 mm.
Lubrication. Semi dry sump.
Carburettor. 248 c.c. Amal 25/32" bore. 348 c.c. Amal ⅞" bore.
Gear Box. Burman 4 speed, positive stop foot change.
  Ratios. 248 c.c. 24.00, 15.50, 9.50 and 7.25 to 1.
          348 c.c. 21.75, 14.00, 8.75 and 6.75 to 1.
Clutch. Neoprene in oil.
Transmission. Primary. Chain ½" x .305".
  Secondary. Chain ⅝" x ¼".

Ignition. Lucas magneto. Manually controlled.
Lighting. Lucas 40 watt dynamo.
Petrol Capacity. 1½ gallons.
Oil Capacity. 2½ pints.
Tyres. Dunlop, Universal, 2.75" x 21" front. 4.00" x 19" rear.
Brakes. Internal expanding. 6" front, 8" rear.
Frame and Suspension. Dowty Oleomatic forks and rigid frame.
Saddle. Lycett or Terry.   Height from ground 26¾"
Wheelbase. 54".   Ground Clearance. 6".
Overall Length. 83".   Width over bars. 29".
Weight (dry) 273 lb.
Finish. Chrome tank, cream panelled, lined red and black, chrome rims, centred cream, lined red. Frame stove enamelled black. Buffed aluminium alloy mudguards.
Equipment. Speedometer, number plates, tool kit, rear stand and lighting
Extra or optional equipment. Pillion seat and rests.

Royal Enfield

THE ENFIELD CYCLE COMPANY LTD.
REDDITCH · WORCS.

U.S.A. Distributor:
INDIAN SALES CORPORATION
29 Worthington St.
Springfield, Mass.

Royal Enfields have had a long and honourable history in the motor cycle world. The famous slogan—"Made like a Gun," has become almost a household word in this country, and Enfield machines were in the forefront several decades ago.

Associated with the name of Enfield is a tradition of sound workmanship and conventional design which has produced a series of motor cycles of outstanding reliability, capable of an enormous amount of hard work, and continuously tried and tested in trials and scrambles so that the marque figures consistently in the list of awards of very many of the premier events held in this country and abroad.

Founded in 1892, the Enfield Company was at first associated with the Townsend Needle Company at Redditch. The manufacture of cycles soon absorbed the entire works, and in 1906 these were moved to the present site. The first powered machine produced by the company was a quadricycle in 1899, and the first motor cycle appeared in 1901. This had the engine on the front fork, and was produced, with various improvements, until 1903. In 1910, a 2¼ h.p. twin appeared. Between 1910 and the Great War, the company produced a 2¾ h.p. machine with all-chain drive and two-speed gears, and the 3 h.p. twin, incidentally the first internal combustion engine to have dry sump lubrication. Other interesting machines were 6 h.p. and 8 h.p. "Big Twins" for solo and sidecar work. During World War 1 was begun the manufacture of the first Enfield two stroke, a 225 c.c. machine.

The development of the Royal Enfield concern continued unchecked between the two wars, and the Redditch works now cover some 24 acres. Tens of thousands of machines were supplied to the Services during the last war, including a 125 c.c. machine for the Airborne Forces.

The current range of Enfield machines comprises a 125 c.c. lightweight, a 346 c.c. and 499 c.c. o.h.v. single, a 496 c.c. vertical twin, and the 346 c.c. o.h.v. "Bullet" model, which is offered in no less than three forms:—the standard machine and two specially modified models designed for trials and scrambles respectively.

The 125 c.c. lightweight model is a remarkably well finished machine and includes a number of interesting features. The Enfield two-stroke engine of 53.79 x 55 mm. has a deflectorless piston of heat-treated low expansion aluminium alloy with two compression rings and a fully floating gudgeon pin. The aluminium alloy cylinder head is detachable. The main shafts are carried on ball bearings and a roller bearing big end is fitted. The crankcase is of aluminium.

The gearbox is cast integrally with the engine crankcase but is a separate unit as regards lubrication. It provides 3 speeds with a hand controlled lever. All gears are in constant mesh, changes being effected by robust dog clutches, and a kick starter is fitted. A fully enclosed flywheel magneto supplies a 6 volt, 24 x 24 watt double filament bulb, and a standard dry battery is fitted in the headlamp for parking. A handlebar controlled dipper switch is fitted.

A new design of telescopic front fork has been fitted to this model. The upper tubes of the fork are fixed, and the lower sliding tubes operate outside them. A single helical spring which controls impact and rebound is enclosed in each fork leg. As the legs are filled with lubricating oil on assembly, no further maintenance is necessary. The total movement allowed is 4" (or 2" on compression and 2" on rebound). 4" front and 5" rear internal expanding brakes are provided. Improvements made to current models are a larger tank and 2.75" x 19" tyres. The exhaust system has a special streamlined expansion chamber close to the cylinder, and a large easily cleaned silencer at the end of the exhaust pipe. A Smith's illuminated speedometer and a central stand are standard fittings and the model is attractively finished in silver-grey enamel. Legshields are available at an extra charge.

The 346 c.c. o.h.v. Model G follows normal Enfield practice. The engine has a bore and stroke of 70 mm. x 90 mm. with valves, rocker gear and push rods totally enclosed and automatically lubricated. A form-turned, heat treated oval piston of low expansion aluminium alloy and a hiduminium RR 56 aluminium alloy connecting rod are employed. The big end bearing incorporates a special floating bush and the main shafts are on roller bearings. The timing gear, with separate cams operates direct on to large diameter flat base tappets running in an oil bath. The single port cylinder head is detachable.

Lubrication is on the Enfield dry-sump system, and is entirely automatic and positive in action. The oil compartment is integral with the crankcase and ensures a full rate of circulation immediately after starting the engine. Oil is fed positively to the big end, the rear of the cylinder and to the rocker gear and timing gear. A large felt oil filter ensures a clean supply at all times. A large air filter is fitted to the carburettor.

A Lucas gear driven 6 volt magdyno with automatic voltage control supplies the headlamp, which has a dipper switch, the tail lamp and the electric horn. The Royal Enfield patent telescopic forks have long flexible springs combined with oil damping, which is light in the normal position but becomes progressively more effective towards the end of the fork travel. The bearings are automatically lubricated by oil in the fork.

The 4 speed gearbox has positive stop foot change, and all gears are in constant mesh, changes being effected by dog clutches. An ingenious neutral finder is fitted, enabling neutral to be positively selected from 2nd gear when the machine is at rest, or from top, third or second gear when the machine is moving. The 4 plate clutch is handlebar controlled.

The well known Royal Enfield cush drive with rubber blocks is fitted to the rear wheel. By loosening only four nuts the entire rear mudguard can be lifted away, giving access to practically the whole of the tyre. A detachable two-piece rear spindle also allows an inner tube to be withdrawn through the gap between the hub and the fork end, without disturbing the brake, chain adjustment or alignment of the wheels. The internal expanding brakes are fitted with a finger adjustment. The low level exhaust pipe has an efficient silencer. A high level system can be supplied to order and legshields can also be supplied at an extra charge.

The 499 c.c. Model J 2 follows the specification of the Model G outlined above. The engine has a bore and stroke of 84 mm. x 90 mm. and minor differences are altered gear ratios (sidecar ratios are also available), the provision of a 3.50" x 19" tyre, and an additional tool box.

The engine has a twin port head, and the standard low level exhaust system can be replaced by a high level type. Legshields are also available for this model, and sidecar forks with stronger springs and a reduced trail can be supplied.

The 346 c.c. o.h.v. "Bullet" was developed from the machine used in the 1948 International Six Days Trial, and is a thoroughly sporting "350" that will appeal to experienced riders. The high efficiency engine has a light alloy cylinder head and connecting rod. The cylinder head has wide angle valves and cast-in inserts for the valve seats and sparking plug. Valves, rocker gears and push rods are totally enclosed and automatically lubricated.

Like the Enfield twin, the Bullet has a fully sprung frame with hydraulically damped coil spring rear suspension. A full-lift central stand and a prop stand are provided. The petrol tank holds 3¼ gallons. The exhaust system is upswept at the rear, but high level pipes can be supplied to order. A neat cast aluminium facia contains the speedometer.

The Bullet is available as a scrambles or trials edition, with racing magneto, special close or wide ratio gearbox, high level or straight through exhaust pipes and competition tyres. High compression pistons suitable for petrol, petrol-benzol or alcohol fuels are available, as well as special racing cams on the scrambles model.

The 496 c.c. o.h.v. vertical twin has separate cylinder barrels with separate light-alloy heads and is housed in a Bullet type frame. The crankcase has a half-gallon oil compartment at the rear. Each barrel is spigotted to a depth of 3" into the crankcase, and the massive one-piece crankshaft is integral with the central flywheel. Plain bearing big ends are fitted, with ball and roller main bearings. Two chain driven high level camshafts operate valves through large diameter flat base tappets and short push-rods. Heat treated pistons of low expansion aluminium alloy, and connecting rods of Hiduminium RR 56 alloy are fitted.

Lubrication is on the dry sump system by two double acting, oscillating plunger pumps. Oil is fed through internal drilled passages to the big end bearings, overhead rockers, camshafts and timing gear and to the rear of the cylinder.

A fully sprung frame with telescopic forks and swinging arm rear suspension, with hydraulically damped enclosed coil springs is provided.

The usual Enfield features of detachable mudguards, two piece rear spindles and cush drive rear hub are found on this machine. Both central and prop stands are fitted. The 4 speed positive stop foot gear change gearbox is bolted directly to the back of the crankshaft and incorporates the Enfield neutral finder. The 4 plate clutch is handlebar controlled. A twin low-level exhaust system is fitted and the speedometer is housed in a facia panel, similar to the Bullet model.

Royal Enfield
125 c.c. Two Stroke
Model R.E.

Royal Enfield
496 c.c. o.h.v.
Vertical Twin

SPECIFICATION.

125 c.c. Model R.E.

Engine. Make. Royal Enfield.
Bore and Stroke. 53.79 x 55 mm. 125 c.c.
Compression Ratio. 5.5 to 1.
B.H.P. 3½ at 4,500 r.p.m.
Single cylinder, air cooled, single port, two stroke. Deflectorless heat treated low expansion aluminium alloy piston. Detachable aluminium alloy cylinder head. Roller bearing big end.
Sparking plugs. 14 mm.
Lubrication. Petroil system.
Carburettor. Amal needle type, with air cleaner.
Gearbox. Integral with engine crankcase. 3 speed. Hand control.
Ratios. 22.4, 12.4 and 7.6 to 1.
Clutch. Cork lined clutch, handlebar controlled.
Transmission. Primary. Chain ⅜" pitch, in oilbath chain case.
Secondary. Chain ½" pitch.
Ignition. Fully enclosed Flywheel magneto.
Lighting. Flywheel magneto. Headlamp 6 volt. 24 x 24 watt double filament bulb. Tail light. Provision for parking battery in headlamp.
Petrol Capacity. 1⅞ gallons Petroil.
Oil Capacity. Petroil system,
Tyres. Dunlop 2.75" x 19", front and rear,
Brakes. Internal expanding, 4" front, 5" rear.
Frame and Suspension. Rigid frame, all welded construction, alloy steel tubes. Oil lubricated telescopic front forks.
Saddle. Spring seat. **Height from ground.** 26½".
Wheelbase. 48". **Ground clearance.** 6.75".
Overall Length. 6′ 3". **Width over bars.** 2′ 2".
Weight (dry). 135 lb.
Finish. Silver Grey enamel. Bright parts chromium plated.
Equipment. Toolbox, pump. Smith's Chronometric Speedometer.
Extra or optional equipment. Legshields available.
Maximum Speed. 1st 18 m.p.h. 2nd 30 m.p.h. 3rd 40–45 m.p.h.
Petrol consumption (at 30 m.p.h.) 130 m.p.g.
Braking (from 30 m.p.h. to rest). 32′ 6".

SPECIFICATION.

346 c.c. o.h.v. Model G. 499 c.c. o.h.v. Model J2.

Engine. Make, Royal Enfield.
Bore and Stroke. 70 mm. x 90 mm. 346 c.c. (Model G.)
84 mm. x 90 mm. 499 c.c. (Model J2).
Compression Ratio 6.5 to 1 (Model G). 5.75 to 1 (Model J2).
B.H.P. G. 15 at 5,500 r.p.m. J2. 21 at 4,750 r.p.m.
Single cylinder air cooled, o.h.v. single port (J2 twin port). Aluminium alloy piston, detachable cylinder head. Valves, rocker gear and push rods totally enclosed. Hiduminium RR56 aluminium alloy connecting rod.
Sparking plugs. 14 mm.
Lubrication. Dry sump. Twin double acting oscillating plunger pumps.
Carburettor. Amal needle type.
Gearbox. Four speed, positive stop, foot change, with patent neutral finder. Constant mesh gears.
Ratios. Model G. 15.6, 10.1, 7.3 and 5.6 to 1.
J2. 14.2, 9.2, 6.6 and 5 to 1.
Sidecar J2. 16.6, 10.7, 7.7 and 5.95 to 1.
Clutch. 4 plate, with handlebar control.
Transmission. Primary. Chain ½" pitch in oilbath case.
Secondary Chain ⅝" pitch. Cush drive in rear hub.
Lighting. Lucas 6 volt magdyno, 60 watt output. Automatic voltage control 30 watt headlamp.
Petrol Capacity. 2¾ gallons.
Oil Capacity. ½ gallon.
Tyres. Model G. Dunlop 3.25" x 19" ribbed, front. Universal, rear.
J2. Dunlop 3.25" x 19" ribbed-front. 3.50" x 19". Universal rear.
Brakes. Internal expanding, 6" front and rear. J2. 7" rear.
Frame and Suspension. Cradle type rigid frame of chrome molybdenum alloy steel tubing. Enfield patent Telescopic oil lubricated front forks.
Saddle. Large spring seat. **Height from ground.** G. 29". J2 28¾".
Wheelbase. G. 53½". J2. 54½". **Ground Clearance.** G. 5¼" J2. 4¾".
Overall Length. G. 7′. J2. 7′ 1". **Width over bars.** 2′ 6".
Weight (dry). G 370 lb. J2 395 lb.
Finish. Black enamel. Bright parts chromium plated. Tank chromium plated, panelled in frosted silver with blue and red lining.
Equipment. Toolboxes. (One on Model G, two on J2.) Tools. Tyre pump. Smith's Speedometer. (120 m.p.h. dial on J2.)
Extra or optional equipment. Legshields.
Maximum Speed. 1st 30 m.p.h. 2nd 43 m.p.h.(G). 3rd 60 m.p.h.(G). 4th 70–75 [m.p.h.(G).
2nd 46 m.p.h. (J2). 3rd 65 m.p.h. (J2). 4th 80–85 m.p.h. (J2).
Petrol consumption (at 30 m.p.h.) 95 m.p.g. (G). 80 m.p.g. (J.2).
Braking (from 30 m.p.h. to rest). 30 ft.

SPECIFICATION.

500 c.c. TWIN

Engine. Make, Royal Enfield.
Bore and Stroke. 64 mm. x 77 mm. 496 c.c.
Compression Ratio. 6.5 to 1.
B.H.P. 25 at 5,750 r.p.m.
Vertical twin cylinder, air cooled, twin port, o.h.v. Separate cylinders with separate light alloy cylinder heads. One piece crankshaft integral with central flywheel. Aluminium alloy pistons. Chain driven high level camshafts.
Sparking plugs. 14 mm.
Lubrication. Dry Sump. Twin double acting, oscillating plunger pumps.
Carburettor. Amal needle type.
Gearbox. 4 speed, positive stop foot change. Patent neutral finder. All gears in constant mesh.
Ratios. 13.9, 9.0, 6.5 and 5 to 1.
Clutch. 4 plate clutch with handlebar control.
Transmission. Primary. Chain ⅜" pitch, duplex. Oilbath chaincase.
Secondary. Chain ⅝" pitch. Cush drive in rear hub.
Ignition. Lucas Dynamo and coil.
Lighting. Lucas Dynamo 75 watt output. Automatic voltage control. 30 watt headlamp, pilot light, tail lamp and electric horn.
Petrol Capacity. 3¼ gallons.
Oil Capacity. ½ gallon.
Tyres. Dunlop. 3.25" x 19" ribbed, front. 3.50" x 19" Universal-rear.
Brakes. Internal expanding, 6" front and rear.
Frame and Suspension. Alloy steel tubing, fully sprung frame, with swinging arm rear frame. Telescopic forks.
Saddle. Large spring seat. **Height from ground.** 29½".
Wheelbase. 54". **Ground clearance.** 5½".
Overall Length. 7′ 0½". **Width over bars.** 2′ 6".
Weight (dry) 400 lb.
Finish. Silver-grey enamel. Bright parts chromium plated. Tank chromium plated, panelled in frosted silver, with red and blue lining.
Equipment. Two tool boxes. Tools. Tyre pump. Smith's illuminated speedometer with 120 m.p.h. dial.
Extra or optional equipment.
Maximum Speed. 1st 35 m.p.h. 2nd 52 m.p.h. 3rd 70 m.p.h. 4th 85–90 [m.p.h.
Petrol consumption (at 30 m.p.h.) 70 m.p.g.
Braking (from 30 m.p h. to rest). 30 ft.

Royal Enfield 350 c.c. BULLET

SPECIFICATION.

Engine. Make, Royal Enfield.
346 c.c. Bore and Stroke.
70 mm. x 90 mm.
Compression Ratio. 6.5 to 1.
B.H.P. 18 at 5, 750 r.p.m.
Single cylinder, o.h.v. air cooled, single port. Light alloy detachable cylinder head, wide angle valves, Valves, rocker gear and push rods totally enclosed. Aluminium alloy piston, Hiduminium connecting rod. Big end bearing incorporates special floating bush.
Sparking plugs. 14 mm.
Lubrication. Dry sump. Twin double acting, oscillating plunger pump.
Carburettor. Amal needle type.
Gearbox. 4 speed, foot controlled, positive stop. Patent neutral finder.
Ratios. 15.8, 10.2, 7.37 and 5.67 to 1.
Clutch. 4 plate with handlebar control.
Transmission. Primary. ⅜" duplex chain in oil bath case.
Secondary. ⅝" pitch chain.
Ignition. Lucas Gear driven magdyno.
Lighting. Lucas 6 volt gear driven magdyno. 60 watt output. Automatic voltage control. 30 watt headlamp, tail lamp and horn.
Petrol Capacity. 3¼ gallons.
Oil Capacity. ½ gallon.
Tyres. Dunlop, 3.25" x 19" front, ribbed. 3.25" x 19" Universal-rear.
Brakes. Internal expanding, 6" front and rear.
Frame and Suspension. Fully sprung of alloy steel weldless tubing. Swinging arm sprung rear suspension. Telescopic forks.
Saddle. Large spring seat. **Height from ground.** 29½".
Wheelbase. 54". **Ground clearance.** 6¼".
Overall Length. 7′ 0½". **Width over bars.** 2′ 6".
Weight (dry) 350 lb.
Finish. Silver-grey enamel. Bright parts chromium plated. Tank chromium plated, panelled in frosted silver, with blue and red lining.
Equipment. Two tool boxes. Tools. Pump. Smith's illuminated speedometer, mounted in facia panel.
Maximum Speed. 1st 30 m.p.h. 2nd 45 m.p.h. 3rd 62 m.p.h. 4th 75–80 m.p.h.
Petrol consumption (at 30 m.p.h.) 85 m.p.g.
Braking (from 30 m.p.h. to rest). 30ft.
Modifications TRIALS MODEL.
Lucas or B.T.H. gear driven racing magneto. No lights provided. Bulb horn.
Gearbox. Special wide ratios. 22.8, 16.3, 10.65 and 7.6 to 1.
Folding kickstarter. No neutral finder.
Exhaust System. High level.
Tyres. Dunlop Universal. 3.00" x 21", front. 4.00" x 19" rear.
Security bolts fitted. Chromium plated light narrow mudguards.
Ground clearance. 7". **Weight** 310 lb.
Equipment. Crankcase shield. One toolbox with kit. Mudguard pad. Carburettor intake shield in lieu of air filter.

SCRAMBLES MODEL

High compression pistons suitable for petrol, petrol-benzol or alcohol fuels available and special racing cams.
High compression pistons. 7½ to 1—Petrol.
8½ to 1. Petrol-benzol.
11 to 1—Alcohol fuel.
Ignition. Lucas or B.T.H. racing gear driven magneto. No lights or horn.
Gearbox. Standard ratios. 19.7, 12.7, 9.2 and 7.08 to 1.
Special close ratios. 15.4, 11.8, 9.2 and 7.08 to 1.
Exhaust system. Straight through open exhaust pipe.
Tyres. Dunlop sports. 3.00" x 21" front. 4.00" x 19" rear.
Security bolts fitted. Chromium plated light narrow guards.
Ground clearance. 7". **Weight.** 300 lb.
Equipment. Crankcase shield. Mudguard pad. Tool kit. Carburettor intake shield in lieu of air filter.

Scott

**SCOTT MOTOR CYCLE COMPANY
SHIPLEY · YORKS**

Scotts have exercised a strong fascination for the motor cycle enthusiast for over 30 years, for the Scott has always been a unique machine with its own devoted band of admirers to whom the four stroke cycle is a heresy and the ownership of any other make of machine unthinkable.

The Scott has undoubtedly a charm of its own, for the water cooled two-stroke parallel twin, with its crank throws at 180° has an exceptionally smooth torque, magnificent roadholding, a first class performance and an absence of clatter and vibration, and the familiar powerful purr of the Scott exhaust note is one of its more endearing features. Needless to say a strong spirit of camaraderie exists among Scott riders, who can almost be described as a clan.

The latest 596 c.c. 1950 model Scott retains the characteristic layout and appearance of previous machines and is still known as the "Flying Squirrel." The Scott twin cylinder powerplus replica type engine is water cooled, has wide roller bearings throughout and a detachable high efficiency alloy cylinder head. The bore is 73 mm. with a stroke of 71.4 mm. giving a power output of 16 b.h.p. at 2,500 r.p.m. and 30 b.h.p. at 5,000 r.p.m. A central Amal downdraught carburettor is fitted.

Coil ignition has now been adopted in place of the magneto, and as the magneto chain drive has now been discarded, it has been possible to give better enclosure to the primary chain between the two crankcases, and this is carried out by shields and light alloy castings. A Lucas 6 volt, 70 watt dynamo is mounted on the outside of the crankcase and is driven by the crankshaft which also drives the vertically mounted distributor. The ignition is controlled by automatic advance and retard mechanism.

The gearbox is a Scott 3 speed, constant mesh type with wide ratio gears and positive stop foot change. Standard ratios are 4.18, 5.50 and 8.90 to 1, and 5.12, 6.72 and 13.30 to 1 for sidecar work. Wide ratio gears can be fitted if required. The foot change mechanism is integral with the gear box end cover.

The well-known Scott Duplex frame, triangulated in every plane is retained and this frame has always been notable for its low centre of gravity, rock steady steering and freedom from vibration. Scott Telescopic front forks are now fitted, giving 6" of progressive springing, with oil damping. An adjustable friction type steering damper is included.

Twin 6" diameter brakes are fitted to the front wheel, one each side of the hub and balanced by compensating mechanism neatly housed on the front mudguard. The hub shell is of light alloy, deeply finned for cooling. Ball journal bearings are fitted. The rear wheel has an extra heavy hub, with a powerful internal expanding brake, 8" diameter, finger adjusted and thoroughly weatherproof. The drive is taken on a very large and efficient cushioning device in the hub which has deep-groove, non-adjustable ball journals. The hub shell again, is of light alloy and finned for cooling.

The petrol tank, which has a capacity of 3½ gallons, forms a unit with the quickly detachable frame tube and has a two level tap with self cleaning filter. A separate oil tank holds 5 pints of oil, and the primary chain is lubricated by means of an adjustable drip feed from the tank. The two-in-one exhaust pipe is fitted with an efficient silencer.

Equipment includes a high frequency horn, 80 m.p.h. internally illuminated speedometer, a front and a central roll-on type stand and a full complement of tools and the model is finished in chrome and black. Engine shield and chain covers are in polished aluminium. A 5" front and 6" rear mudguard are fitted and the rear guard hinges from stays; it can be quickly detached to facilitate wheel removal.

This fascinating motor cycle has a cruising speed of from 60-65 m.p.h. with a maximum of from 75-80 m.p.h., with a petrol consumption in the region of 70-80 miles per gallon.

STOP PRESS
Sidecar ratios are 13.30, 6.72 and 5.12 to 1.

Scott. 596 c.c. Twin Two Stroke

SPECIFICATION.

SCOTT "Flying Squirrel" 596 c.c. twin two stroke.
Engine. Make Scott.
    Bore and Stroke. 73 mm. x 71.4 mm.
    Compression Ratio. 6.9 to 1.
    B.H.P. 30 at 5,000 r.p.m.
    Twin cylinder water cooled two stroke. Detachable alloy cylinder head.
    Sparking plugs. 14 mm.
Lubrication. Twin mechanical pump.
Carburettor. Amal downdraught.
Gearbox. Scott 3 speed, constant mesh. Close ratio, Positive foot change.
    Ratios. Solo 8.90, 5.50 and 4.18 to 1.
        Sidecar, 13.30, 6.72 and 4.62 to 1.
Clutch. Multi-plate.
Transmission. Primary. Chain ⅜" x .305".
    Secondary. Chain ⅝" x .38".
Ignition. Lucas coil. Automatic advance and retard.
Lighting. Lucas 6 volt, 70 watt dynamo. Constant voltage control. Electric horn.
Petrol Capacity. 3½ gallons.
Oil Capacity. 5 pints.
Tyres. Front, 3.25" x 19". Rear, 3.50" x 19".
Brakes. Front, Two 6" internal expanding. Rear, one 8" internal expanding.
Frame and Suspension. Telescopic forks and duplex triangulated rigid frame.
Saddle. Flexible top type.   Height from ground. 30".
Wheelbase. 57".   Ground clearance. 5".
Overall Length. 7' 4".   Width over bars. 28½".
Weight (dry) 376 lb.
Finish. Black enamel. Bright parts chromium plated.
Equipment. Front and central stands. 80 m.p.h. internally illuminated speedometer. Steering damper, tool box, number plate and tools.
Extra or optional equipment.
Maximum Speed. 75—80 m.p.h.
Petrol consumption (at 30 m.p.h.) 70—80 m.p.g.

Sun

SUN CYCLE & FITTINGS CO. LTD.
ASTON BROOK STREET . BIRMINGHAM, 6

The Sun Company have been manufacturing lightweight motor cycles for some considerable time. Their machines were reintroduced at the 1948 Motor Cycle Show in the form of a 98 c.c. Auto-cycle and a 98 c.c. Motor cycle. This was in the nature of a "Show Surprise."

At the 1949 show a further model was introduced, although it is not yet (at the time of writing) in active production, and to begin with will be produced primarily for export. This is a 122 c.c. Villiers engined lightweight of exceptionally attractive appearance and well finished.

All three machines have, of course, many features in common, and are fitted with the latest type Villiers two-stroke engines. The 98 c.c. Auto-cycle is fitted with the Villiers Mark2F engine of 47 mm. bore x 57 mm. stroke. The engine has an aluminium detachable cylinder head and an aluminium flat topped piston, and develops 2.0 b.h.p. at 3,750 r.p.m. A Villiers single lever carburettor is fitted and the clutch is of the two plate cork insert type. A Villiers flywheel magneto supplies the headlamp, which includes a parking bulb, and the tailamp. A parallel ruler front fork with pressed steel blades is fitted, and the machine has 4" internal expanding brakes front and rear, 21" x 2.25" Dunlop tyres and a 1½ gallon petroil tank. The auto-cycle type frame gives a low and comfortable riding position, enabling the rider to place both feet on the ground. Equipment is very complete, and includes a soft top saddle, a rear stand to facilitate easy removal of the rear wheel, a useful carrier, tool kit and pump. The machine is well finished, the frame being rust-proofed and stove enamelled maroon, whilst the tank is attractively finished in maroon with gold lines. The exhaust system and other bright parts are chromium plated.

The frame of the 98 c.c. motorcycle has been redesigned for 1950. Previously, part-welded construction was employed, but the latest models have frames built up of separate tubes and cast lugs, thus enabling damaged frame members to be replaced without renewing the complete frame. The engine on the 98 c.c. motorcycle is the Villiers Mark 1F, developing a b.h.p. of 2.8 at 4,000 r.p.m. A Villiers single lever carburettor and flywheel magneto is fitted, and the Villiers 2 speed gearbox has a folding kickstarter, the gear change control being fitted on the handlebar. Centre coil spring type front forks and a 1½ gallon petroil tank are fitted on this model, and 4" internal expanding brakes, front and rear. Dunlop 2.50" x 19" tyres are however fitted on the motor cycle. Equipment includes central stand, soft top saddle, rear carrier, headlamp with parking light, and tail lamp. The finish—maroon with gold lines, is similar to the auto-cycle.

As mentioned above, a third model was exhibited at the 1949 Motor Cycle Show, and, it is hoped, will be in production later this year. Full details are not yet available. The engine will be the Villiers Mark 10D, 50 mm. bore x 62 mm. stroke, developing 4.8 b.h.p. at 4,400 r.p.m., with the usual Villiers features of flat topped deflectorless piston and detachable alloy cylinder head. The Villiers unit construction 3 speed foot change gearbox is fitted, with a 2 plate cork insert type clutch running in oil. A neat looking telescopic front fork is fitted, and ignition will be by Villiers flywheel magneto and lighting by either flywheel magneto or by battery rectifier. A 5" headlamp and electric horn will be provided. Dunlop 2.50" x 19" tyres are fitted to this model, and a 1½ gallon petrol tank. Finish, it is understood, will be similar to the 98 c.c. models. The initial production of this machine will be devoted primarily to export.

STOP PRESS
122 c.c. and 197 c.c. Villiers engined models have telescopic forks, plunger type rear springing, battery and rectifier sets, electric horn and rear carrier as standard. Tank capacity 2¼ gals. Tyres 3.00 x 19. 5" brakes. 98 c.c. motor cycle—link action tubular forks now fitted.

Sun 98 c.c. Autocycle

SPECIFICATION.
SUN 98 c.c. Autocycle.
Engine. Make. Villiers Mark 2F.
Bore and Stroke. 47 mm. x 57 mm. 98 c.c.
Compression Ratio. 8 to 1.
B.H.P. 2.0 at 3,750 r.p.m.
Single cylinder, air cooled two stroke. Aluminium detachable cylinder head, aluminium flat top piston.
Sparking plugs. 14 mm.
Lubrication. Petroil.
Carburettor. Villiers single lever.
Gearbox. Single speed.
Ratios.
Clutch. Two plate cork insert type.
Transmission. Primary. Chain.
Pedal. Chain.
Ignition. Villiers flywheel magneto.
Lighting. Villiers flywheel magneto. Headlamp 6 volt, 12 watt main bulb. 4 volt 3 amp, parking bulb. Tail lamp, 4 volt, 3 amp.
Petroil Capacity. 1½ gallons.
Oil Capacity.
Tyres. Dunlop, 21" x 2.25", front and rear.
Brakes. 4" internal expanding, front and rear.
Frame and Suspension. Forks-girder type. Rigid frame.
Saddle. Special soft top saddle.
Wheelbase. 48".
Overall Length. 76".
Weight (dry). 115 lbs.
Height from ground. 39".
Ground clearance. 4".
Width over bars. 25".
Finish. Tank maroon with gold lines. Frame stove enamelled maroon. Bright parts chromium plated.
Equipment. Rear stand, pump, tools, horn, number plates.
Optional equipment. Engine shields.

Sun 98 c.c. Motor Cycle

SPECIFICATION.
SUN 98 c.c. Motorcycle
Engine. Make, Villiers Mark 1F.
  Bore and Stroke. 47 mm. x 57 mm. 98 c.c.
  Compression Ratio. 8 to 1.
  B.H.P. 2.8 at 4,000 r.p.m.
  Single cylinder, air cooled two stroke. Aluminium detachable cylinder head. Aluminium flat top piston.
  Sparking plugs. 14 mm.
Lubrication. Petroil.
Carburettor. Villiers single lever.
Gearbox. Villiers two speed. Hand gear control. Kickstarter with folding pedal. Ratios.
Clutch. 2 plate cork insert type.
Transmission. Primary. Chain.
  Secondary. Chain.
Ignition. Villiers flywheel magneto.
Lighting. Villiers flywheel magneto. Headlamp 6 volt, 12/12 watt. 6 volt 3 watt parking light. 6 volt 3 watt tail lamp.
Petrol Capacity. 1½ gallons.
Oil Capacity.
Tyres. Dunlop. 2.50" x 19", front and rear.
Brakes. 4" internal expanding, front and rear.
Frame and Suspension. Centre coil spring type girder forks. Rigid frame.
Saddle. Special soft top saddle. Height from ground. 38".
Wheelbase. 48". Ground clearance. 4½".
Overall Length. 74". Width over bars. 26".
Weight (dry). 120 lbs.
Finish. Tank—maroon with gold lines: Frame stove enamelled black. Bright parts chromium plated.
Equipment. Rear stand, pump, tools, horn, number plates.
Maximum Speed. 35-40 m.p.h.
Petrol consumption (at 30 m.p.h.) 120 m.p.g.

Sunbeam

**SUNBEAM CYCLES LTD.
BIRMINGHAM, 11**

U.S.A. East Coast Distributors:
RICH CHILD CYCLE CO., INC.
639 Passaic Ave., Nutley, N.J.

U.S.A. West Coast Distributors:
HAP ALZINA
3074 Broadway, Oakland, Calif.

Before the last war, the familiar black and gold colours of the Sunbeam were considered as a hall mark of quality—not to say aristocracy in the motor cycle world. The machine's reputation had been built up over a number of years by their outstanding performances in racing and trials, their high efficiency engines, and the first class workmanship to be found in all their models, not least those designed for the everyday rider. Such famous motorcycles as the 600 c.c. o.h.v. Model 9, the 500 o.h.v. Model 95, the 250 o.h.v. "little 95" and the Lion Model, were, like the Scott, held in reverence by a band of devotees who would not have dreamed of riding any other marque. The Marston Sunbeams had indeed an enviable reputation, and details of their design, such as the long stroke engine and the fitting of hairpin valve springs, distinguished them from their competitors.

There are probably those who look back with a certain nostalgia on the Sunbeams of the past, and regret the disappearance of the famous black and gold, for the change in Sunbeam design has been a radical one since the war. It is sufficient to say however, that the present Sunbeam is a motor cyclists dream, and does not stand in any danger whatsoever of diminishing the reputation of its predecessors.

The new Sunbeam, a 487 c.c. o.h.c. shaft-driven, in-line vertical twin was introduced in 1946, and, with certain modifications, remains substantially the same. In 1948 it was joined by another stable companion, the Model S8, a faster and lighter machine based on the design of the S7. Both models have a luxurious but practical specification and are notable for their exceptionally clean and handsome appearance.

The power unit is a unit construction vertical twin of 70 mm. bore x 63.5 mm. stroke. The crankcase and cylinders are in a one piece aluminium alloy casting and austenitic cylinder liners are fitted. The one piece cylinder head is also of aluminium alloy. The overhead camshaft is driven by a chain with an automatic tensioner. Since its introduction in 1946 the design of rockers and camshafts has been slightly modified. The cam and rocker gear is totally enclosed and adequately lubricated, and the light alloy connecting rods have indium flashed lead-bronze big end bearings. The power unit is fully floating, and mounted on rubber with high frequency vibration damper. The sump is generously finned, a feature which adds to the efficient and workmanlike appearance of the engine, and a streamlined air cleaner is fitted to the Amal carburettor. It incorporates a shroud to prevent water reaching the filter elements.

The car type wet sump engine lubrication system is used, with a separate oil supply for the gearbox and rear drive. The direct drive is taken from the engine, through a single plate car type dry clutch to the four speed positive stop foot change gearbox. Shaft drive transmits the power from the gearbox layshaft to the rear wheel through one shock absorber and one needle bearing universal joint. Final drive from the shaft to the rear wheel is by totally enclosed worm gear. Suitable gearing for sidecar machines can be provided by a reduction in the worm drive ratio. Ignition is by Lucas coil, and the Lucas "pancake" dynamo, which is mounted in front of the crankcase, has been lengthened on the latest models to give increased output. Solo ratios are 14.5, 9.0, 6.5 and 5.3 to 1.

The tubular duplex cradle frame has Telescopic front forks with automatic hydraulic damping, and both models have totally enclosed plunger springs at the rear, which are lubricated by grease gun. Integral sidecar lugs are fitted at the front and rear of the frame, for left hand or right hand sidecar attachment. The wheels on both models are instantly detachable, and on Model S7, both detachable and interchangeable. The rubber mounted petrol tank has a capacity of 3 gallons, with half a gallon reserve. The domed and valanced mudguards are hinged at the rear.

The specification includes an easy action central stand, a folding prop stand, an 8" headlamp with integral speedometer, ignition and oil warning lights, and coil ignition with automatic advance. The coil, cut-out, switch, ammeter and spare bulb holder are housed in a box on the offside of the machine, and adequately protected from the weather. The battery, mounted on rubber buffers is in a box on the nearside. The twist grip throttle, front brake and horn button are fitted on the right handlebar; the clutch and dip switch on the left bar. Both handlebars, footrests and saddle are adjustable to suit the rider.

Compression ratio is 6.5 to 1 or 6.8 to 1 as opposed to 7.2 to 1 on export models.

Model S8, which was introduced early in 1948, differs from S7 in detail. Smaller section tyres are fitted on Model S8. As against a 4.50" x 16" Dunlop ribbed front and 4.75" x 16" rear studded tyre on the S7, the S8 has a 3.25" x 19" studded front and a 4.00" x 18" studded rear. This modification in tyre sizes has resulted in a redesigned exhaust system to allow extra ground clearance for cornering. Silencers are of the cast aluminium baffle type, those on the larger (S7) machine being of the absorption type, chromium plated. Brakes are 8" diameter front and rear on S7 models, and 7" front and 8" rear on the S8. A redesigned fork has been fitted on this machine to suit the narrower section tyre, and the mudguards are of narrower, valanced type, the rear mudguard hinging for easy wheel removal. A normal type saddle is supplied in place of the large adjustable sprung-cradle mounted seat on the S7. The S8 saddle has three point attachment. Finish on the S7 is mistgreen, with black frame and chromium plated exhaust system, whilst the S8 is in black lustre with chromium plated exhaust system and bright parts. Weights are:— S7 435 lbs., S8 400 lb.

Both models attracted well merited attention and admiration at the 1949 Motor Cycle Show.

SUNBEAM 487 c.c. o.h.c. Models S7 and S8.

SPECIFICATION

Engine. Make Sunbeam.
    Bore and Stroke. 70 mm. x 63.5 mm. 487 c.c.
    Compression Ratio. 6.5 to 1 or 6.8 to 1.
        Export 7.2 to 1.
    B.H.P. S7 25 at 5,800 r.p.m. S8 26, at 5,800 r.p.m.
    Twin cylinder, air cooled, vertical twin, overhead camshaft drive by chain.
    Crankcase and cylinders in one piece aluminium alloy casting.
    Sparking plugs 14 mm. Champion NA 8.
Lubrication. Wet sump.
Carburettor. Amal 276DO/3A.
Gear Box. 4 speed, positive stop foot change.
    Ratios. Solo 14.5, 9.0, 6.5, and 5.3 to 1.
        Sidecar 16.6, 10.3, 7.4, and 6.13 to 1.
Clutch. Single plate, car type dry clutch.
Transmission. Shaft drive to worm and worm wheel.
Ignition. Lucas coil.
Lighting. Lucas 6 volt. 60 watt. dynamo. 8" headlamp.
Petrol Capacity. 3¼ gallons.

Oil Capacity. ½ gallon.
Tyres. S7 Dunlop 4.50" x 16", ribbed-front. 4.75" x 16" rear.
    S8 Dunlop 3.25" x 19", studded front. 4.00" x 18" rear.
Brakes. S7 8" internal expanding, front and rear. S8 7" front, 8" rear.
Frame and Suspension. Tubular duplex cradle frame. Telescopic front forks with automatic hydraulic damping. Rear suspension by enclosed plunger springs.
Saddle. Adjustable on S7.   **Height from ground.** S7 30½". S8 30".
Wheelbase. S7 56". S8 57".   **Ground Clearance.** S7 4½". S8 5¼".
Overall Length. 86".   **Width over bars.** 27¼".
Weight (dry). S7 435 lb. S8 400 lb.
Finish. S7 Mistgreen with black frame. Bright parts chromium plated.
    S8 Black lustre. Bright parts chromium plated.
Equipment. Electric horn, tool kit, tyre pump, licence holder, prop stand, speedometer.
Extra or optional equipment. Saddle type pillion seat. Pillion footrests.
Maximum Speed. S7 75—80 m.p.h. S8 80—85 m.p.h.
Petrol Consumption (at 30 m.p.h.) 70—75 m.p.g.
Braking (from 30 m.p.h. to rest). 30 ft.

Swallow

**THE SWALLOW COACHBUILDING CO. (1935) LTD.
THE AIRPORT · WALSALL, STAFFS.**

The Swallow "Gadabout" is an extremely practical motor scooter of exceptionally interesting design. This machine has become increasingly popular lately, and this is not surprising, since this little machine offers reasonably rapid transport (the cruising speed is 30 m.p.h.) with great comfort and a marked degree of cleanliness at a petrol consumption of approximately 95 miles per gallon.

Although economical in performance, the machine is very well equipped and a great deal of thought has obviously gone into the design. Further detail refinements have been added for the present year.

The scooter type chassis consists of one single unit, of welded tubular construction, to which is attached the steering head carrying the one inch diameter tubular handlebars. The front wheel is mounted on forks which incorporate a torsion bar, and the suspension is by means of rubber bushes in torsion, the rubber bushes being loaded when the front wheel receives an impact. This tubular front fork is resilient, giving a soft and easy movement. The small diameter pressed steel wheels carry 4.00 x 8 tyres, are of disc pattern, and have detachable rim flanges to facilitate tyre removal. Attached to the upswept front end of the chassis is a metal shield, which gives weather protection to the rider, and (a most thoughtful provision, this) has a parcel net attached to its inner side. Immediately behind this shield, on the platform, is located the battery, with two foot controls, the rear brake and the gear change, placed on either side. The sheet steel bodywork is reinforced for rigidity, and the rear portion of the body fairing, which incidentally, is very attractively styled, hinges forward to give access to the rear wheel, above which is mounted the 2½ gallon petrol tank. The power unit is located just in front of the rear wheel, and is housed inside another metal fairing, which is quickly detachable, and gives easy access to the engine. A filler cap on the petrol tank provides a useful oil measure.

The engine is the Villiers Mark 10D of 122 c.c., with a single exhaust and two transfer ports, an aluminium detachable cylinder head, and an aluminium flat top piston, with two compression rings. As the engine is enclosed, cooling is provided by a two-bladed fan, driven from the flywheel at 1½ times engine speed. The latest "Mark II" model is equipped with a 3 speed gear box, incorporating a foot change, but a hand gear change can be fitted for those who prefer it. The drive from the engine to the two plate, cork insert type clutch, which has a finger control adjustment, is by roller chain running in oil. The kick starter folds back when not in use. Bowden cable operated brakes are provided, a hand lever controlling the front brake, and a foot pedal the rear. The throttle is controlled by a twist grip, and a hand control clutch lever is fitted to the handlebar.

One of the most interesting features of the design is that the exhaust gases from the power unit pass into the rear portion of the main chassis tubes of the machine, which act as silencers. A Villiers flywheel magneto provides the ignition, and, through a rectifier, supplies a 6 volt battery, which runs a 5½" diameter headlamp, which is equipped with an ammeter and a dipper switch. Illumination is also provided for the speedometer, which is driven by the front wheel. A hinged rear stand is provided.

The Mark II Swallow is also available with an attractive box commercial sidecar, with a capacity of 11 cubic feet and a maximum payload of 2 cwt. This box carrier can be fitted either right or left, and when fitted to the right, a hand starter is provided. Suitable gear ratios are supplied for sidecar use, and the outfit has a maximum speed of 32 m.p.h., with a fuel consumption of 75 m.p.g. It should prove a very attractive proposition for the small tradesman.

The machines are pleasingly finished in Black, Cream, Blue or Amaranth red. Equipped as they are, with modern and practical features, they fully justify the manufacturers motto—"Ahead of time."

SPECIFICATION.
SWALLOW "GADABOUT" MARK II.

Engine. Make. Villiers Mark 10D.
Bore and Stroke. 50 mm. x 62 mm. (1.968" x 2.440") 122 c.c.
Compression Ratio. 8 to 1.
Single cylinder, two stroke, fan cooled, single port, aluminium detachable cylinder head, aluminium flat top piston.
Three ball races to crankshaft, two roller races to crankpin.
Sparking plug. 14 mm.
Lubrication. Petroil system.
Carburettor. Villiers.
Gearbox. 3 speed unit construction. Positive stop foot change mechanism.
Folding kickstarter.
Ratios. 14.7, 7.7, 4.53 to 1. (Solo).
19.63, 10.27, 6.04 to 1. (Sidecar).
Clutch. 2 plate cork insert type, finger adjustment.
Transmission. Primary. Chain ½" x .205".
Secondary. Chain ½" x ⅜".
Ignition. Villiers Flywheel Magneto.
Lighting. Villiers Flywheel magneto with rectifier. 6 volt battery. 5½" headlamp with dipper switch. Rearlamp.
Petroil Capacity. 2½ gallons.
Oil Capacity. Petroil system.
Tyres. Dunlop. 4.00" x 8", front and rear. Pressed steel disc wheels.
Brakes. Internal expanding. 5" front and rear.
Frame and Suspension. Single unit, tubular welded one piece rigid frame.
Torsion bar forks, with rubber bushes in tension.
Saddle. Squab type. Height from ground. 27½".
Wheelbase. 50". Ground clearance. 4".
Width over bars. 2' 0". Overall length. 6' 0".
Weight (dry). Mark II. 199 lb. Commercial model 300 lb.
Finish. Finished in black, cream, blue or amaranth red. Bright parts chromium plated.
Equipment. Illuminated speedometer. Electric horn. Dipper switch.
Rear hinged stand. Lifting handle. Tail lamp.
Optional equipment. Hand gear change.

The Swallow Gadabout Mark II.

STOP PRESS Mark II Commercial now fitted with 197 c.c. engine.

Tandon

TANDON MOTORS LTD.
29 LUDGATE HILL · LONDON, E.C.4

Amongst the lightweights exhibited at the Motor Cycle Show last year were two which attracted a very considerable amount of attention on account of their originality of design and interesting features. The Tandon concern is certainly enterprising, and the two machines shown were up to the minute in every way.

Both the Tandon lightweights are powered by Villiers engines, the De Luxe with model 10D, and the Milemaster with the earlier 9D hand-change unit.

The newest machine—the Tandon "De Luxe" is exceptionally well equipped. The specification includes the Villiers 3 speed foot change gearbox, with final drive ratios of 20.08, 10.57 and 7.55 to 1. This machine is fitted with Tandon telescopic forks. These forks are spring loaded for main and rebound springing, giving added comfort to the rider. A simple, but ingenious system of rear suspension is fitted to this model. The pivoting chainstays at the rear of the machine are linked by a bell crank and rod to a rubber buffer type cylinder unit, 4" long, which lies horizontally below the Villiers engine-gear unit. The rubber is compressed as the rear wheel moves upwards and 2" of wheel movement is allowed for. The frame itself is of the duplex type, formed from chrome molybdenum steel. Solid steel stays are fitted to give extra strength to the front and rear mudguards, and a centre stand, with patent spring, allows either wheel to be lifted from the ground with ease.

A sensible provision on this machine is the compartment in the petrol tank designed for the storage of the tool kit. The compartment, which is readily accessible, is covered over by a chrome plated petrol tank plate. Lighting, too, has received a great deal of careful thought.

On the "De Luxe" model, lighting is rectified through a Westinghouse rectifier. A Lucas 7" headlamp, incorporating switch and ammeter is fitted, whilst the horn is operated by a special 6 amp accumulator. The wiring is connected to a junction box which has been neatly mounted in the petrol tank recess at the rear of the tank. The battery is mounted below the saddle.

Tyres on this model are Dunlop 3.00" x 19", ribbed, front and Universal rear. A wide choice of finishes is available in various colours of Polychromatic stove enamel or black. Chromium plating is standard for the handle bars, tank top, exhaust pipe and silencer, and the wheel rims are also chromium plated, the centres being enamelled and lined to match. All machines are bonderized for protection against rust and all nuts and bolts are heavily cadmium plated for the same purpose. A Smith's speedometer is supplied.

Very similar in general design, the Tandon "Milemaster" has the Villiers 122 c.c. engine, and the Tandon Telescopic forks. Rear wheel springing is not provided on this model however, and the 3 speed gearbox is hand controlled. A straight tube, full duplex, cradle frame is employed, which is assembled to Elektron castings and frame clip lugs in a special assembly jig and the castings are through bolted and pinned. The steering head lug spindle is constructed from 40 ton tensile steel and is of very robust design. The steering head ball races are fully adjustable. In designing this machine, special attention has been given to weight and light alloys have been used wherever possible, resulting in an all up weight of 154 lbs. Elektron alloy is used for the steering head lugs, frame clip lugs, handle bar clip lugs and the brake pedal.

Direct lighting on this model is by Villiers flywheel magneto. The Milemaster incorporates the Tandon petrol tank tool compartment. Brakes are 4" diameter, front and rear, and tyres are Dunlop 2.75" x 19", front and rear. The machine can be supplied in a number of polychromatic finishes, or in black, and equipment includes Smith's speedometer.

Tandon 122 c.c. 'Milemaster'

SPECIFICATION.
TANDON 122 c.c. "Mile Master."

Engine. Make Villiers Model 9D.
 Bore and Stroke. 50 mm. x 62 mm. 122 c.c.
 Compression Ratio. 8.0 to 1.
 Single cylinder, two stroke air cooled. Flat topped deflectorless piston.
 Detachable alloy cylinder head.
 Sparking plugs. 14 mm.
Lubrication. Petroil.
Carburettor. Villiers.
Gearbox. Villiers 3 speed. Hand change.
 Ratios. 20.08, 10.57 and 7.55 to 1.
Clutch. 2 plate, cork insert type, running in oil.
Transmission. Primary. Chain ¼" x .205".
 Secondary. Chain ¼" x .205".
Ignition. Villiers flywheel magneto.
Lighting. Villiers flywheel magneto.
Petrol Capacity. Petroil, 2 gallons.
Tyres. Dunlop, 2.75" x 19", front and rear.
Brakes. 4" internal expanding, front and rear.
Frame and Suspension. Rigid duplex cradle frame. Tandon telescopic forks.
Saddle. Terry. **Height from ground.** 25¼".
Wheelbase. 48". **Ground clearance.** 4½".
Overall Length. 6' 4". **Width over bars.** 26".
Weight (dry). 154 lbs.
Finish. Polychromatic enamels or black. Bright parts chromium plated.
Equipment. Smith's Speedometer.
Maximum Speed. 1st 19 m.p.h. 2nd 31 m.p.h. 3rd. 45 m.p.h.
Speed at end of quarter mile from rest. 43 m.p.h.
Petrol Consumption (at 30 m.p.h.) 112 m.p.g.
Braking (from 30 m.p.h. to rest). 33' 6".

Tandon 122 c.c. 'De Luxe'

SPECIFICATION.
TANDON 122 c.c. "De Luxe."

Engine. Make, Villiers Mark 10D.
Bore and Stroke 50 mm. x 62 mm. 122 c.c.
Compression Ratio. 8 to 1.
B.H.P. 4.8 at 4,400 r.p.m.
Single cylinder, two stroke air cooled, single port. Flat top, deflectorless piston. Detachable alloy cylinder head.
Sparking plugs. 14 mm.
Lubrication. Petroil.
Carburettor. Villiers.
Gearbox. Unit construction. Villiers 3 speed, foot change. Kickstarter
Ratios. 20.08, 10.57 and 7.55 to 1.
Clutch. 2 plate, cork insert type, running in oil.
Transmission. Primary. Chain ½" x .205".
Secondary. Chain ½" x .205".
Ignition. Villiers Flywheel Magneto.
Lighting. Lucas Battery-rectifier. 7" headlamp, type MU42. Electric horn.
Petrol Capacity. 2¼ gallons.
Tyres. Dunlop, 3.00" x 19" ribbed, front. 3.00" x 19", "Universal" rear.
Brakes. 4" internal expanding, front and 5" rear.
Frame and Suspension. Duplex frame with swinging arm rear springing. Tandon telescopic forks.
Saddle. Wrights.
Wheelbase. 50".
Overall Length. 6' 3".
Weight (dry). 160 lbs.
Height from ground. 27".
Ground clearance. 6¾".
Width over bars. 26".
Finish. Polychromatic stove enamel (various colours), or black Handlebars, tank top, exhaust pipes and silencer. Chromium plated. Wheel rims chromium plated.
Equipment. Smith's Speedometer.
Maximum Speed. 1st — 2nd 35 m.p.h. 3rd 48 m.p.h.
Speed at end of quarter mile from rest. 31.9 m.p.h.
Petrol Consumption (at 30 m.p.h.) 128 m.p.g.
Braking (from 30 m.p.h. to rest). 33 ft.

STOP PRESS
New model—Supaglid Supreme—with Villiers 197 c.c. engine, offered for 1951.

Triumph

TRIUMPH ENGINEERING CO. LTD.
MERIDEN WORKS · COVENTRY

U.S.A. Eastern Distributor:
THE TRIUMPH CORPORATION
Towson,
Baltimore 4, Maryland

U.S.A. Western Distributor:
JOHNSON MOTORS, INC.
267 W. Colorado Blvd.
Pasadena, California

The first Triumph motorcycle was built in 1903 but the company had been in existence many years before this, manufacturing high grade bicycles. 1885 was in fact the year in which this great organisation had its beginnings. In the early days of the century the motorcycle industry was not exactly flourishing, machines generally were unreliable and their riders were regarded as being slightly eccentric. It was however realised that the motor cycle could be a pleasant and reliable means of transport, and Triumph, with other manufacturers, was responsbile for building up the British motorcycle industry to the unassailable position which it holds today. It is interesting to recall that Triumph popularised the high tension magneto, an instrument which virtually ended the bugbear of unreliable ignition—one of the major troubles of early motorcycles.

Just as in recent times, Triumph have been in the forefront with high performance twin cylinder types, so before the first world war, the Triumph 3½ h.p. single cylinder machine set a high standard in its day, and the company's single cylinder machines have upheld this reputation until the arrival of the famous Triumph Speed Twin in 1937.

With the outbreak of war in 1914, Triumph set to work to provide the armed forces with motorcycles. The famous 3½ h.p. belt drive three speed Triumph became a familiar sight on battlefields everywhere. Over 30,000 machines were supplied to the Army alone and many thousands more to Allied Governments. Well known models of the "between wars" period made by Triumph included the 4 valve Ricardo which achieved many notable successes on road and track, the Model "P," a 500 c.c. side valve, at a price never approached previously, and the L.W. "Baby Two stroke" which had a fine reputation among utility riders.

The Triumph has always had a great sporting reputation and its high performance has gained it many laurels in the competition world. As long ago as 1908 the Senior T.T. in the Isle of Man was won on a Triumph, and in more recent times, 1946 and 1948, the Manx Grand Prix has seen a Triumph victory at record speeds. In the International Six Days Trial the Triumph team has completed both post war events without losing a single mark and is the only team, British or Foreign, to do this. Practically every other big trade supported trial has been won by Triumph at one time or another since the war.

In 1937 Triumph introduced a machine which was destined to cause a major design revolution in the motorcycle industry. This was the famous 500 c.c. Speed Twin. A vertical twin of advanced design, it had a formidable performance and rapidly achieved such popularity that since the war no single cylinder machines have been built by Triumph. This type of machine is now the accepted British 500 c.c. high performance sports model, practically every leading manufacturer having introduced a model on similar lines. A super sports version, the "Tiger 100" was added to the range in 1939 and this was followed in 1945 by a 350 c.c. vertical twin, the "3T de Luxe" which achieved considerable fame on account of its silence and sweet running. This smaller engine incidentally was based on a design developed during the war for the services and which had come through the strenuous official 10,000 mile test with flying colours.

In the recent war the Triumph works were once more turned over to the manufacture of machines for the services. Something over 40,000 machines was the total figure reached by the end of the war, and this would have been considerably higher had not the Coventry factory been completely destroyed by enemy bombing in 1941. Temporary premises were taken where at first spares for service machines and later on complete machines were turned out. In the meantime the site for a new factory had been selected and work begun on it. By early 1943 it was completed and in full production. This was the magnificent modern works which has been the Triumph home ever since. Situated outside the city, it is a light, airy and efficient factory, in very pleasant surroundings. From this factory in 1945 came the first announcement by a British manufacturer of his post war range, which in this case were not wartime designs in peacetime colours, but a complete range of modern high performance twin cylinder types beautifully made and finished.

The latest model to be added to this fine range of twins is the new 650 c.c. "Thunderbird." This was introduced in a sensational manner in 1949 when the first three machines off the assembly line were ridden to Montlhery track near Paris where each covered 500 miles at 92 m.p.h. with final flying laps in excess of 100 m.p.h. The machines were fully equipped for the road and immediately after the demonstration were ridden back to Coventry. This model was introduced to meet a demand from overseas for a machine with an even higher performance than the "Tiger 100" and one which could cruise indefinitely at the highest possible speeds. To prove this latter point was the object of the Montlhery demonstration.

The range now comprises six machines, the 3T de Luxe, (350 c.c.), the Speed Twin and Tiger 100 (both 500 c.c.), the Thunderbird (650 c.c.), a special trials machine, the Trophy (500 c.c.) and the road racing Grand Prix model (500 c.c.) All are fitted with the overhead valve vertical twin cylinder engines, four speed gearboxes, and the Triumph spring wheel rear suspension system is available on all models if required. Telescopic forks with hydraulic damping are used throughout and detail design and finish is to the extremely high standard always associated with this marque.

Some of the more outstanding individual features of this range are of interest. The Triumph Telescopic fork, which has 6" of hydraulically damped movement, sets a high standard of controllability and comfort. Long supple fork springs are enclosed inside the stanchions, which enables these vital components to be of maximum diameter and strength. No adjustments of any kind have to be made by the rider.

Fitted to all machines, except the Grand Prix, is a very neat and useful chromium plated tank-top fitting parcel grid, which is particularly valuable to the long distance solo rider. Triumphs have also developed a very attractive and streamlined instrument "nacelle." This is integral with the top of the forks and is therefore fully sprung, and the handlebars pass through it, thereby giving the whole assembly a neat and "finished" appearance. All instruments and switchgear are grouped where they can most easily be seen, and the nacelle incorporates the headlamp (with adjustable rim) speedometer, ammeter, lighting switch, cut-out button and horn. All instruments are rubber mounted and internally illuminated. This nacelle is fitted to all machines except the Trophy and Grand Prix Models.

Triumph "Thunderbird" 650 c.c. o.h.v. Vertical Twin

Triumph "Trophy" 498 c.c. o.h.v. Vertical Twin

Another interesting feature is the Triumph design patented Vokes air cleaner. The efficient oil-wetted muslin filament is readily detachable for cleaning and the filter fits snugly between the oil tank and the battery. A spring loaded Triumph prop stand is also available as an extra on all models.

Finally there is the well known Triumph patent spring hub. This is available as an extra on all models except the Grand Prix, on which it is a standard fitment. The massive aluminium alloy hub shell totally encloses all moving parts and has a powerful eight inch brake attached. It is mounted in the frame exactly like a normal wheel. In operation the spindle remains stationary, bolted into the frame as usual, while the wheel and hub move on a curved path taken from the centre of the gearbox sprocket. The chain tension remains constant, and movement is controlled by springs, two below the spindle and two above.

Turning now to the machines themselves, the smallest in the range, the 3T de Luxe has a vertical twin cylinder engine with a bore of 55 mm. and a stroke of 73.4 mm. (349 c.c.) developing a b.h.p. of 19 at 6,500 r.p.m. The compression ratio is 6.3 to 1. The overhead valve engine has a rocker box integral with the cylinder head. Plain big ends are fitted and the crankshaft has a central flywheel. Lubrication is on the dry sump system, with positive feed to big-ends and valve gear. An auto-advance magneto and separate dynamo are provided. A Triumph 4 speed gearbox, with positive stop foot change is fitted, the primary chain runs in a polished aluminium oil-bath case and the rear chain is positively lubricated and protected on both runs. Triumph Telescopic front forks and the Triumph nacelle are fitted. Wide "D" section mudguards are supplied, the rear portion being readily detachable. Equipment includes Dunlop 3.25" x 19" tyres, Triumph air cleaner and parcel grid, Lucas 6 volt., 60 watt dynamo and Smith's 85 m.p.h. chronometric speedometer. The machine is finished in black enamel.

The 500 c.c. o.h.v. "Speed Twin" and 500 c.c. o.h.v. "Tiger 100" are similar in general specification. Both have vertical twin cylinder engines with two gear driven camshafts. The bore of 63 mm. and stroke of 80 mm. give a cubic capacity of 498 c.c. The overhead valves are totally enclosed and positively lubricated, the high tensile aluminium alloy crankcase is exceptionally rigid, and "H" section connecting rods in RR. 56 hiduminium alloy with patented plain big ends are fitted. The crankshaft is mounted on massive ball and roller bearings with a central flywheel. Lubrication is on the dry sump system, plunger type pumps giving a positive feed to big ends and valve gear. A pressure indicator is provided on the timing cover. The auto advance magneto and separate dynamo are gear driven. The Amal carburettor is controlled by a Triumph quick action twist grip.

The primary chain runs in a polished aluminium oil bath case and the Triumph 4 speed positive stop foot change gearboxes have hardened nickel and nickel chrome steel shafts and gears and integral speedometer drive. A large diameter multiplate clutch is fitted.

The frame is of the brazed full cradle type with large diameter tapered front down tube and incorporates sidecar lugs on either side. Triumph Telescopic forks and the Triumph nacelle are fitted to both machines. 7" internal expanding brakes are fitted front and rear, and the front brake anchor plate is polished. Brakes have finger adjustment back and front. The 4 gallon tank has a quick opening filler cap, a two way tap with reserve and incorporates the Triumph parcel grid. Oil tanks have accessible filters, a drain plug and separate vent and a screw down leak proof filler cap. Equipment includes Dunlop 3.25" x 19" front and 3.50" x 19" rear tyres, Lucas 6 volt. 60 watt dynamo, rubber knee grips. Smith's 120 m.p.h. chronometric speedometer, with

**Triumph
"Tiger 100"
500 c.c. o.h.v.
Vertical Twin**

**Triumph
"3T. De Luxe"
349 c.c. o.h.v.
Vertical Twin**

r.p.m. scale and internal illumination, electric horn, Vokes air cleaner and completely detachable rear mudguards. Spring hubs can be fitted to both machines, and the Speed Twin is finished in amaranth red, the Tiger 100 in silver sheen.

Compression ratio is 7 : 1 for the Speed Twin and 7.8 1 for the Tiger 100, the Speed Twin developing 27 b.h.p. at 6,300 r.p.m. whilst the Tiger 100 develops 30 b.h.p. at 6,500 r.p.m. Tiger 100 engines differ in detail from the Speed Twin, having cylinder heads, ports and all moving parts highly polished, special high compression pistons of silicon low expansion alloy and highly polished rocker boxes and push rod tubes. Both engines employ Duplex aero valve springs.

Reference has already been made to the new Triumph "Thunderbird," a machine which has undoubtedly made its mark and gained the admiration of motor cyclists everywhere. Of similar design to the Speed Twin and Tiger 100 models, the engine capacity has been increased to 649 c.c. (Bore 71 mm., Stroke 82 mm.) The standard compression ratio is 7 : 1 and at 6,300 r.p.m. a maximum b.h.p. of 34 is developed. Certain modifications have been made to this new machine and the connecting rods have been strengthened and are of a similar type to that used in the Grand Prix racing machine. The engine has also been more generously finned and an external drain pipe is provided from the rocker gear. Gear ratios have been modified to suit the more powerful engine, and the clutch carries a fifth plate to take the extra load. A stronger redesigned gearbox designed for this model is standard throughout the Triumph range. The Thunderbird is finished in a most attractive shade styled "Thunder Blue" and this distinctive machine will be easily recognised. It includes the usual features of instrument nacelle, Telescopic forks, parcel grid, air cleaner and the chromium Triumph motif. Lucas 6 volt. 60 watt lighting is standard and a Smith's 120 m.p.h. speedometer is fitted.

For the trials rider, Triumph have produced the 498 c.c. "Trophy" model, which scored such a success in the International Six Days Trial, P. H. Alves, S. B. Manns and A. F. Gaymer completing the course without loss of marks and gaining the Manufacturers Team Award. Based on the familiar Triumph twin engine, the machine has certain modifications for trials work. The vertical twin engine, with gear driven double high camshafts, has a bi-metal cylinder and head with cast-in liners and valve inserts. The usual features of duralumin pushrods and high tensile aluminium alloy crankcase and hiduminium alloy connecting rods are repeated. A manually operated B.T.H. waterproof magneto is fitted. The primary chain is in a polished light-alloy oil bath case and a four speed positive stop foot change wide ratio gearbox with folding kickstarter is fitted. Ratios are 15.25, 11.58, 7.46, and 5.25 to 1. The narrow 2½ gallon capacity petrol tank has a quick release filler, twin racing type taps and a parcel grid. A special competition frame, light in weight and with 6½" ground clearance gives light and accurate steering at all speeds and over rough going and has a 70 degree steering lock. Telescopic forks are fitted. Fully adjustable competition pattern handlebars, light alloy mudguards with tubular stays, a saddle adjustable at front and rear and a two-in-one exhaust pipe with a tubular silencer are other features of the machine. Dunlop 3.00" x 20" front and 4.00" x 19" rear tyres are standard and a quick release plug is supplied for easy removal of the headlamp. Finish is chromium plate and silver sheen and the weight (less lighting set) is 295 lbs.

Finally there is the "Grand Prix" racing machine which is designed to enable non-professional riders to compete on level terms in all types of long and short circuit road racing. The machine embodies many interesting technical developments but is essentially simple and straightforward in design and responds readily to familiar tuning methods. Each machine is carefully and individually assembled and each engine is brake tested and has a specified power output.

The o.h.v. all alloy vertical twin cylinder engine has two gear driven racing lift curve camshafts, and a bi-metal cylinder and head with cast-in liners and valve inserts. Cylinder head, ports and all moving parts are mirror polished and high duty alloy pistons can be supplied for Pool petrol, Petrol-Benzol or Alcohol fuels. Special forged connecting rods in R.R. 56 hiduminium alloy with plain bearing big ends and a forged extra stiff built up crankshaft in case hardened nickel chrome steel mounted on heavy duty roller bearings, with a central flywheel and dry sump lubrication with large capacity plunger type pumps with positive feeds to big ends and valve gear are other salient features of the specification. The carburettors are twin Amals with flexible feed pipes and remote float chamber. A B.T.H. T.T. type gear driven magneto with handlebar control is fitted and the exhaust pipes are fitted with megaphones. The Triumph 4 speed gearbox has special nickel chrome shafts and gears dogged for easy gear changing, in conjunction with a lightweight multiplate clutch with Ferodo inserts. The frame is made from high quality alloy steel tubes, and Triumph Telescopic forks and spring hub are fitted. The racing type brakes are 8" diameter.

The 4½ gallon petrol tank and one gallon oil tank have quick action caps and a Vokes full flow type oil filter is fitted in the scavenge oil line. Racing pattern alloy steel handlebars, light alloy narrow section mudguards and Dunlop light alloy racing type rims and tyres, a Smith's 80 x 100 revolution counter, Terry saddle and sponge rubber mudguard pad are fitted to this model. The timing cover, rocker boxes and gearbox end cover are all highly polished. Machines are finished in silver sheen, lined in blue.

All machines are delivered ready for immediate racing, and this model has already scored a considerable number of successes. One of these machines on a dry tarmac road and running on Pool petrol has attained speeds in excess of 120 m.p.h. (7,100 r.p.m.)

TRIUMPH 649 c.c. "Thunderbird." Model 6T.

SPECIFICATION

Engine. Make Triumph.
Bore and Stroke. 71 mm. x 82 mm. 649 c.c.
Compression Ratio. 7 to 1.
B.H.P. 34 at 6,500 r.p.m.
Vertical twin cylinder air cooled o.h.v., with two gear driven camshafts. RR. 56 alloy connecting rods. Central flywheel. High tensile aluminium crankcase.
Sparking plugs 14 mm.
Lubrication. Dry sump, with plunger pumps.
Carburettor. Amal. Type 6, with air cleaner.
Gear Box. Triumph 4 speed, positive stop foot change.
Ratios. 11.2, 7.75, 5.45, and 4.57 to 1.
12.8, 8.85, 6.24 and 5.24 to 1. (Sidecar).
Clutch. 5 plate.
Transmission. Primary. Chain ½" x .305".
Secondary. Chain ⅝" x ⅜".
Ignition. Lucas or B.T.H. magneto.
Lighting. Lucas gear driven dynamo, 6 volt. 60 watt. Electric horn.
Petrol Capacity. 4 gallons.
Oil Capacity. 6 pints.
Tyres. 3.25" x 19", ribbed (front). 3.50" x 19", Studded, (rear), Dunlop.
Brakes. 7" internal expanding, front and rear.
Frame and Suspension. Cradle type frame, incorporating sidecar lugs. Triumph Telescopic forks. Rear springing optional extra.
Saddle. Adjustable De Luxe saddle. **Height from ground.** 29½".
Wheelbase. 55". **Ground Clearance.** 6".
Overall Length. 84". **Width over bars.** 28½".
Weight (dry). 370 lb.
Finish. Frame, forks, tank, wings, etc., in "Thunder" blue. Chromium motif on tank. Wheels chromium plated with blue centres. Bright parts chromium plated.
Equipment. Electric horn, Kneegrips. Parcel carrier. Smith's 120 m.p.h. chronometric speedometer internally illuminated with r.p.m. scale. Tools and pump.
Extra or optional equipment. Prop stand. Triumph spring rear wheel. Twin-seat.

TRIUMPH 498 c.c. "Speed Twin." Model 5T.

SPECIFICATION

Engine. Make Triumph.
Bore and Stroke. 63 mm. x 80 mm. 498 c.c.
Compression Ratio. 7 to 1.
B.H.P. 27 at 6,300 r.p.m.
Vertical twin cylinder, air cooled, two gear driven camshafts, overhead valves. R.R. 56 alloy connecting rods, crankshaft mounted on ball and roller bearings with central flywheel.
Sparking plugs 14 mm.
Lubrication. Full dry sump, with plunger type pumps.
Carburettor. Amal type 6. Main jet 140 with air cleaner.
Gear Box. Triumph 4 speed, positive stop foot change.
Ratios. 12.2, 8.45, 5.95 and 5.0 to 1. (Solo).
14.13, 9.8, 6.90 and 5.8 to 1. (Sidecar).
Clutch. Large diameter multiplate clutch.
Transmission. Primary. Chain ½" x .305".
Secondary. Chain ⅝" x ⅜".
Ignition. B.T.H. or Lucas magneto. Gear driven.
Lighting. Lucas 6 volt. 60 watt dynamo.
Petrol Capacity. 4 gallons. Two way tap reserve.
Oil Capacity. ¾ gallon.
Tyres. Dunlop 3.25" x 19" (front). 3.50" x 19" (rear).
Brakes. Internal expanding, 7" front and rear.
Frame and Suspension. Full cradle type frame, incorporating sidecar lugs. Triumph Telescopic forks with 6" movement. Rear springing optional extra.
Saddle. Adjustable, De Luxe. **Height from ground.** 29½".
Wheelbase. 55". **Ground Clearance.** 6".
Overall Length. 84". **Width over bars.** 28½".
Weight (dry). 365 lb.
Finish. Frame and forks in dark red lacquer. Chromium motif on petrol tank. Chromium plated wheels, with red hubs and rim centres (lined gold). Bolts and nuts cadmium plated. Bright parts chromium plated.
Equipment. Kneegrips. Smith's 120 m.p.h. chronometric speedometer with r.p.m. scale and internal illumination. Electric horn.
Extra or optional equipment. Triumph Spring Rear Wheel. Prop stand. Twin-seat.

TRIUMPH 498 c.c. o.h.v. "Tiger 100." (T100).

SPECIFICATION

Engine. Make Triumph.
Bore and Stroke. 63 mm. x 80 mm. 498 c.c.
Compression Ratio. 7.8 to 1
B.H.P. 30 at 6,500 r.p.m.
Vertical twin cylinder air cooled o.h.v. with two gear driven camshafts. Cylinder heads, ports and all moving parts highly polished. Special high compression pistons of silicon low expansion alloy. RR. 56 alloy connecting rods.
Sparking plugs 14 mm.
Lubrication. Full dry sump, with plunger type pumps.
Carburettor. Amal type 6 with air-cleaner.
Gear Box. Triumph 4 speed, positive stop foot change gearbox.
Ratios. 12.2, 8.45, 5.95, and 5.0 to 1. (Solo.)
14.13, 9.8, 6.90 and 5.8 to 1. (Sidecar).
Clutch. Large diameter, multiplate clutch.
Transmission. Primary. Chain ½" x .305".
Secondary. Chain ⅝" x ⅜".
Ignition. B.T.H. or Lucas magneto.
Lighting. Lucas 6 volt, 60 watt dynamo. Large diameter headlamp.
Petrol Capacity. 4 gallons. Twin two way taps. Reserve.
Oil Capacity. ¾ gallon.
Tyres. Dunlop 3.25" x 19", front. 3.50" x 19", rear.
Brakes. 7" internal expanding, front and rear.
Frame and Suspension. Full cradle type frame, incorporating sidecar lugs. Triumph Telescopic forks with 6" movement. Rear springing optional, extra.
Saddle. Adjustable, De Luxe. **Height from ground.** 29½".
Wheelbase. 55". **Ground Clearance.** 6".
Overall Length. 84". **Width over bars.** 28½".
Weight (dry). 365 lb.
Finish. Petrol tank in silver sheen, with chromium motif. Mudguards in silver sheen, with black centre strip. Wheel rims chromium plated with rim centres in silver sheen, lined blue.
Equipment. Smith's 120 m.p.h. Chronometric speedometer, with r.p.m. scale and internal illumination. Electric horn.
Extra or optional equipment. Triumph Spring rear wheel. Prop stand. Twin-seat.

TRIUMPH 498 c.c. o.h.v. "Trophy" Model. TR5.

SPECIFICATION

Engine. Make Triumph.
Bore and Stroke. 63 mm. x 80 mm. 498 c.c.
Compression Ratio. 6 to 1.
B.H.P. 25 at 6,000 r.p.m.
O.H.V. vertical twin, with gear driven double high camshafts. Bi-metal cylinder and head with cast-in liners and valve inserts. Totally enclosed and positively lubricated valve gear. Duralumin pushrods. High tensile aluminium alloy crankcase.
Sparking plugs 14 mm.
Lubrication. Dry sump with plunger pumps, positive feed to big ends and valve gear.
Carburettor. Amal type 6 with air cleaner.
Gear Box. Triumph 4 speed positive stop foot change. Wide ratio. Folding kickstarter.
Ratios. 15.25, 11.58, 7.46 and 5.25 to 1.
Clutch. Multiplate, Large diameter.
Transmission. Primary. Chain ½" x .305".
Secondary. Chain ⅝" x ⅜".
Ignition. B.T.H. or Lucas gear driven magneto. Manually operated.
Lighting. Lucas 6 volt dynamo lighting set with voltage control. Quick release plug for easy removal of headlamp.
Petrol Capacity. 2½ gallons.
Oil Capacity. ¾ gallon. Drain plug and separate vent.
Tyres. Dunlop 3.00" x 20" (front) 4.00" x 19" (rear).
Brakes. 7" internal expanding, front and rear.
Frame and Suspension. Full cradle type. Triumph Telescopic forks, hydraulically damped. Rear springing optional extra.
Saddle. Adjustable for height front and rear. **Height from ground.** 31".
Wheelbase. 53". **Ground Clearance.** 6½".
Overall Length. 80". **Width over bars.** 29".
Weight (dry) 295 lb. (without lighting set).
Finish. Petrol tank chromium plated with silver sheen panels lined in blue. Mudguards in silver sheen with black central strip. Wheel rims chromium plated with rim centres in silver sheen, lined blue.
Equipment. Smith's 120 m.p.h. chronometric speedometer. Lucas horn.
Extra or optional equipment. Triumph spring rear wheel.

TRIUMPH. Model 3T. 349 c.c. Twin.
SPECIFICATION

Engine. Make Triumph.
    Bore and Stroke. 55 mm. x 73.4 mm. 349 c.c.
    Compression Ratio. 6.3 to 1.
    B.H.P. 19.0 at 6,500 r.p.m.
    Vertical twin cylinder, o.h.v. rocker box integral with cylinder head, plain big ends.
    Sparking plugs 14 mm.
Lubrication. Full dry sump with positive feeds to big ends and valve gear.
Carburettor. Amal. Type 5 with air cleaner.
Gear Box. 4 speed, positive stop foot change.
    Ratios. 14.13, 9.8, 6.90 and 5.8 to 1.
Clutch. Multiplate.
Transmission. Primary. Chain $\frac{3}{8}$" x .305". Oil bath chain case.
    Secondary. Chain $\frac{5}{8}$" x $\frac{3}{8}$".
Ignition. Lucas or B.T.H. Magneto.
Lighting. Lucas Dynamo, 6 volt. 60 watt.
Petrol Capacity. 3$\frac{1}{4}$ gallons.
Oil Capacity. $\frac{3}{4}$ gallon.
Tyres. Dunlop, front, 3.25" x 19". (and rear).
Brakes. 7" front and rear.
Frame and Suspension. Full cradle type with large diameter front down tube. Rear springing optional extra. Triumph Telescopic forks.
Saddle. Adjustable De Luxe.   **Height from ground.** 28$\frac{1}{2}$".
Wheelbase. 53$\frac{1}{2}$".   **Ground Clearance.** 6".
Overall Length. 82$\frac{1}{2}$".   **Width over bars.** 28$\frac{1}{4}$".
Weight (dry). 325 lb.
Finish. Hard black enamel, with chromium tank motif. Black wheel centres, lined ivory. Chromium plated rims.
Equipment. Smith's 85 m.p.h. Chronometric speedometer. Tools. Electric horn.
Extra or optional equipment. Rear spring wheel, prop stand, pillion seat.

TRIUMPH 498 c.c. o.h.v. "Grand Prix" Model.
SPECIFICATION

Engine. Make Triumph.
    Bore and Stroke. 63 mm. x 80 mm. 498 c.c.
    Compression Ratio to suit various fuels as required.
    B.H.P. approx. 45.
    O.H.V. all alloy vertical air cooled twin cylinder, with two gear driven racing lift curve camshafts. Bi-metal cylinder and head with cast-in liners and valve inserts. Cylinder head ports and all moving parts mirror polished. High duty alloy pistons.
    Sparking plugs K.L.G. 689. Lodge R49. Champion LA15.
Lubrication. Dry sump with plunger pumps, positive feed to big ends and valve gear.
Carburettor. (Two) Amal type 6 (modified).
Gear Box. Triumph, 4 speed, positive stop, foot change. Nickel chrome shafts and gears.
    Ratios. 7.93, 6.58, 5.01 and 4.57 to 1. 24T (Std)
              8.26, 6.88, 5.24 and 4.78 to 1. 23T   Engine
              8.67, 7.20, 5.48 and 5.00 to 1. 22T   Sprocket
Clutch. Lightweight multiplate with Ferodo inserts.
Transmission. Primary. Chain $\frac{3}{8}$" x .305".
    Secondary. Chain $\frac{5}{8}$" x $\frac{3}{8}$".
Ignition. B.T.H. Magneto, T.T. type, gear driven, handlebar controlled.
Petrol Capacity. 4$\frac{1}{4}$ gallons. Quick action cap, separate vent.
Oil Capacity. 1 gallon, drain plug, separate vent and quick action cap. Vokes full flow type oil filter.
Tyres. Dunlop racing, 3.00" x 20", front, ribbed. 3.50" x 19", rear, studded.
Brakes. 8", internal expanding, front and rear.
Frame and Suspension. Cradle type frame. Triumph Telescopic forks and patent Triumph spring rear wheel.
Saddle. Terry.   **Height from ground.** 29$\frac{1}{4}$".
Wheelbase. 55".   **Ground Clearance.** 6".
Overall Length. 84".   **Width over bars.** 28".
Weight (dry). 314 lb.
Finish. Petrol tank in silver sheen, lined blue. Mudguards in silver sheen, with black centre strip. Highly polished timing cover, rocker boxes and gearbox end cover.
Equipment. Smith's 80 x 100 Revolution Counter, rubber mounted Terry saddle. Sponge rubber mudguard pad.

STOP PRESS

Grand Prix model discontinued. Racing conversion kit available (£35) enables Tiger 100 to be converted into a racing mount. Redesigned engine now gives 32 b.h.p.

Velocette

VELOCE LIMITED
HALL GREEN, BIRMINGHAM, 28

U.S.A. Distributor:
LOU BRANCH MOTORS
2019 W. Pico Blvd.
Los Angeles 6, Calif.

The Velocette company is a happy example of a family concern, which, founded over half a century ago, has consistently enhanced its reputation, until today it is in the first flight of the motor cycle industry.

The firm began by building ordinary cycles, and the Goodman brothers and sister, who are still the present directors, built their first power driven machine—a 499 c.c. side valve, in 1909. The same direction has inspired the development of the many well-known models of the years between the two wars. The fact that the company is still very much on its toes has been amply demonstrated since the last war by the introduction of the revolutionary and very successful Velocette Model L.E.—probably the most interesting all-British lightweight to be produced up to the present time.

The earliest models were marketed under the name of "Veloce," and were four stroke machines, and the title of "Velocette" was adopted on the introduction of the first two-stroke machine. The first T.T. entry was a 250 c.c. machine with an O.H. inlet valve. The marque first came into prominence, however, with the arrival of the two-stroke models, which showed their capabilities by winning the Team Prize in the 1920 Six Days Trial. Velocettes rapidly established a reputation with two-stroke enthusiasts, and production from 1920 to 1925 was concentrated on that very popular model, the G.T.P. utility.

In 1925 the first overhead camshaft machine appeared, and was the forerunner of a line of machines which were to establish Velocette as a name known in racing circles the world over. After a false start in the 1925 T.T., Alec Bennett won the 1926 event in flying style. This was indeed a milestone in the history of the company, orders for the production version of the famous machine flowed in, and output was stepped up to unprecedented levels within a matter of months. In 1928 Bennett again won the T.T. on an O.H.C. Velocette, to be followed by F. Hicks' victory in 1929. Although success in the T.T. eluded Velocettes for some years after this, the racing reputation of the breed was made. The inimitable Stanley Woods rode a great race to win the 1938 Junior T.T. and repeated his success in the 1939 race. 1947 saw Velocette once more out in front, with Bob Foster winning the Junior T.T. Freddie Frith scored victories in the same event in 1948 and 1949. It would be monotonous to repeat the number of successes scored by this machine in road racing events all over the world, since its introduction, and the space at our disposal precludes it. One of the more recent successes however was the Dutch T.T. in 1948 (Kenneth Bills, first and Freddie Frith, second).

Despite the magnificent record of this model, Velocettes have not been content to rest on the laurels which it has won for them. In fact their latest production, designed for "Everyman," instead of the racing man, has probably diverted a great deal of attention from the "K.T.T. 348 c.c. job." This is not surprising, for the 149 c.c. L.E. Velocette has probably caused more discussion, and achieved more publicity than any machine of its type since the last war. That the machine has been completely successful is proved by the increasing number of these models to be seen on the roads, and the praiseworthy reputation which it has already achieved.

The "L.E." represents the achievement of an ideal—a reliable economical, quiet, foolproof and weather-proof motorcycle for the million. But the manufacturers have avoided one trap, into which others who have had this idea in mind before have fallen. They have not built "down" to a price, but up to a carefully worked out specification. As lightweights go, the Velocette is not the cheapest—as value for money it is undoubtedly outstanding.

Some of the ideas which dictated this novel design, and their solution, will probably be of interest. As mentioned above, the model was designed for the everyday rider, and the aims were:

To produce a machine which would run for 20,000 miles without a major overhaul.

A maximum of around 50 m.p.h., with a cruising speed of 40 m.p.h.

Comfort—fully sprung, engine enclosed—for quietness and easiness of cleaning.

Instant starting (particularly important for women). Smooth and noiseless running, with sufficient power to climb almost any hill, and to carry a pillion passenger.

Fully accessible and easy to clean, and capable of running for long periods without decarbonising.

As may well be imagined, the answer to all these requirements was not easy to find, and the problem was solved only by a radical change in design.

First of all, to achieve the desired smoothness and silence, the two-stroke engine was discarded. A horizontally opposed twin was chosen for its absence of vibration —of side valve design for simplicity and reliability. This engine also has easy starting characteristics, and since the proposed design aimed at the elimination of chains, the mounting of such an engine across the frame makes it suitable for operation with shaft drive. To improve silencing, give a long life to the valves and increase the periods between decarbonising, water-cooling was adopted. A new 3 speed, easy change gearbox and shaft drive were then designed to work in conjunction with the new engine.

To aid easy starting, coil ignition is standard, and a simple hand starting lever is fitted. A further safeguard for the non-mechanical rider, is the provision of a permanent magnet in the ignition system, which supplies sufficient starting current, by-passing the battery, and provides a get-away should the battery be flat.

There remained two further problems, to design a carburettor which would allow the engine to tick-over happily at any speed, and not need constant "blipping" at traffic lights etc., and to further increase mechanical silence. Eventually a very small five-jet carburettor was evolved, which gave very satisfactory results, but this was found to be sensitive to dirt, so that a special filter was designed to fit it. The frame construction consists of a tubular cradle, holding the engine, and connected to the steering head and rear wheel, and, on top of this, to complete triangulation, fits the pressed steel body, covering petrol tank and rear wheel. It was found that this method of construction acted as a "sound box" and amplified the noise. To overcome this, the engine has been mounted on rubber to deaden the vibration. Finally, to cut down gear noise, all the gear wheels have been specially "shaved"—a process rarely found on motor-cycles and the cheaper cars.

Incidentally, Velocettes have always built their own engines and gearboxes, and to produce the L.E. models have one of the most modern assembly lines and array of machine tools in the business, and the experience gained during the war on aircraft work has given greater facilities for precision work to extremely fine limits than before. So successful has the " L.E." proved, that present production is devoted in very great part to it, the production of the other two models—the 349 c.c. M.A.C. o.h.v. and 348 K.T.T. o.h.c. being correspondingly reduced.

The design of the L.E. has many interesting features. The side valve twin engine has a bore of 44 mm. and a stroke of 49 mm. The two-throw crankshaft is carried on four main bearings, and the roller bearing big ends have single row races. The Y alloy die-cast pistons carry two compression rings and an oil control ring, gudgeon pins are fully floating and the connecting rods are of 85 ton tensile steel. The pistons are of the split-skirt type. The cast iron cylinder barrel is deeply spigotted into the crankcase, and the positioning of the valves allows both sets to be operated by one camshaft and also aids the water cooling by allowing of circulation around the valve seats. The cylinder head is of aluminium alloy. An extremely neat and compact B.T.H. generator, which incorporates the h.t. coil, contact breaker, distributor, cut-out and condenser is mounted in front of the flywheel. A "dry" type two plate clutch is fitted and the gearbox has six pinions—all ratios being indirect. The propeller shaft is fitted inside the swinging arm of the spring frame,—the neatest transmission fitted to any motor-cycle today, and thus drives the bevel gears at the rear wheel. The starting handle, on the offside of the machine, is also designed to raise the double propstands —one fitted at each side of the machine. Telescopic front forks are fitted, with one spring in each leg. Coil type swinging arm rear suspension is fitted, its action being specially designed to avoid distortion of the driving shaft. The rear suspension is adjustable to suit the load carried.

The wide front mudguards are stayless, easily cleaned, and surround the front forks. Very adequate legshields and comfortable footboards are fitted, and at the top of each leg shield is fitted a small instrument panel, one carrying the speedometer, the other the ignition, and lighting switches and the ignition warning lamp. Other points have evidently received careful attention. The battery, which is neatly mounted in the pressed steel frame, insulated from shock and shielded from the weather, is instantly accessible by tilting forward the saddle. The tool box is most sensibly mounted at the forward end of the tank, behind the handlebars, and is formed by a compartment of the tank itself. The handlebars are exceptionally clean, built in clutch and front brake levers being fitted. The footboards provide two levels, so that the position of the feet can be changed, and the provision of two built-on pannier bags at the rear of the machine is a most practical feature which will be much appreciated by shoppers.

The " L.E." really does provide car type comfort, with the ability to go anywhere, including 1 in 4 gradients, with a petrol consumption of from 100-120 m.p.g. and a top speed of 50 m.p.h.

The ever popular 349 c.c. o.h.v. Model M.A.C. is being produced alongside the L.E., and a very handsome and efficient looking machine it is. The single port push-rod engine has a bore of 68 mm. and a stroke of 96 mm. and a compression ratio of 6 to 1. The valve gear and valve stems are totally enclosed. Lubrication is by dry sump and gear pump and ignition by magneto. A Velocette 4 speed twin-top gearbox is fitted, with foot gear change and a folding kickstarter. A seven plate clutch is provided and the gear ratios are 14.1, 9.6, 7.3 and 5.5. to 1. The frame is rigid, and of conventional design, 7" brakes are fitted front and rear and the rear wheel is quickly detachable. A 6 volt dynamo supplies the 8¼" diameter headlamp, the electrical system including a dip-light, parking light, rear light and illuminated speedometer dial. A 2½ gallon petrol tank is supplied and 3.25" x 19" tyres, front and rear. The performance is attractive, with a top speed in the region of 70 m.p.h.

Finally there is the world famous 348 c.c. Velocette Model KTT., with the well known Velocette overhead camshaft engine. This is an out and out racing job, with a compression ratio of 10.94 to 1 for Petrol Benzol or 7.8 to 1 for Pool petrol. The latest model, styled the Mark VIII has Webb girder forks and Oleomatic rear springing, and has a true thoroughbred racing appearance enhanced by the huge 4 gallon petrol tank and the megaphone exhaust system. 7" internal brakes are fitted, front and rear, and tyres are 3.00" x 21" front and 3.25" x 19" rear. Ignition is by B.T.H. racing magneto, and the 4 speed positive stop foot change gearbox gives ratios of 9.6, 7.3, 5.55 and 5.05 to 1. Finish, like the M.A.C. Model is in the well-known Velocette black and gold.

Velocette 348 o.h.c. Model KTT.

VELOCETTE 149 c.c. Side Valve. Model L.E.

SPECIFICATION

Engine. Make Velocette.
　　Bore and Stroke. 44 mm. x 49 mm. 149 c.c.
　　Compression Ratio. 6 to 1.
B.H.P. 6.
　　Horizontally opposed twin cylinder, four stroke, side valve. Water cooled by thermo-syphon system and forward mounted radiator. Roller bearing big ends, ball and plain bearings supporting crankshaft. Light alloy pistons and cylinder heads.
　　Sparking plugs 10 mm.
Lubrication. Gear pump. Wet sump pressure system.
Carburettor. Amal, with air cleaner.
Gear Box. 3 speed, hand gear change control.
　　Ratios. 21.1, 13.1, and 7.1 to 1.
Clutch. 2 plate, friction type.
Transmission. Enclosed universal joint and shaft to bevel gears driving rear wheel.
Ignition. B.T.H. coil with automatic advance.
Lighting. B.T.H crankshaft driven, 6 volt. 30 watt. generator, 13 a.h. accumulator. 6" diameter headlamp, 24 watt. bulb, 3 watt parking light. Dipper switch.
Petrol Capacity. 1¼ gallons.
Oil Capacity. 1¼ pints.

Tyres. Dunlop 3.00" x 19". Ribbed front, studded rear.
Brakes. Internal expanding, 5" front and rear.
Frame and Suspension. Frame, light steel pressing, incorporating rear mudguard, battery and tool box. Velocette Telescopic front forks, swinging arm, coil spring, rear suspension.
Saddle. Pan seat, waterproof cover. **Height from ground.** 28".
Wheelbase. 51¼". **Ground Clearance.** 5¼".
Overall Length. 6' 10". **Width over bars.** 25".
Weight (dry). 260 lb.
Finish. Silver-grey, black and chromium.
Equipment. Prop stand, licence holder, speedometer, electric horn, footboards, legshields, pannier bags.
Maximum Speed. 1st 18 m.p.h. 2nd 30 m.p.h. 3rd 50 m.p.h.
Speed at end of quarter mile from rest. 40 m.p.h.
Petrol Consumption (at 30 m.p.h.) 120 m.p.g.
Braking (from 30 m.p.h. to rest). 30 ft. on dry tarmac.

STOP PRESS
1951 model LE200 will have 192 c.c. power unit. Bore 50 m.m., stroke 49 m.m. Specification otherwise mainly as 149 c.c. L.E.

VELOCETTE 349 c.c. Model M.A.C.

SPECIFICATION

Engine. Make Velocette.
　　Bore and Stroke. 68 mm. x 96 mm. 349 c.c.
　　Compression Ratio. 6 to 1.
B.H.P. 14.
　　Single cylinder, air cooled, single port, push rod, o.h.v. Totally enclosed valve gear and valve stems.
　　Sparking plugs 14 mm.
Lubrication. Dry sump, and gear pump.
Carburettor. Amal.
Gear Box. Velocette 4 speed twin top. Foot gear change. Kickstarter with folding crank.
　　Ratios. 14, 9.6, 7.3 and 5.5 to 1.
Clutch. 7 plate.
Transmission. Primary. Chain ½" x .305". Oil bath chain case.
　　Secondary. Chain ½" x .305".
Ignition. B.T.H. Magneto, gear driven.
Lighting. Miller dynamo, 6 volt. with voltage control. 13 a.h. accumulator. 8½" diameter headlamp, with diplight, parking light, rear light and illuminated speedometer dial.

Petrol Capacity. 2½ gallons.
Oil Capacity. ¾ gallon.
Tyres. 3.25" x 19", front and rear.
Brakes. 7" internal expanding, front and rear.
Frame and Suspension. Dowty oleomatic forks and rigid frame.
Saddle. Flexible top, adjustable. **Height from ground.** 27½".
Wheelbase. 52¼". **Ground Clearance.** 5".
Overall Length. 7'. **Width over bars.** 27½".
Weight (dry). 320 lb.
Finish. Black and chromium. Tank black and gold.
Equipment. Tool kit, speedometer, rear and prop stands, electric horn, licence holder, pillion seat and pillion footrests.
Extra or optional equipment.
Maximum Speed. 1st 30 m.p.h. 2nd 44 m.p.h. 3rd 57 m.p.h. 4th 75 m.p.h.
Speed at end of quarter mile from rest. 47 m.p.h.
Petrol Consumption (at 30 m.p.h.) 80 m.p.g.
Braking (from 30 m.p.h. to rest). 30 ft. on dry tarmac.

The VELO SOLEX

The motor cycle or motorised bicycle of under 100 c.c. is a recent development in this country, although the 50 c.c. engine has received much greater attention in France, where several types of machine are in production.

A motorised bicycle—the Velo Solex, was produced as a prototype in 1940, and production was begun in 1945. Several thousand machines have now been manufactured and are being ridden in widely differing conditions all over the world.

SOLEX (CYCLES) LTD.
223 MARYLEBONE RD.
LONDON, N.W.1

The Velo Solex is not a bicycle with a small power unit attached, but has been designed as a complete machine to include both cycle and engine in one balanced whole. It is claimed that a cycle which has been *designed* to be motor driven is better balanced, more controllable and capable of standing up to the strains and stresses imposed by the engine, than a unit which has been simply added to an existing cycle. In the same way the motor has been designed as an integral part of the frame.

The engine of the Velo Solex, although extremely small, is lightly stressed, a feature which makes for reliability, absence of vibration and long life. The single cylinder Solex two stroke engine has a bore of 38 mm. and a stroke of 40 mm. (45 c.c.) and gives .4 horsepower at 2,000 r.p.m. Lubrication is by petroil. A flywheel magneto provides the ignition and lighting. The rubber mounted engine has a crankshaft mounted on two ball races. A positive drive direct from the crankshaft operates a specially designed roller on the front wheel. A Solex carburettor and depression operated Solex fuel pump are provided. The engine is mounted and balanced astride the front wheel. Coil spring suspension is used. The open swan neck frame is assembled from four separate groups to reduce replacement time and cost.

A single control—a throttle-decompressor lever, is mounted on the handlebars. Other features of note are the well-sprung saddle, caliper brakes, powerful headlamp and parking lamp. The petrol tank holds a supply for a 60 mile range and the filler cap forms the oil measure for mixing fuel. Front and rear hubs and bottom bracket are grease packed, no lubrication being necessary, and cables are concealed inside the frame. The free wheel is reinforced, a light chain guard is provided and an efficient silencer and exhaust pipe.

Equipment includes a strong luggage carrier with provision for pannier bags, a metal tool box, tools and tyre pump and rear number plate.

The Velo Solex can claim to take the work out of cycling at minimum cost, whilst retaining the simplicity, safety and balance of a good bicycle. It takes up no more space than a pedal cycle and weighs only 55 lb. With a petrol consumption of approximately 300 m.p.g., and a cruising speed of 16 m.p.h. it will prove a most attractive proposition to a large section of the public.

SPECIFICATION.

ENGINE. Make. Solex. Bore and Stroke, 38 mm. × 40 mm. 45 c.c. Compression Ratio 6.4. Approximate b.h.p. .4 at 2,000 r.p.m. Single cylinder, air cooled, two stroke Crankshaft mounted on two ball races. Sparking plug 14 mm.
LUBRICATION. Petroil system.
CARBURETTOR. Solex 7 LL.
GEAR RATIO. Friction drive.
TRANSMISSION. Positive drive, direct from crankshaft by specially designed roller on front wheel.
IGNITION. S.E.V. Flywheel magneto.
LIGHTING. Direct lighting (battery operated parking lights).
PETROL CAPACITY. Tank. 1 litre petroil.
TYRES. Make. 26" × 1¾" × 1½".
BRAKES. Caliper rim type.
FRAME AND SUSPENSION. Open swan neck cycle type. Cycle type forks.
Height from ground. 2' 9".
WHEELBASE. 3' 8". Ground clearance. 5½".
WEIGHT (dry). 55 lb.
EQUIPMENT. Luggage carrier, with provision for pannier bags. Tool box, tools and tyre pump. Headlamp, rear lamp and number plate. Bulb horn. Speedometer—extra.

Villiers

**THE VILLIERS ENGINEERING CO. LTD.
WOLVERHAMPTON**

As the majority of two stroke machines described in this book are fitted with the Villiers engine, it is felt that a brief description of the latest power units will be of general interest to the reader.

Villiers have undoubtedly reached an unassailable position in the two stroke world, and in addition to motor cycles, a large number of agricultural and horticultural machines have adopted their products. The Villiers Company have been making motor cycle engines for 36 years, and during this time have produced over a million engines. The company manufactures itself all castings, forgings, pressings and machined parts and the factory at Wolverhampton covers 16 acres.

Late in 1948 Villiers introduced a complete new range of Auto-cycle and Motor Cycle engines consisting of four models, two of 98 c.c. the Mark 1F, two speed Ultra lightweight motor cycle engine, and the Mark 2F Single speed Auto-cycle engine, the Mark 10D 122 c.c. and Mark 6E 197 c.c. motor cycle models. All the new models have single port exhaust systems and redesigning of the porting has given increased power output. In accordance with modern practice the two larger engines have positive stop foot change gear boxes, and a new magneto providing current for either " Direct " or " Rectifier " lighting.

Dealing firstly with the Mark 2F engine for autocycles it should be observed that this has superseded the Junior de Luxe model, and is now mounted within the frame of the machine, instead of in a horizontal position beneath the bottom bracket, as was the case with the Junior de Luxe model. The cylinder centre line of the new engine is nearly vertical. It has a bore of 47 mm. and a stroke of 57 mm. and develops approximately 2 b.h.p. at 3,750 r.p.m. The latest engine has an aluminium alloy detachable cylinder head. A 14 mm. sparking plug is fitted at the rear and a compression release valve at the front. The combustion chamber is hemispherical in shape. The head is retained by four high tensile steel bolts and direct jointing is used between head and cylinder, no gasket being provided. A flat topped die cast aluminium alloy piston has two pegged compression rings. Phosphor bronze bushes in the gudgeon pin bosses accommodate the fully floating gudgeon pin, which is parallel in diameter and retained by circlips, and the piston skirt itself is suitably relieved in the area of the gudgeon pin bosses. The connecting rod is of nickel molybdenum steel and contains a phosphor bronze bush at the small end. The " Big end " of the connecting rod consists of two rows of uncaged $\frac{3}{16}"$ x $\frac{3}{16}"$ steel rollers.

The cast iron cylinder itself is retained to the crankcase by four studs. Re-designing of the porting has placed the inlet port at the rear, the single exhaust port at the front of the cylinder and the two transfer ports are placed one on each side. The transfer passages originate as cutaways in the crankcase, the passages proper are formed by the cylinder spigot and then continue through the cylinder casting. The outlets of these passages in the cylinder are so designed that an outward and rearward swirl is given to the incoming charge, directing it towards the cylinder head to facilitate complete scavenging. Journal ball races support the built-up crankshaft on both sides. A steel stamping forms each crank web and shaft. A parallel diameter crankpin of carbon steel which is an interference fit in the web bosses joins the webs together. The crankshaft carries on the right hand side the engine sprocket and the flywheel magneto on the taper end. On the left hand side the crankshaft is sufficiently long to fit into the ball race only and is 25 mm. in diameter.

The inner half of the primary chaincase and the boss for the clutch shaft bearing are an integral part of the die cast aluminium alloy crankcase. On the left hand side of the crankcase a compression retaining plate is provided which is held in place by countersunk screws and contains at the base a bolt, which forms the crankcase drain plug. This plate carries the crankshaft ball race.

The ratio of engine to clutch is 1-2.47 and the drive is taken by an endless chain of $\frac{3}{8}"$ pitch. The two plate cork insert type clutch is designed to operate in oil. One friction plate is formed by the sprocket itself and a further friction plate has five tongues which are located in slots in the sprocket face. Three plain steel driven plates are fitted to splines on the clutch shaft. A single coil spring is fitted. The clutch shaft itself is supported at both ends by ball races. The clutch thrust lever and thrust mechanism adjustment are mounted on the primary chain case cover in a casting. At the opposite end of the clutch shaft the 11 tooth driving sprocket is keyed. An aluminium-alloy cover protects the sprocket from the ingress of oil. All the clutch operating mechanism is totally enclosed.

The Mark 2F engine is fitted with the Villiers Junior pattern single lever carburettor incorporating a starting strangler and a wire mesh air filter. A six pole flywheel magneto incorporating ignition and lighting coils is provided, the principle of revolving magnets and stationary coils being used, the contact breaker cam being integral with the flywheel boss. The contact breaker is on the armature back plate.

The engine portion of the Mark 1F two speed unit is of almost identical design to the auto-cycle unit. No compression release valve is fitted on the cylinder head however. The major difference lies in the provision of the gear box and kickstarter. The clutch thrust lever and thrust rod adjustment are fitted on the sprocket cover on the left hand side of the engine however. Reduction between engine and gear box remains the same, i.e. 1: 2.47. A constant mesh gearbox with case hardened pinions is provided. The main shaft supports the clutch and the kickstarter ratchet pinion and also carries the sliding dogs and bottom gear pinion. At the right hand side the mainshaft runs in a ball race. The kick starter is mounted in a cover on the outer half of the primary chain case and engages with a ratchet pinion on the mainshaft of the gear box. The kick starter pedal can be folded inwards when not in use. The gears are operated by a control lever mounted on the handlebar. The magneto has built-in lighting coils providing alternating current, which is rectified for charging a 6 volt accumulator.

The Mark 10D (50 mm. x 62 mm.) 122 c.c., and Mark 6E (59 mm. x 72 mm.) 197 c.c. engine gear units have few detail differences. In fact the positive stop foot change, clutch mechanism, kick starter and gear boxes are identical.

Cylinder head design differs however, the 122 c.c. engine having a "half pear" shaped combustion chamber with a 14 mm. plug at the rear, and no compression release valve. On the Mark 6E engine the combustion chamber is hemispherical in shape and the sparking plug is fitted on the right hand side, with a compression release valve fitted on the left. The 197 c.c. engine also has a larger crankcase to take the greater crank throw.

Both engines have cast iron cylinders with detachable light alloy heads and flat topped pistons. Porting is as described for the 98 c.c. engines. The carburettor inlet stub on the engine is a light alloy casting, fixed on the cylinder lug by two studs, whereas on the 98 c.c. engines it is in one piece with the cast iron cylinder. A Villiers single lever lightweight carburettor with air filter and strangler is fitted on the Mark 10D and a Middleweight two lever pattern on the 6E engine. Crankcases are die-cast aluminium alloy. The left hand crankshaft in both the larger engines is fitted with two 20 mm. spaced ball races and carries the engine sprocket. On the right hand side a single ball race is provided and the flywheel magneto is fitted on the tapered end of the shaft. The crankpin itself is hollow and parallel in diameter and is an interference fit in the crankshaft webs. In the end of the pin hardened taper plugs are fitted. The big end bearing consists of two rows of uncaged $\frac{1}{4}''$ x $\frac{1}{4}''$ rollers and a phosphor bronze bush is fitted at the small end. The gudgeon pin is hollow, fully floating, and is held in the piston boss bushes by circlips.

A $\frac{3}{8}''$ pitch endless primary chain is fitted on the 122 c.c. engine. Engine to gear box reduction is 2.83 to 1.

The 197 c.c. engine has a $\frac{1}{2}''$ pitch primary chain and engine to gearbox reduction is 2 to 1. Gearbox ratios are the same for both engines (top, 1:1, second 1.4:1, and bottom 2.66:1) and the clutch is of the two plate cork insert type running in oil. These two-friction plate clutches have six springs and the thrust lever is carried in the outer end cover of the gear box, the thrust rod operating through the centre hole of the mainshaft. The pivot pin has an adjuster for hand setting, adjustment being maintained by a flat spring which locates in four cutaways in the adjuster.

A separate 3 speed, constant mesh type gearbox is bolted to the rear of the crankcase. Although self contained it virtually forms part of the engine when assembled. The gear pinions are case hardened. The mainshaft at the cover end, and the layshaft at both ends, are carried by phosphor bronze bushes. The other end of the mainshaft rotates without a bush directly in the top gear sleeve, ample lubrication being provided by a spiral groove in the mainshaft journal. A 25 mm. ball race forms the top gear sleeve bearing. An oil filler of ample dimensions is provided in the top of the gear box case and an accessible dip stick is fitted.

A pawl type kickstarter is fitted, engaging with internal ratchet teeth in the layshaft bottom gear pinion, and the kickstarter and the foot change mechanism are carried by the gear box inner end cover. The kick starter crank is splined to its spindle and is fitted with a spring loaded folding pedal.

The positive stop foot change mechanism consists of a spindle mounted in the end cover, the spindle carrying a floating operating plate. A stop in the cover prevents this plate from turning. A pawl plate, spring loaded from the rear by a coil spring, is splined to the spindle and cants over when the gear lever is moved. The pawl plate is thus brought into engagement with the operating lever, which operates the selector forks in its turn. A spring loaded plunger locates the selector quadrant.

Lighting, of course, is by the Villiers six pole flywheel magneto, which is fitted with lighting coils, from which the alternating current can be taken direct to the lamps or alternatively rectified to direct current for charging a battery. When the "direct" system is used a 36 watt headlamp bulb is fitted and in the case of the "rectifier" set a 24 watt bulb is used.

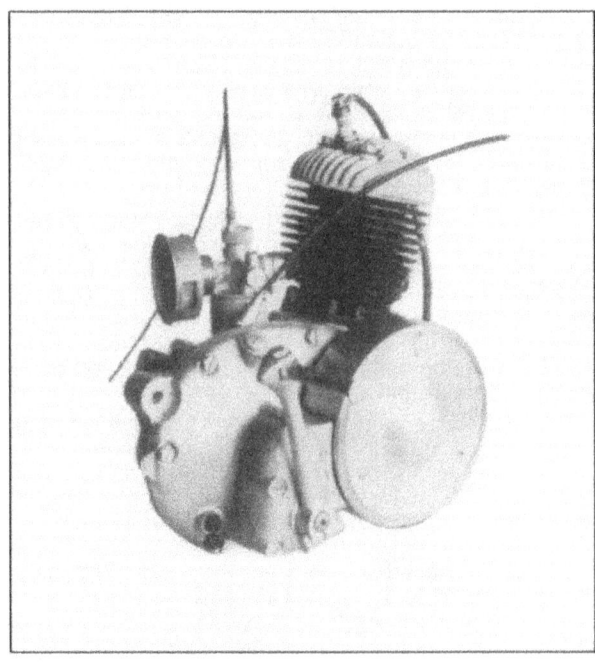

Villiers Mk. 1F.

Villiers Mk. 2F.

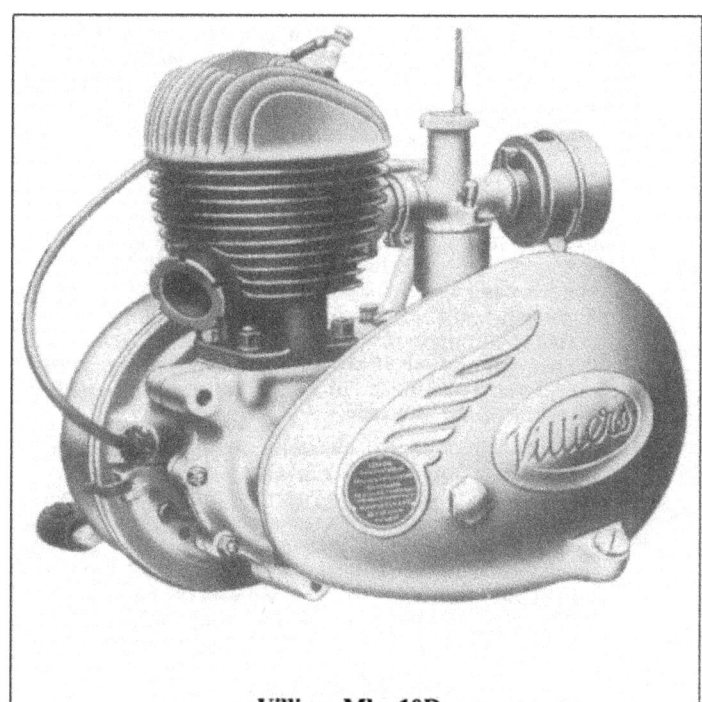
Villiers Mk. 10D.

Villiers Mk. 6E.

ABRIDGED SPECIFICATIONS OF VILLIERS ENGINES.

MARK 1F.

Bore and Stroke.	47 mm. (1.85") x 57 mm. (2.24"). 98 c.c. (5.98 cu. in.)
Cylinder Head.	Aluminium, detachable. 14 mm. sparking plug.
Piston.	Aluminium, flat top, two compression rings.
Gudgeon Pin.	Fully floating, held in place by circlips.
Bearings.	Ball bearings to crankshaft and clutchshaft. Roller bearing big end.
Clutch.	Two plate cork insert type, running in oil bath chain case.
Ratios.	Engine to clutch. 1-2.47. Gearbox top gear 1-1, low gear 1.54-1. Final drive sprocket 14 teeth x ½" pitch to suit Coventry chain No. 112045. Chainline 2½".
Two Speed Gear.	Constant mesh gears, sliding dog operated by control lever on handlebar.
Starting.	By kickstarter with folding pedal.
Carburettor.	Villiers " Junior " single lever control, latest type air cleaner with strangler for easy starting.
Magneto.	Villiers latest pattern flywheel magneto providing current for ignition and lighting. Magneto has built in lighting coils giving alternating current which is rectified by charging a 6 volt accumulator.
Lighting Set.	12/12 W. headlamp with dipswitch. 3 W. tail and parking lights. A stop tail lamp can be supplied.
Lubrication.	Engine—one part Castrol XL oil (SAE. 30) to 16 parts petrol. Gearbox and chaincase—Castrol " D " oil (SAE. 140) filled to level plug.
Weight.	Unit complete with magneto and carburettor. Approx. 38 lbs.
Fuel Consumption.	Approx. 140 m.p.g.
B.H.P.	2.8 at 4,000 r.p.m.

MARK 2F.

Bore and Stroke.	47 mm. (1.85") x 57 mm. (2.24") 98 c.c. (5.98 cu. in.)
Cylinder Head.	Aluminium, detachable. 14 mm. sparking plug. Compression realease valve.
Piston.	Aluminium, flat top. Two compression rings.
Bearings.	Ball bearings to crankshaft and clutchshaft. Roller bearing big end.
Clutch.	Two plate cork insert type running in oil bath chaincase.
Carburettor.	Villiers " Junior " single lever control, with hand operated strangler for easy starting. Air filter fitted.
Magneto.	Villiers latest pattern flywheel magneto with both ignition and lighting coils.
Lighting Set.	Headlamp with 6V., 12W. main bulb, and 4V., .3A parking bulb. Tail lamp with 4V., .3A bulb.
Lubrication.	Engine—one part Castrol XL oil (SAE. 30) to 16 parts petrol Chain and Clutch case. Castrol " D " oil (SAE. 140) filled to level plug.
Weight.	Complete with flywheel magneto and carburettor. 31 lb. approx.
B.H.P.	2 at 3,750 r.p.m.
Fuel Consumption.	Approx. 120 m.p.g.

MARK 10D.

Bore and Stroke.	50 mm. (1.968") x 62 mm. (2.440") 122 c.c. (7.44 cu. in.)
Cylinder Head.	Aluminium, detachable. 14 mm. sparking plug.
Pistons.	Aluminium, flat top. Two compression rings.
Bearings.	Three ball bearings to crankshaft. Roller bearing big end.
Clutch.	Two plate cork insert type. Finger control to adjustment.
Ratios.	Engine to clutch 1:2.83. Gearbox, Top Gear 1:1. Middle 1.4:1. Low, 2.66:1. Final drive sprocket—15 teeth x ½" pitch to suit Renold chain No. 110044.
Starting.	By kickstarter with folding pedal.
Carburettor.	Villiers single lever, suitable for lever or twist grip control. Latest type air cleaner with strangler for easy starting.
Magneto.	Villiers flywheel magneto type providing current for ignition and lighting. For direct lighting from magneto to lamps or for charging a battery through a rectifier.
Lighting Set.	Either 24 watt battery and rectifier set or 30 watt direct lighting set.
Weight.	Unit complete with carburettor and magneto. Approx. 50lbs.
Lubrication.	Engine—one part Castrol XL oil (SAE. 30) to 16 parts petrol. Gearbox and chaincase. Castrol " D " Gear oil (SAE. 140) to level plug fitted.
B.H.P. (Max.)	4.8 at 4,400 r.p.m.
Fuel Consumption.	Approx. 110 m.p.g.

MARK 6E.

Bore and Stroke.	59 mm. (2.322") x 72 mm. (2.834") 197 c.c. (11. 71 cu. in.)
Cylinder Head.	Aluminium, detachable. 14 mm. sparking plug. Compression release valve.
Piston.	Aluminium, flat top. Two compression rings.
Bearings.	Three ball bearings to crankshaft. Roller bearing big end.
Clutch.	Two plate cork insert type, finger control to adjustment.
Ratios.	Engine to clutch 1:2. Gearbox top gear 1:1. Middle 1.4:1. Low, 2.66:1. Final drive sprocket. 15 teeth x ½" pitch to suit Renold chain No. 110044.
Gearbox.	Constant mesh gears, positive stop foot change, lever adjustable for position.
Starting.	By kickstarter with folding pedal.
Carburettor.	Villiers two lever with latest type air cleaner. Suitable for lever or twist grip control.
Magneto.	Villiers flywheel magneto type providing current for ignition and lighting. For direct lighting from magneto to lamps or for charging a battery through a rectifier.
Lighting Set.	Either 24 watt battery and rectifier set or 30 watt direct lighting.
Lubrication.	One part Castrol XL oil to 16 parts petrol. Gearbox and chaincase. Castrol " D " oil.
B.H.P. (Max.)	8.4 at 4,000 r.p.m.
Weight.	Complete with magneto and carburettor, approx. 59 lbs.
Fuel Consumption.	Approx. 90 m.p.g.

Vincent

THE VINCENT H.R.D. CO. LTD.
STEVENAGE · HERTS.

U.S.A. Distributor:
INDIAN SALES CORPORATION
29 Worthington St.
Springfield, Mass.

It has often been remarked that figures are dull. This contention can scarcely have been put forward by the proud owner of a Vincent "Rapide." Such astonishing figures as 6.5 seconds from a standing start to 60 m.p.h., 90 m.p.h. in 14 seconds or 120 m.p.h. in 45 seconds from rest leave one rather breathless, to say the least. Add the fact that a standard production model broke the U.S. National Speed Record in 1948, with a speed of 150.313 m.p.h. for the flying mile, and it will be realised that here is something in a class apart as far as motorcycles are concerned.

The Vincent Company state that they manufacture the World's fastest standard motor cycle. Notice that they state this, not "claim" it, and go on to add " This is a fact—not a slogan." They have indeed proved it very handsomely.

The original H.R.D. Company, founded by Howard R. Davies, was reformed in 1928, by Mr. P. C. Vincent, with works at Stevenage, Herts. From the beginning, the company were pioneers in the use of spring frames, and they have been amply justified by the adoption of spring frames for high-speed and racing work by all of the world's manufacturers. The first Vincent-H. R. D. designed engine made its appearance in 1935. This engine, which powered the " Comet " model incorporated a number of unique features, including the method of valve operation still used in all Vincent engines. In 1937, as an experiment, two " Meteor " cylinders (the " Meteor " was a development of the " Comet ") were grafted on to a special crankcase, producing a 50° Vee Twin—the original Series 'A' Rapide.

The war years saw the factory turning out many types of delicate equipment, such as rocket and bomb fuses. At the end of the war, the attention of the designers was turned to a new conception, the Series ' B ' Rapide. No longer in wheelbase than the average 500 c.c. machine with superb cornering, steering and road-holding qualities, the Rapide has fulfilled the vision of its creators.

Studying the Vincent range it will be seen that the " Black Lightning " Rapide Racing Model has a maximum speed of 150 plus in top gear. Next there is the " Black Shadow " Rapide Sports Model, with a maximum of a mere 125 m.p.h.—as Vincents say " It gives a performance in touring trim above all but a select few of the most specialised racing machines." Taking another step down the performance scale we reach the standard " Rapide," which has been deliberately tamed to a maximum of 110 m.p.h., in order to endow it more fully with the many charming attributes that the tourist demands of his favourite mount. Nevertheless this tractable and reliable machine is still faster than any other standard motor cycle in the world (except of course the " Black Lightning " and " Black Shadow.")

Two single cylinder machines complete the range. The 500 c.c. Comet has a maximum of 90-95 m.p.h., and a 500 c.c. racing machine—the " Grey Flash," is the latest addition to a very thoroughbred stable.

To produce such a magnificent series of machines obviously calls for superb designing, unremitting research, minute attention to detail and assembly, a determination to use only the very highest grade materials no matter the cost, and an ultimate faith in the rightness of the machine for its job.

Before describing the range in more detail, a number of points of interest in the general design will not be out of place, and many of these features are exclusive to Vincent machines.

To begin with, it is interesting to note, in view of the modern tendency to equip models with spring frames, that every Vincent machine has had a spring frame— no rigid framed model has ever been made !

Declining to adopt the growing practice of fitting telescopic forks, Vincents, as the result of several years of applied thought, have produced the Girdraulic front fork, a design which gives complete lateral rigidity and freedom from twist in all connecting members between the two wheels. This fork provides the maximum travel that Vincent designers will permit for perfect high speed handling, in fact it provides considerably more travel than the usual girder fork. It is hydraulically damped and has hydraulic limit stops to prevent metallic "bottoming" in both directions, while the trail and the effective spring strength can be adjusted to suit sidecar or solo work in a few minutes.

Noteworthy features of the Rapide twins are the unique big-end design, with six rows of rollers, and the exclusive " Vincent " valve design, with guides above and below the rocker collar. The transmission is by a triple primary chain to a " Vincent " patented servo clutch, and a massive Vincent gearbox. The rear chain can be adjusted without tools.

The frame of the machine has largely disappeared, a short box-type girder, used as the oil tank, forms the spine of the machine, connecting the top of the head lug with the rear cylinder head. By detaching this oil tank from the rear cylinder head, and the connecting bracket from the front cylinder head, the petrol tank and complete steering and front wheel assemblies can be wheeled away, leaving the engine readily accessible for decarbonising or maintenance.

The wheels may be easily removed without tools and the rear wheel is reversible, allowing for easy change of gear ratios by fitting a second sprocket. All models are fitted with the Feridax dualseat, supported at the rear by a patented suspension.

For fifteen years all Vincent models have been fitted with four internal expanding brakes of 7" diameter. The spreading of the braking stresses spread over four brakes gives an extremely high standard of controllability and safety. A recent " Motor Cycling " test— of a " Black Shadow " gave the astonishing stopping distance of 22' 6" from 30 m.p.h., the usually accepted figure for 100 per cent. braking efficiency is 30 feet ! Needless to say, overheating of the brakes is virtually unknown, on account of the large cooling area, and the life of the linings is quite abnormal.

The current range of models incorporates five distinctive engine types, yet through rational design the great

Vincent "Black Shadow" 1000 c.c. Twin. Series "C"

majority of the components of these engines are identical and interchangeable. The five engine types consist of two 500 c.c. (30.50 cu. in.) singles, the Comet sports and Grey Flash racing models. The twins consist of the Standard Rapide touring, Black Shadow Rapide sports and Black Lightning Rapide racing engines. All models are fitted with the Girdraulic forks previously mentioned and in addition a two-way hydraulic shock absorber identical with that used on the front forks, is mounted between the twin spring units of the spring frame at the rear. The friction dampers incorporated in the Feridax dualseat mounting are retained, thus giving dual damping.

Dealing first with the twin cylinder engines, it should be noted that the cylinder head and valve gear are made from Aluminium Alloy RR53B aircraft specification, heat treated, and have inclined o.h. valves with twin valve guides. The 1.8″ diameter inlet valve is of silichrome steel, the 1.67″ diameter exhaust valve of DTD 49B steel. The valve seats are shrunk in, the inlet seat being of austenitic cast iron, the exhaust seat of aluminium bronze. The o.h. rockers are forged from KE 805 steel, are entirely enclosed and lubricated and run in duralumin bearings. The rockers operate against a hardened contact collar placed on the valve stem between the upper and lower guides. Totally enclosed duplex helical valve springs are fitted, and are seated on the top of the cool upper valve guide, which in turn is separated by a large air space from the top of the hot exhaust port, on which the springs are seated on conventional design engines. All exhaust ports face forward, are liberally finned and positioned to receive the best cooling airstream, this finning being made possible by the positioning of the separate rocker boxes. It should be noted that the duplex helical valve springs are supplemented on Black Shadow and Black Lightning models by an additional inner spring which provides higher spring loading.

The cylinder barrel consists of a detachable high grade cast iron liner shrunk into a finned aluminium cylinder jacket. The aluminium alloy piston has two Wellworthy pressure rings and one scraper ring, a $\frac{7}{8}$″ diameter rigid taper-bored gudgeon pin, fully floating and retained by circlips. The pistons are available to give a wide range of compression ratios but maintaining a constant relationship in the positioning of the rings relative to the gudgeon pin height. Standard Rapide Models are sent out with 6.8 to 1 compression ratio, the Black Shadow ratio is 7.3 to 1 and ratios on the Black Lightning are supplied to customers requirements. These ratios can be reduced by fitting lower compression pistons and/or compression plates. The cylinder bore is 84 mm. and the piston stroke 90 mm., the total engine capacity being 998 c.c.

Forged connecting rods of 65 ton nickel chrome steel (75-80 tons on the Black Lightning) are fitted and have a polished finish on Black Lightning and Black Shadow models. The big end liners are of EN 31 carbon chrome steel, hardened, ground and honed. There are 3 rows of 3 mm. diameter x 5mm. long rollers in each connecting rod's big end, separated and guided by hardened, ground and lapped rings between each row of rollers. The $1\frac{9}{16}$″ diameter crank pin is of EN 36 case hardened nickel chrome steel. Drilled oilways in pin, flywheel and mainshaft ensure a copious supply of oil to the big end.

The timing gear consists of a separate camshaft for each cylinder mounted high in the timing case with 6″ push rods operating within stainless steel push rod tubes. A mechanical rotary breather valve is provided, but the design differs in detail between the singles and the twins, as does the exhaust valve lifter mechanism. The Lucas magneto is driven from the timing gear through a

Vincent "Black Lightning" 1000 c.c. Twin. Series "C"

Lucas automatic advance and retard unit (except the Black Lightning, which has manual control).

The crankcase is cast in DTD424 aircraft specification alloy, and is massively ribbed. A housing for the large oil filter is cast integral with the timing side case. Very massive anchorage bosses are provided for the 65 ton cylinder head bolts. For additional rigidity, the cylinder liner extension below the jacket is spigotted into the massive upper throat of the crankcase. The oil pump is housed in an accurately bored cylinder formed in the lower part of the timing case and feeds the oil direct through a drilled passage into the filter housing. Four large diameter crankcase main bearings are provided, two to each mainshaft. Three of these are roller bearings and the fourth is a ball bearing for endwise location of the crankshaft.

The upper faces of the paired crankcases are machined to accept two cylinders at 50° in Vee formation, the rear cylinder being offset $1\frac{1}{4}$" towards the timing gear for improved cooling. The timing case is shaped and machined to accept the camshafts for both cylinders and their appropriate operating gear. The twins, having a unit construction gearbox, the gearbox housing and the inner half of the oilbath for the primary chain are cast integral with the crankcase.

The flywheels are specially machined and balanced to suit the characteristics of the Vee twin engine. Forged in 40 ton carbon steel, they are machined all over and jig drilled for consistent balance and are polished on the Black Lightning model. The nickel chrome steel mainshafts are drive side splined to accept a 3 lobe engine shock absorber sprocket, carried on a separate hardened sleeve. The timing side carries the oil pump drive worm and half time pinion. The mainshafts are a tight pressed fit in the flywheels and the outside diameter and one raised face flange on each flywheel are subsequently ground off the mainshaft centres to bring them exactly true to the shafts themselves. These ground locations are then used to position the flywheels for the boring and facing of the crankpin holes; thus ensuring an astonishing degree of accuracy in the true running of the flywheel assembly, long life for the main bearings and smoothness of running. Both mainshafts and both ends of the crankpin are an accurate and parallel fit in the flywheels, obviating the disadvantages of taper fits.

Lubrication is on the dry sump system, a large double acting rotary plunger pump being worm driven from the timing side mainshaft. It draws oil from a 6 pint oil tank through a gauze filter and a large bore pipe, pumps it through a 54" square full flow Tecalemit filter, and hence direct to the big end assembly, camshaft bearings and the rear of the cylinder walls. Return oil is scraped from the flywheels and pumped back to the tank. By-pass jets from the return pipe to the tank lubricate the valve gear.

A unit construction, 4 speed constant mesh gearbox of Vincent design is fitted. The shafts are very rigid and are supported by large diameter ball bearings. All gears are of casehardened nickel chrome EN 36 steel. The end cover is of circular design and spigots accurately into the case, relieving the studs of all transmission stresses. The external gear indicator lever can be used to select neutral or change by hand. The foot change mechanism and kick starter are mounted in a separate, easily detachable cover. The kick starter can be mounted on the left hand side of the machine when a right hand sidecar is fitted. The starter crank is of special design, giving great leverage and is fitted with a folding footpiece. The gearbox is driven by a Renolds Triplex $\frac{3}{8}$" pitch chain, the tension of which is controlled by a stiff leaf spring tensioner and the whole primary transmission is contained in an oilbath case cast integral with the crankcase and gearbox, with a detachable aluminium cover. An accessible external screw varies the curvature of the spring, and hence the chain adjustment. The engine sprocket of 35 teeth, drives a 56 tooth clutch sprocket.

The engine shaft shock absorber is of the 3 lobe cam type with 36 light coil springs, which give it smooth action. The cam slides on a separate hardened and splined sleeve, so that in the event of wear, the sleeve alone can be detached and replaced. The single plate clutch is contained in a separate oiltight housing in the chaincase cover, and provides the expanding pressure to work a pair of shoes in a nickel chrome alloy cast iron ribbed drum.

The final drive sprocket has 21 teeth but 22 teeth sprockets are available for providing extra high gear ratios for racing. The rear chain is Renold $\frac{5}{8}"$ x $\frac{3}{8}"$ and the chain line is sufficiently wide to permit the fitting of larger tyres. Final drive is changed by altering the rear wheel sprocket which has 46 teeth as standard for solo use. Where desired a second sprocket can be fitted to the other brake drum and ratios quickly changed by reversing the wheel. A finger adjustment is provided for chain tension. Standard Rapide gearbox reductions are 1, 1.19, 1.61 and 2.6 to 1, giving with the standard sprockets overall ratios of 3.5, 4.2, 5.6, and 9.1 to 1. Black Shadow ratios are the same, except that bottom gear is raised to 2.07 (7.2 to 1).

Black Lightning models are provided with the same ratios as the Black Shadow, but the engaging dogs have greater backlash in the interests of quicker gear changing.

The Girdraulic Forks use forged light alloy blades of tapered oval section and preserve the maximum of rigidity by using one-piece forged links. Very long springs, in telescopic cases are mounted between the bottom of the crown lug and the fork ends. A two-way hydraulic shock absorber with hydraulic limit stops is fitted. The steel spindles run in oil-impregnated bearings.

The frame consists of an exceptionally strong head lug which bolts to a forged steel bracket on the front cylinder head. A strong triangulated oil tank stays it against a similar lug on the rear cylinder head. The only other important frame members are the rigid triangulated rear forks and the plates which secure this fork to the rear end of the engine unit. The rear springing provides a long soft action of about 6" travel, controlled by the Girdraulic type hydraulic damper. There is only one bearing in the springing system, which pivots on 2 large S.K.F. taper roller bearings. The four powerful 7" diameter brakes work in nickel chrome alloy cast iron drums. On "Black Shadow" and "Black Lightning" models the drums are deeply finned for cooling. On the "Black Lightning" only, cast magnesium brake plates are used, with Duplex airscoops on the front brakes.

The wheels run on large diameter S.K.F. taper roller bearings, and are detachable in less than a minute without using any tools. The rear wheel may be mounted either way round in the machine for equalising tyre wear, or, if two sprockets of different sizes are fitted, for speedy changing of gear ratios. The brake drums may be removed without disturbing the spokes. Rapide models are fitted with one security bolt and two balance weights. On the "Black Lightning" solo model Aluminium alloy racing rims and security bolts are fitted as standard.

On Standard Rapides and Black Shadows, two $1\frac{3}{8}"$ exhaust pipes join and run direct into the silencer. On Black Lightnings special straight through pipes are supplied.

Some performance characteristics of this magnificent range of machines are given below:-

Characteristic	Black Lightning	Black Shadow	Standard Rapide	Comet	Meteor	Units of measurement
Power to Weight Ratio	480	280	222	150	130	Brake-horse power per ton
Dry Weight	380 172	458 207	455 206	390 176	380 172	Pounds Kilogrammes
Petrol Consumption	— — —	55 to 65 50 to 60 5 to 6	55 to 65 50 to 60 5 to 6	75 to 80 70 to 75 4 to 5	75 to 80 70 to 75 4 to 5	Miles per Imp. Gall. ,, Amer. ,, Litres per 100 kilos.
Oil Consumption	—	1,500 500	1,500 500	2,000 650	2,000 650	Miles per gallon Kilos. per litre.
Cruising Speed	—	100 160	85 136	65 104	60 96	Miles per hour Kilos. ,,
Maximum Speed	150 + 240 +	125 200	110 175	90 to 95 144 to 152	80 to 85 128 to 136	Miles per hour Kilos. ,,
Minimum Speed in top gear	—	18 29	18 29	19 31	19 31	Miles per hour Kilos. ,,
Maximum Safe Speeds in Indirect Gears	According to Gearing	110 85 65 175 136 104	96 80 50 154 127 80	77 55 38 123 88 60	70 50 34 112 80 55	3rd 2nd miles per 1st hour 3rd kilos. per 2nd hour 1st
Acceleration through gears as recorded in "Motor Cycling" Road Tests	Not yet tested	3½ secs. 6¼ ,, 10 ,, 21 ,, 31 ,, 44 ,,	1½ secs. 6 ,, 12 ,, 24 ,, 35 ,, —	Not yet tested	Not yet tested	0–30 miles per hour 0–48 kilos. ,, 0–60 miles ,, 0–96 kilos. ,, 0–80 miles ,, 0–128 kilos. ,, 0–100 miles ,, 0–160 kilos. ,, 0–110 miles ,, 0–175 kilos. ,, 0–120 miles ,, 0–192 kilos. ,,

Vincent "Comet" 500 c.c. Single. Series "C"

Single Cylinder Machines.

The specification of these machines follows very closely that of the twins.

The crankcases, of course, differ in having provision for only one cylinder inclined forward at 25°, and for one set of timing gear. These castings do not incorporate oilbath or gearbox housing, as these units are separate on 500 c.c. models. The flywheels are specially machined and balanced to suit the single cylinder model.

A separate 4 speed Burman gearbox and clutch are fitted, driven by a $\frac{1}{2}''$ x $\frac{5}{16}''$ Renold chain in an oilbath. The shock absorber is of the same design and all details of the final drive (except that the gearbox sprocket has 18 teeth and the chain is on the opposite side of the machine) are the same as for the Rapides. Standard gear ratios are 4.64, 5.94, 8.17 and 12.4 to 1. The Miller dynamo is gear driven from the timing case, instead of from the primary chain and sprocket, as is the case with the twins.

The Comet has a compression ratio of 6.8 to 1, and a single Amal 29 mm. ($1\frac{1}{8}''$) carburettor. Compression ratios on the Grey Flash racing model are to order and a special racing Amal carburettor is fitted.

The frame on the singles is to the same design as the twins, but is stayed at the rear against the cast aluminium rear seat stay in lieu of the rear cylinder head lug. A single port exhaust system is supplied on 500 c.c. Models.

SPECIFICATION.
499 c.c. " Comet " Model.

Engine. Make, Vincent.
  Bore and Stroke. 84 mm. x 90 mm. 499 c.c.
  Compression Ratio. 6.8 to 1.
  B.H.P. Approximately 26.
  Single cylinder, o.h.v. air cooled, single port, enclosed push rod operated valves, cylinder barrel; cast iron liner shrunk into finned aluminium cylinder jacket. Aluminium alloy piston. Triple helical valve springs. Forged nickel chrome steel connecting rod. Individually balanced flywheel Sparking plug. 14 mm. L.R.
Lubrication. Dry sump. Double acting rotary plunger pump.
Carburettor. Amal 289 (29 mm. 1⅛" choke).
Gearbox. Burman 4 speed. Foot change.
  Gear ratios. 12.4, 8.17, 5.94 and 4.64 to 1.
Clutch. Burman clutch.
Transmission. Primary. Chain ½" x ⅜".
  Secondary. Chain Renold ⅝" x ⅜".
Ignition. Gear driven Lucas magneto.
Lighting. Miller 50 watt dynamo, gear driven from timing gear train. 6 volt. 13 a.h. Exide battery. Stop light. Lucas Altette horn.
Petrol Capacity. 3½ gallons. Pressed steel tank. Twin petrol taps, quick action filler caps. Dropped rear end traps water or dirt.
Oil Capacity. Six pints. Oil tank forms upper frame member.
Tyres. Avon Speedster, ribbed. 3.00" x 20" front.
  Avon Supreme studded. 3.50" x 19" rear.
Brakes. Four internal expanding. 7" diameter.
Frame and Suspension. Fully triangulated laterally rigid spring frame. Patent Girdraulic forks. Hydraulically damped rear suspension.
Saddle. Feridax Dunlopillo Dualseat. **Height from ground.** 31".
Wheelbase. 56". **Ground clearance.** 6".
Weight (dry). 390 lb. **Length overall.** 85¼".
Finish. All enamelled parts Bonderised and stove enamelled. Bright parts polished stainless steel, aluminium or chromium plate. Tank, black enamel, finished gold leaf.
Equipment. Rear tubular stand. Twin prop stands (together form front stand Smith's chronometric 3" dial. 120 m.p.h. speedometer.

SPECIFICATION.
499 c.c. " Grey Flash " Model.

Generally based on Comet Model, but produced to Black Lightning standard, with the following main alterations.
Engine. Head with specially enlarged streamlined and polished ports, triple valve springs, lightened and polished rockers and cam followers, special racing camshaft, compression ratio to customer's requirements. 85 ton nickel chrome steel highly polished conrod., polished flywheels.
Carburettor. Special racing Amal 32 mm. choke.
Magneto. Lucas or B.T.H. manual control racing type.
Gearbox. Fourspeed close ratio. Albion type.
Forks. Girdraulic. Specially lightened.
Frame. Drilled for lightness with Girdraulic rear suspension.
Brakes. Ribbed drums. Magnesium plates with dual airscoops.
Wheels. Aluminium alloy rims. Special Avon racing tyres. 3.00 x 21 front, 3.50 x 20 rear.
Weight Stripped. Under 300 lbs.
Finish. Mainly dull chrome. Fork blades and certain aluminium parts anodized grey. Crankcase, timing cover and oil bath, fine shot blast aluminium.
Note—This model can be supplied with full road equipment, as Comet model, or less lighting set, horn, speedometer silencer, and fitted with racing type mudguards, footrests, exhaust pipe etc. Alternatively the machine can be supplied with both sets of equipment. Smith's revolution counter extra.

SPECIFICATION.
998 c.c. Black Shadow Model. Series "C"

Engine. Make. Vincent.
  Bore and Stroke (twin). 84 mm. x 90 mm. 998 c.c.
  B.H.P. Approximately 55.
  Compression Ratio. 7.3 to 1.
  Twin cylinder, o.h.v. air cooled, enclosed push rod operated valves, cylinder barrel—cast iron liner shrunk into finned aluminium cylinder jacket. Aluminium alloy piston, Triple helical valve springs. Polished connecting rods, individually balanced flywheel.
  Sparking plug. 14 mm. L.R.
Lubrication. Dry sump. Double acting rotary plunger pump.
Carburettors. Twin Amals, type 289 (29 mm. 1⅛" choke.) Air filters optional extra.
Gearbox. Vincent 4 speed, foot change.
  Gear ratios. 7.2, 5.6, 4.2, 3.5 to 1.
Clutch. Vincent patent Servo type.
Transmission. Primary. Renold ⅜" pitch Triplex chain.
  Secondary. Renold Chain ⅝" x ⅜".
Ignition. Gear driven Lucas magneto, specially laboratory tested.
Lighting. Miller 50 watt dynamo, driven from primary chain. 6 volt, 13 a.h. Exide battery. Miller 7" headlamp. Stop light.
Petrol Capacity. 3¾ gallons. Pressed steel tank. Twin petrol taps. Quick action filler caps. Dropped rear end traps water or dirt.
Oil Capacity. Six pints. Oil tank forms upper frame member.
Tyres. Avon Speedster, Ribbed, 3.00" x 20", front.
  Avon Supreme, studded, 3.50" x 19", rear.
Brakes. Four internal expanding, 7" diameter. Drums finned for cooling.
Frame and Suspension. Fully triangulated, laterally rigid spring frame.
  Series C. Patent Girdraulic Forks. Hydraulically damped rear suspension.
Saddle. Feridax Dunlopillo dual seat. **Height from ground.** 31".
Wheelbase. 56". **Ground clearance.** 6".
Weight (dry) 458 lb.
Finish. All enamelled parts bonderised and stove enamelled. Bright parts polished stainless steel, aluminium or chromium plate. Tank, black enamel, finished gold leaf. Both wheels fitted with one security bolt and two balanced weights. Special light alloy, highly polished mudguards. Rear guard hinged for easy wheel removal. Rear tubular stand. twin prop stands. Pillion footrests. Power unit Pyluminised and enamelled glossy black.
Equipment. Smith's Chronometric 5" dial, 150 m.p.h. Speedometer mounted on top of fork girder.

SPECIFICATION.
998 c.c. Standard Rapide Models. Series "C"

Engine. Make. Vincent.
  Bore and Stroke (twin). 84 mm. x 90 mm. 998 c.c.
  Compression Ratio. 6.8 to 1.
  B.H.P. Approximately 45.
  Twin cylinder, o.h.v. air cooled, enclosed push rod operated valves, cylinder barrel—cast iron liner shrunk into finned aluminium cylinder jacket. Aluminium alloy piston. Duplex helical valve springs. Forged nickel chrome steel connecting rod. Individually balanced flywheel.
  Sparking plug. 14 mm. L.R.
Lubrication. Dry Sump. Double acting rotary plunger pump.
Carburettors. Twin Amals, type 276. (27 mm. (1 1/16") choke). Air filters optional extra.
Gearbox. Vincent 4 speed, foot change.
  Gear ratios. 9.1, 5.6, 4.2, 3.5 to 1.
Clutch. Vincent patent Servo type.
Transmission. Primary. Renold Triplex ⅜" pitch.
  Secondary. Renold ⅝" x ⅜".
Ignition. Gear driven Lucas magneto.
Lighting. Miller 50 watt dynamo, driven from primary chain. 6 volt. 13-a.h. Exide battery. Miller 7" Head lamp. Stop light.
Petrol Capacity. 3¾ gallons. Pressed steel tank. Twin petrol taps. Quick action filler caps. Dropped rear end traps water and dirt.
Oil Capacity. Six pints. Oil tank forms part of frame.
Tyres. Avon Speedster, ribbed, 3.00" x 20", front.
  Avon Supreme, studded, 3.50" x 19" rear.
Brakes. Four internal expanding, 7" diameter.
Frame and Suspension. Fully triangulated laterally rigid spring frame.
  Series C. Patent Girdraulic forks. Hydraulically damped rear suspension.
Saddle. Feridax Dunlopillo dual seat. **Height from ground.** 31".
Wheelbase. 56". **Ground clearance.** 6".
Weight (dry) 455 lb. **Length overall** 85½".
Finish. All enamelled parts bonderised and stove enamelled. Bright parts polished stainless steel, aluminium or chromium plate. Tank, black enamel, finished gold leaf. Both wheels fitted with one security bolt and two balance weights. Special light alloy, highly polished mudguards (valanced type on export model). Rear guard hinged for easy wheel removal. Rear tubular stand. Twin prop stands. Pillion footrests.
Equipment. Smith's Chronometric 3" dial, 120 m.p.h. speedometer.

SPECIFICATION.
998 c.c. "Black Lightning" Model.

Engine. Make. Vincent.
  Bore and Stroke (twin) 84 mm. x 90 mm. 998 c.c.
  Compression Ratio. To customer's requirements.
  B.H.P. Approximately 85 on alcohol fuel.
  Twin cylinder, o.h.v. air cooled, enclosed push rod operated valves, cylinder barrel—cast iron liner shrunk into finned aluminium cylinder jacket. Aluminium alloy piston. Triple helical valve springs. Forged connecting rods (75—80 tons) polished finish. Individually balanced, polished flywheel.
  Sparking plugs. 14 mm. L.R.
Lubrication. Dry sump. Double acting rotary plunger pump.
Carburettors. Twin racing Amals, 1 5/32" or 32 mm. choke.
Gearbox. Vincent 4 speed, foot change.
  Gear ratios. 7.2, 5.6, 4.2 and 3.5 to 1.
Clutch. Vincent patent Servo type.
Transmission. Primary. Triplex ⅜" pitch Renold chain.
  Secondary. Renold chain ⅝" x ⅜".
Ignition. Lucas. Gear driven from timing gear, manually controlled.
Lighting. Not supplied.
Petrol Capacity. 3¾ gallons. Pressed steel tank. Twin petrol taps. Quick action filler caps. Dropped rear end traps water or dirt.
Oil Tank. 6 pints capacity. Forms upper frame member.
Tyres. Special Avon racing, with rayon cases, 3.00" x 21", front.
  3.50" x 20" rear. Special racing inner tubes.
  Alternative sizes available for sidecar racing.
Brakes. Four internal expanding, 7" diameter. Deeply finned, cast magnesium brake plates, duplex airscoops on front brakes.
Frame and Suspension. Fully triangulated, laterally rigid spring frame. Patent Girdraulic forks. Hydraulically damped rear suspension.
Saddle. Feridax Dunlopillo Racing seat. **Height from ground.** 31".
Wheelbase. 56". **Ground clearance.** 6".
Weight (dry) 380 lb. **Length overall** 85½".
Finish. All enamelled parts bonderised and stove enamelled. Bright parts polished stainless steel, aluminium or chromium plate. Tank, black enamel, finished gold leaf. Both wheels fitted with one security bolt and two balance weights. Aluminium alloy racing rims (solo machine). Special light alloy highly polished mudguards. Rear tubular stand (no prop stands fitted). No pillion footrests. Sprint handlebars available to special order. Power unit Pyluminised and enamelled glossy black. Separate straight through exhaust pipes.
Equipment. Smith's Chronometric 3" dial, 180 m.p.h. speedometer. 8,000 r.p.m. tachometer.

ARE YOU:
INTERESTED IN EUROPEAN, IMPORT & EXOTIC AUTOMOBILES?

DO YOU:
DO YOUR OWN MAINTENANCE?

If you answered yes to either of these questions, then you should check out our automobile books and manuals. We have included a sample listing of some of our featured marques. However, for complete details and the most up-to-date information, please visit our website.

—— www.VelocePress.com ——

The fastest growing specialist USA publisher of niche market automotive books and manuals.

All VelocePress titles are available through your local independent bookseller, Amazon.com or direct from VelocePress. Wholesale customers may also purchase direct or from the Ingram Book Group.

AUTOBOOKS WORKSHOP MANUALS

ALFA ROMEO GIULIA 1300, 1600, 1750, 2000 1962-1978 WSM
AUSTIN HEALEY SPRITE, MG MIDGET 1958-1980 WSM
BMW 1600 1966-1973 WSM
BMW 2000 & 2002 1966-1976 WSM
BMW 2500, 2800, 3.0 & 3.3 1968-1977 WSM
BMW 316, 320, 320i 1975-1977 WSM
BMW 518, 520, 520i 1973-1981 WSM
FIAT 1100, 1100D, 1100R & 1200 1957-1969 WSM
FIAT 124 1966-1974 WSM
FIAT 124 SPORT 1966-1975 WSM
FIAT 125 & 125 SPECIAL 1967-1973 WSM
FIAT 126, 126L, 126 DV, 126/650 & 126/650 DV 1972-1982 WSM
FIAT 127 SALOON, SPECIAL & SPORT, 900, 1050 1971-1981 WSM
FIAT 128 1969-1982 WSM
FIAT 1300, 1500 1961-1967 WSM
FIAT 131 MIRAFIORI 1975-1982 WSM
FIAT 132 1972-1982 WSM
FIAT 500 1957-1973 WSM
FIAT 600, 600D & MULTIPLA 1955-1969 WSM
FIAT 850 1964-1972 WSM
JAGUAR E-TYPE 1961-1972 WSM
JAGUAR MK 1, 2 1955-1969 WSM
JAGUAR S TYPE, 420 1963-1968 WSM
JAGUAR XK 120, 140, 150 MK 7, 8, 9 1948-1961 WSM
LAND ROVER 1, 2 1948-1961 WSM
MERCEDES-BENZ 190 1959-1968 WSM
MERCEDES-BENZ 220/8 1968-1972 WSM
MERCEDES-BENZ 220B 1959-1965 WSM
MERCEDES-BENZ 230 1963-1968 WSM
MERCEDES-BENZ 250 1968-1972 WSM
MERCEDES-BENZ 280 1968-1972 WSM
MG MIDGET TA-TF 1936-1955 WSM
MINI 1959-1980 WSM
MORRIS MINOR 1952-1971 WSM
PEUGEOT 404 1960-1975 WSM
PORSCHE 911 1964-1973 WSM
PORSCHE 911 1970-1977 WSM
RENAULT 16 1965-1979 WSM
RENAULT 8, 10, 1100 1962-1971 WSM
ROVER 3500, 3500S 1968-1976 WSM
SUNBEAM RAPIER, ALPINE 1955-1965 WSM
TRIUMPH SPITFIRE, GT6, VITESSE 1962-1968 WSM
TRIUMPH TR2, TR3, TR3A 1952-1962 WSM
TRIUMPH TR4, TR4A 1961-1967 WSM
VOLKSWAGEN BEETLE 1968-1977 WSM

BROOKLANDS BOOKS & ROAD TEST PORTFOLIOS (RTP)

AC CARS 1904-2009
ALFA ROMEO 1920-1933 ROAD TEST PORTFOLIO
ALFA ROMEO 1934-1940 ROAD TEST PORTFOLIO
BRABHAM RALT HONDA THE RON TAURANAC STORY
BUGATTI TYPE 10 TO TYPE 40 ROAD TEST PORTFOLIO
BUGATTI TYPE 10 TO TYPE 251 ROAD TEST PORTFOLIO
BUGATTI TYPE 41 TO TYPE 55 ROAD TEST PORTFOLIO
BUGATTI TYPE 57 TO TYPE 251 ROAD TEST PORTFOLIO
DELAHAYE ROAD TEST PORTFOLIO
FERRARI ROAD CARS 1946-1956 ROAD TEST PORTFOLIO
FIAT 500 1936-1972 ROAD TEST PORTFOLIO
FIAT DINO ROAD TEST PORTFOLIO
HISPANO SUIZA ROAD TEST PORTFOLIO
HONDA ST1100/ST1300 PAN EUROPEAN 1990-2002 RTP
JAGUAR MK1 & MK2 ROAD TEST PORTFOLIO
LOTUS CORTINA ROAD TEST PORTFOLIO
MV AGUSTA F4 750 & 1000 1997-2007 ROAD TEST PORTFOLIO
TATRA CARS ROAD TEST PORTFOLIO

VELOCEPRESS AUTOMOBILE BOOKS & MANUALS

ABARTH BUYERS GUIDE
AUSTIN-HEALEY 6-CYLINDER WSM
BMW 600 LIMOUSINE FACTORY WSM
BMW 600 LIMOUSINE OWNERS HAND BOOK & SERVICE MANUAL
BMW ISETTA FACTORY WSM
BOOK OF THE CARRERA PANAMERICANA - MEXICAN ROAD RACE
COMPLETE CATALOG OF JAPANESE MOTOR VEHICLES
DIALED IN - THE JAN OPPERMAN STORY
FERRARI 250/GT SERVICE AND MAINTENANCE
FERRARI 308 SERIES BUYER'S AND OWNER'S GUIDE
FERRARI BERLINETTA LUSSO
FERRARI BROCHURES AND SALES LITERATURE 1946-1967
FERRARI BROCHURES AND SALES LITERATURE 1968-1989
FERRARI GUIDE TO PERFORMANCE
FERRARI OPP, MAINTENANCE & SERVICE H/BOOKS 1948-1963
FERRARI OWNER'S HANDBOOK
FERRARI SERIAL NUMBERS PART I - ODD NUMBERS TO 21399
FERRARI SERIAL NUMBERS PART II - EVEN NUMBERS TO 1050
FERRARI SPYDER CALIFORNIA
FERRARI TUNING TIPS & MAINTENANCE TECHNIQUES
HOW TO BUILD A FIBERGLASS CAR
HOW TO BUILD A RACING CAR
IF HEMINGWAY HAD WRITTEN A RACING NOVEL
JAGUAR E-TYPE 3.8 & 4.2 WSM
LE MANS 24 (THE BOOK THAT THE FILM WAS BASED ON)
MASERATI BROCHURES AND SALES LITERATURE
MASERATI OWNER'S HANDBOOK
METROPOLITAN FACTORY WSM
MGA & MGB OWNERS HANDBOOK & WSM
OBERT'S FIAT GUIDE
PERFORMANCE TUNING THE SUNBEAM TIGER
PORSCHE 356 1948-1965 WSM
PORSCHE 912 WSM
SOUPING THE VOLKSWAGEN
TRIUMPH TR2, TR3, TR4 1953-1965 WSM
VEDA ORR'S NEW REVISED HOT ROD PICTORIAL
VOLKSWAGEN TRANSPORTER, TRUCKS, STATION WAGONS WSM
VOLVO 1944-1968 ALL MODELS WSM

VELOCEPRESS MOTORCYCLE BOOKS & MANUALS

AJS SINGLES 1955-65 350cc & 500cc (BOOK OF)
ARIEL 1939-1960 4 STROKE SINGLES (BOOK OF)
ARIEL LEADER & ARROW 1958-1964 (BOOK OF)
ARIEL MOTORCYCLES 1933-1951 WSM
ARIEL PREWAR MODELS 1932-1939 (BOOK OF)
BMW M/CYCLES R26 R27 (1956-1967) FACTORY WSM
BMW M/CYCLES R50 R50S R60 R69S (1955-1969) FACTORY WSM
BSA BANTAM (BOOK OF)
BSA ALL FOUR-STROKE SINGLES & V-TWINS 1936-1952 (BOOK OF)
BSA OHV & SV SINGLES - 250cc 1954-1970 (BOOK OF)
BSA OHV & SV SINGLES 1945-54 250-600cc (BOOK OF)
BSA OHV SINGLES 350 & 500cc 1955-1967 (BOOK OF)
BSA PRE-WAR MODELS TO 1939 (BOOK OF)
BSA TWINS 1948-1962 (BOOK OF)
BSA TWINS 1962-1969 (SECOND BOOK OF)
CATALOG OF BRITISH MOTORCYCLES (1951 MODELS)
DOUGLAS PRE-WAR ALL MODELS 1929-1939 (BOOK OF)
DOUGLAS POST-WAR ALL MODELS 1948-1957 FACTORY WSM
DUCATI 160cc, 250cc & 350cc OHC MODELS FACTORY WSM
HONDA 50 ALL MODELS UP TO 1970 INC MONKEY & TRAIL (BOOK OF)
HONDA 90 ALL MODELS UP TO 1966 (BOOK OF)
HONDA MOTORCYCLES 125-150 TWINS C/CS/CB/CA WSM
HONDA MOTORCYCLES 250-305 TWINS C/CS/CB WSM
HONDA MOTORCYCLES C100 SUPER CUB WSM
HONDA MOTORCYCLES C110 SPORT CUB 1962-1969 WSM
HONDA TWINS & SINGLES 50cc TO 305cc 1960-1966 (BOOK OF)
HONDA TWINS ALL MODELS 125cc THRU 450cc UP TO 1968 (BOOK OF)
LAMBRETTA ALL 125 & 150cc MODELS 1947-1957 (BOOK OF)
LAMBRETTA LI & TV MODELS 1957-1970 (SECOND BOOK OF)
MATCHLESS 350 & 500cc SINGLES 1945-1956 (BOOK OF)
MATCHLESS 350 & 500cc SINGLES 1955-1966 (BOOK OF)
NORTON 1938-1956 (BOOK OF)
NORTON DOMINATOR TWINS 1955-1965 (BOOK OF)
NORTON MOTORCYCLES 1957-1970 FACTORY WSM
NORTON PREWAR MODELS 1932-1939 (BOOK OF)
ROYAL ENFIELD 736cc INTERCEPTOR FACTORY WSM
ROYAL ENFIELD 250cc & 350cc SINGLES 1958-1966 (SECOND BOOK OF)
SUZUKI 50cc & 80cc UP TO 1966 (BOOK OF)
SUZUKI T10 1963-1967 FACTORY WSM
SUZUKI T20 & T200 1965-1969 FACTORY WSM
TRIUMPH PRE-WAR MOTORCYCLE 1935-1939 (BOOK OF)
TRIUMPH MOTORCYCLES 1937-1951 WSM
TRIUMPH MOTORCYCLES 1945-1955 FACTORY WSM
TRIUMPH TWINS 1956-1969 (BOOK OF)
VELOCETTE ALL SINGLES & TWINS 1925-1970 (BOOK OF)
VESPA 1951-1961 (BOOK OF)
VINCENT MOTORCYCLES 1935-1955 WSM

www.VelocePress.com